ART IN WORLD HISTORY

Mary Hollingsworth
Art in World History
(Original title: *Wealth and Ideas:
A History of World Art*)

From a project by Francesco Papafava
Iconographic Research by Scala Archives,
Florence

Graphics
Carlo Savona

Drawings
Paolo Capecchi

Maps
Rosanna Rea

Managing editor and art consultant
Gloria Fossi

Italian staff editors for the English edition
*Sara Bettinelli, Franco Barbini,
Lucrezia Galleschi*

Page format
Studio Scriba, Bologna

Editing of the original English text
Emily Ligniti

English translation of original Italian maps,
timelines, and glossary
Julia Weiss

The author wishes to thank many friends
and colleagues, above all John Onians
and Daniele Casalino,
and dedicates the book to the memory
of her grandmother.

Library of Congress Cataloging-in-Publication Data

Hollingsworth, Mary.
Art in world history / Mary Hollingsworth.
p. cm.
Includes index.
ISBN 0-7656-8069-6 (set : alk. paper)
1. Art--History. I. Title.
N5300 .H674 2004
709--dc22   2003015510

© 1989, 2003 by Giunti Editore S.p.A, Firenze-Milano
© 2004 by M.E. Sharpe, Inc.

ISBN 0-7656-8069-6

Printed and bound in Italy – Giunti Industrie Grafiche S.p.A. (Prato)

The paper used in this publication meets the minimum requirements of
American National Standard for Information Sciences--Permanence
of Paper for Printed Library Materials, ANSI Z 39.48.1984.

(G) (c) 10 9 8 7 6 5 4 3 2 1

ART IN WORLD HISTORY

MARY HOLLINGSWORTH

Introduction by
GIULIO CARLO ARGAN

VOLUME 1

SHARPE REFERENCE
an imprint of M.E. Sharpe, Inc.

CONTENTS

● **Greece and Rome**

● **Religions and Conquests
Between East and West**

● **The Middle Ages: Time of Faith**

V O L U M E 2

FROM THE SIXTEENTH
TO THE TWENTIETH CENTURY

● The Nineteenth Century

Introduction:

HUMANITY, ART, AND HISTORY

Giulio Carlo Argan

I N EVERY ERA, in every culture, there has always been a desire to do art: groups of artists organized themselves with rules and by-laws; public institutions promoted production, and care was taken to collect and conserve artworks in public museums. We could never write a full history of any era or civilization without including the history of its art that, like science, was a necessary and essential component of the system. The relationships between cities, regions, states, and continents would not have been as frequent, intense, reciprocal, and fertile if art had not served as a powerful factor of communication and exchange. In the ancient religions, art gave form to the gods and goddesses; and the prestige of the states would have been less if art had not given monumental form to their institutions, depicting the facts of their history as exemplary and portraying their heroes. The cities would have been mere places to live or work if art had not given them character and rendered their traditions visible and real. Without the images of art, there would not have been a cult of the dead. Nature itself would not have become a subject of knowledge but merely a cause of disordered, confused feelings if it had not been described using the terms of art: line, shape, color.

Because of its constant relationship with universal values, art seemed like a divine revelation and the artists were considered inspired beings, demiurges, creatures between heaven and earth. In reality, art is the product of human work and techniques that may be more refined but not fundamentally different from those of the crafts. And over the centuries art was the direct or indirect model for handicrafts.

Production was like a pyramid: at the base maximum quantity with minimum quality, at the top, the maximum quality with minimum quantity. Art was pure quality, without quantity: its products were unique and irreproducible. They presupposed the culture and techniques of the times, but in the sense of greater inventiveness, not technical progress. Throughout history, art has represented the metaphysical moment of human endeavor, its ideal goal. Artists have always been the interpreters and spokespeople of a community, and if their works were destined for the few who had the greatest powers, they were considered delegates of a superior, divine power. Therefore, throughout its history, art has been the link between the sphere of power and of labor and thus contributed to the homogeneity of the social body. Through art, in other words, the world of labor participated in power.

Only with the Italian Renaissance and its spread through Europe did art move from the "mechanical" to the "liberal" and artists from the rank of craftspeople to that of intellectuals and hence became part of the governing class. Even earlier, however, artists were never mere "makers": power was not content with their work, it needed their inventive and planning skills. Two examples from an infinity of choices will suffice: Pericles commissioned an artist, Phidias, to build the Parthenon—which was to be the visible fulcrum of Hellenic unity—and decorate it with sculptures; the papacy entrusted artists (Bramante, Raphael, Sangallo, Michelangelo, and later, Bernini) to build St. Peter's Basilica which, in an era of bitter religious conflict, was not supposed to represent, but rather materialize, the doctrine of the Visible Church in its structure. Those artists, like many who came before and after them, were not asked to create a verbal celebration of power and its rituals, or a picturesque framework, but a visualization of its doctrinal essence. Nor was it supposed to be an illustration of written texts: on the contrary, visual art conveyed something that could not be communicated with words. The visual experience has a direct relationship with imagination: an entire chapter in the history of civilization has been built on and from imagination and does not contradict, but rather coincides with the chapter built on rational thought and scientific research. Visual arts are communication through images, as poetry is communication through words and music communication through sounds. It has always been something specific to see, which necessarily assumed an experience more intense than the seen. Art of all times and places is related to the organic association of perception and imagination: artists from different cultures have given visible form to non-visible things, like symbols or symbolic meanings to visible forms. But on what does the power of visual communication depend? Why, in all countries of the world, has religious and political power used visual communication through the work of its artists?

Art, as we have said, is related on the one hand to visual perception and on the other to a technical procedure. For the philosopher or scientist, perception may be the object of rational thought. In the artist, it is a stimulus that triggers a process that uses appropriate techniques for producing "artificial" images that become one with an object, the artwork. In Ancient Greece, where art touched one of the highest peaks of its history, one word (*tecné*) meant both art and technique. In all cultures, art is linked to the concept of doing, of being able to do, of doing with greater power and achieving qualitatively better results. Even today we speak of the technical system of the arts: only recently have we tried to produce things of artistic value using nontraditional techniques taken from industrial technology. Not only with the craftsperson's techniques, but also with farming and tribal techniques, we have tried to achieve ideal results in art: there is folk art, art connected to farming techniques, and an art of primitive peoples. The artistic heritage related to urban techniques is incomparably vaster and more varied. There are ancient cities whose civic history is manifested through the development of artistic, architectural, and other forms, and others in which the image was deliberate and designed by one or a group of artists, such as Vicenza in Italy, Bath in England, St. Petersburg in Russia, and, recently, Brasilia in Brazil.

The type of value produced by art is known as *aesthetic*: it does not preclude or contradict the material, practical, or utilitarian value of artistic objects. It goes beyond presenting itself as purely ideal. Starting in the eighteenth century, an entire philosophy, aesthetics, was built on that type of value. It concerns not only art, but also nature: thus a distinction was drawn between the beautiful in nature and the beautiful in art.

The definition of natural beauty, however, begins from the artistic experience. Ever since Ancient Greece, beauty was conceived as a harmonious relationship of parts: the relationship was not only among plastic shapes, but also among lines and colors. A concept that while not in agreement with, yet not substantially different from beauty, is expressed by Eastern art. Schematically we could say that aesthetics flanks the other two constituents of human thought and action: reason and morals.

The awareness of art's high ideological potential explains the interest, sometimes with negative effects, of constituted power. Most of Ancient Roman art was created to give visible form to the authority of the State. All medieval art aimed at the revelation of religious truths. Considered both a venal and ideal value, art has been war booty: Ancient Rome appropriated the art of its conquests, starting from Greece; Napoleon and Hitler looted Italy; many European countries stripped colonies of their artistic heritage to deprive them of an ideal patrimony and entitlement to independence. In all civilized countries, there are laws and regulations for the conservation and protection of artistic heritage: for years there have been discussions concerning the possibility of international conventions to prevent at least some illegitimate exports and trafficking in stolen items. Scientific studies and researches have been undertaken on the use of the most sophisticated technical tools for the restoration and conservation of artworks. Cataloging, as essential for protection as it is for study, is now done with the most advanced computer technologies. The same can be said for archaeological excavations that are no longer focused on recovering precious objects, but on the scientific reconstruction of ancient civilizations. Since the sixteenth century, collections of antiquities and art objects have been built at royal and princely courts and among the richest noble families. With the advent of liberalism and democracy, these collections have become public museums. Starting in the late nineteenth century, many great museums were established in the United States through the initiatives of industrial capitalism. Established as "temples" of art, today in culturally advanced countries, the museums are agencies for scientific research. Even in the ancient world, both West and East, artists' work was flanked by a literature of chronicles, commentary, criticism, and history. Starting in the fifteenth century, especially in Italy, a theoretical and perceptive activity developed, aimed at protecting the cultural foundations of art and giving artistic production a certain uniformity. In the eighteenth century, as a growing bourgeoisie approached the antique markets, a category of experts or connoisseurs began to develop. Having ascertained the insufficiency and dubious reliability of documents, they developed a criticism based on a direct examination of the artworks. Other currents of historical-artistic research aim at identifying conceptual and ideological contents and iconological processes. Modern criticism refuses to see art as a product of inspiration and uncontrollable impulse: art, always and everywhere, is a product of culture. Cultural anthropology has proved that the same can also be said for so-called primitive art.

During the nineteenth and twentieth centuries, with the rapid development of the economy and industrial technology, the historical circle of the crafts came to a close and in effect the link between art and production systems was broken. The condition of artists, who are no longer integrated, has become increasingly difficult: from isolation they have gone to marginalization, to challenge, to revolt.

Commissions from institutions are becoming increasingly rare and are mainly given to conservative and academic artists. The private clientele is becoming scarce and the market limited to a privileged few. The social class organized by artists has practically disappeared. The probable incompatibility of artistic work with the industrial production system was foreseen and predicted since the beginning of the nineteenth century: Hegel, the early Romantic philosophers, and later Ruskin and Morris discussed a possible crisis and even the death of art. The irreconcilability seems to be becoming more severe: and the final crisis of what is known as the technical system of the arts is objectively certain.

We cannot say the same for aesthetic values that were produced by art. We cannot predict the future: what we can say with certainty is that, as an expression of the individual and as a means of inter-subjective communication, art has not yet been replaced by other values. In fact, the concept of values has entered the crisis along with art.

I.

FROM THE EARLY CIVILIZATIONS
TO THE SIXTEENTH CENTURY

EARLY CIVILIZATIONS

When and how did art begin?
It is difficult to give a precise answer.
We can define the most ancient artifacts
as works of art in contemporary terms
only in a very approximate way.
On the other hand, the further back
in time we go, the narrower
the boundary between archaeology
and art history seems to become.
The objects, the paintings,
the megalithic monuments that
have come down to us are only
a part of what we believe those
ancient civilizations produced.

In any case, the earliest "manual"
evidence of human endeavors can be
found in the tools needed for survival.
They had no decorative, aesthetic,
or symbolic purpose, at least as far
as we can see.

From what is known as "mobile" art,
the earliest statuettes portraying animal
and human female figures, the next step
was cave paintings that were probably
linked to magical-religious experiences.
Then came the anthropomorphic vessels,
terracotta figurines, and finely crafted
gold pieces that can be found in various

cultures. But it was only with the
development of the great river
civilizations (along the Nile, Tigris,
Euphrates, and Yellow Rivers) that man
began to reveal his enormous ability
to create monumental works.

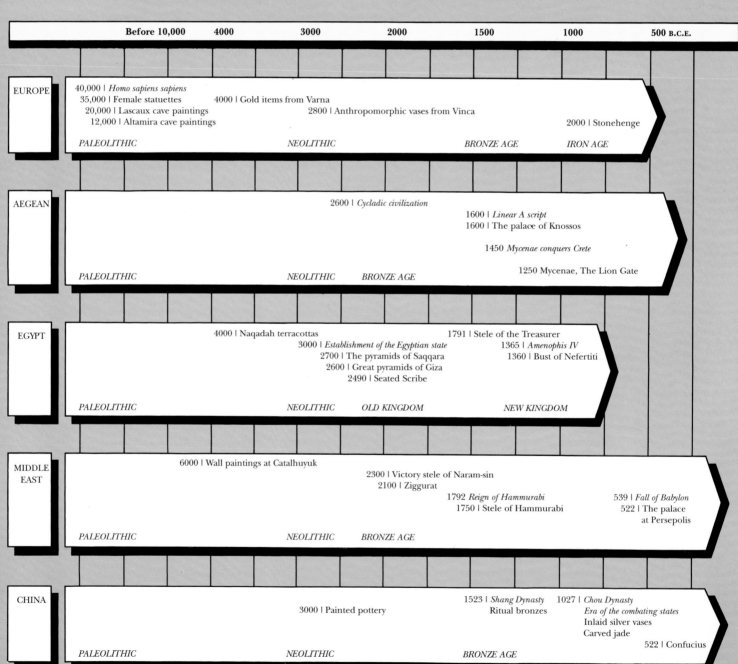

	Before 10,000	4000	3000	2000	1500	1000	500 B.C.E.

EUROPE
40,000 | *Homo sapiens sapiens*
35,000 | Female statuettes   4000 | Gold items from Varna
20,000 | Lascaux cave paintings   2800 | Anthropomorphic vases from Vinca
12,000 | Altamira cave paintings   2000 | Stonehenge

PALEOLITHIC   *NEOLITHIC*   *BRONZE AGE*   *IRON AGE*

AEGEAN
2600 | *Cycladic civilization*
1600 | *Linear A script*
1600 | The palace of Knossos
1450 *Mycenae conquers Crete*
1250 Mycenae, The Lion Gate

PALEOLITHIC   *NEOLITHIC*   *BRONZE AGE*

EGYPT
4000 | Naqadah terracottas   1791 | Stele of the Treasurer
3000 | *Establishment of the Egyptian state*   1365 | *Amenophis IV*
2700 | The pyramids of Saqqara   1360 | Bust of Nefertiti
2600 | Great pyramids of Giza
2490 | Seated Scribe

PALEOLITHIC   *NEOLITHIC*   *OLD KINGDOM*   *NEW KINGDOM*

MIDDLE EAST
6000 | Wall paintings at Catalhuyuk
2300 | Victory stele of Naram-sin
2100 | Ziggurat
1792 *Reign of Hammurabi*   539 | *Fall of Babylon*
1750 | Stele of Hammurabi   522 | The palace at Persepolis

PALEOLITHIC   *NEOLITHIC*   *BRONZE AGE*

CHINA
3000 | Painted pottery
1523 | *Shang Dynasty*   1027 | *Chou Dynasty*
Ritual bronzes   *Era of the combating states*
Inlaid silver vases
Carved jade
522 | Confucius

PALEOLITHIC   *NEOLITHIC*   *BRONZE AGE*

PREHISTORY IS GENERALLY DIVIDED INTO periods that reflect the increasing power of early humans to manipulate and transform their environment. At a very early stage in their development, humans were distinguished from other animals by the ability to use their hands to manufacture tools to suit their particular purposes, rather than rely on stones and other available objects.

Neanderthals, who appeared in Europe and Asia about 70,000 years ago, used flint tools to help hunt, gather, and prepare food. They also developed the ability to use fire, and their remains provide

CHAPTER 1

THE ORIGINS OF ART

Early Artifacts

the first reliable evidence of rituals associated with burial.

The emergence of modern humans, *Homo sapiens sapiens*, occurred about 40,000 years ago. The process by which they evolved remains controversial, but their appearance is known to have coincided with the development of more varied and efficient tools. The new tool kit of *Homo sapiens sapiens*, which included fish hooks and needles fashioned from bone, also featured carved patterns that appear to be decorative but possibly had a symbolic significance. This was soon followed by the manufacture of objects that did not have an immediate

1

practical purpose in the hunting and gathering of food, and which, for want of a better name, we call "art."

Portable Art

As one would expect from their nomadic lifestyle, the artistic endeavors of early humans were for the most part portable. Remains from this early phase in the development of representational art are mainly small statuettes of animals and women made from local materials such as stone, terracotta, bone, or ivory. The carved figures of women show little facial detail and obviously were not intended as portraits. But their exaggerated breasts and buttocks clearly identify them as female. It is generally assumed that the figures served as some form of fertility symbol and, as a result, they are often called "Venus" statues. Many of them were unearthed with a high polish, however, indicating that frequent handling was fundamental to their purpose. Some of them incorporate a conspicuous vulva, a feature also found incised on the walls of caves, and their function may have been related more to the pleasurable aspects of sex than to procreation. Whatever the true purpose of these carved figures, the uncertainty highlights the problems one faces in attempting to understand the origins of art.

Mural Art

Mural art developed somewhat later and suggests that its creators had a more settled lifestyle. Ironically, when the Paleolithic cave paintings at Altamira were discovered during the nineteenth century, they were initially regarded as forgeries on the grounds that they were too good to be prehistoric.

The cave paintings were almost exclusively of animals, including representations

1. Horse with arrows. *Lascaux, Dordogne, France. Rock painting. Ca. 20,000 B.C.E. This image of a horse under attack gave visual expression to the immediate concerns of early humans: survival in hostile surroundings and the search for food.*

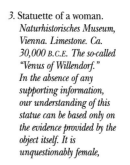

3

2. Statuette of a woman. *Musée de l'Homme, Paris. From Lespugue (Dordogne). Bone. Ca. 20,000 B.C.E. In this stylized interpretation of* the female torso, the carver paid scant attention to the head, arms, and legs, but concentrated on the rounded forms of the female body.

3. Statuette of a woman. *Naturhistorisches Museum, Vienna. Limestone. Ca. 30,000 B.C.E. The so-called "Venus of Willendorf." In the absence of any supporting information, our understanding of this statue can be based only on the evidence provided by the object itself. It is unquestionably female,* but we cannot assume that it had a religious purpose.

4. Carving of a woman. *Musée de l'Homme, Paris. From Laussel (Dordogne). Stone. Ca. 19,000 B.C.E. Conspicuously female, this tactile image has none of the idealization normally associated with cult images.*

2

4

Humans have long been interested in their origins. Explanations have been elaborated in complex mythological and religious accounts. The declining power of the Church in the eighteenth century was reflected in an increasing desire to use rational and intellectual means to find answers to questions that previously had been provided in Judeo-Christian literature. This process gathered pace in the nineteenth century. Charles Darwin's *Origin of the Species* (1859), which traced human ancestry back to the apes, was

THE DISCOVERY OF ALTAMIRA

greeted by a storm of religious protest, but many scientists embraced the theory. Influenced by Darwin, interest in the remains of early humans developed dramatically in the nineteenth century. Archaeologists made important finds of prehistoric portable art in France and elsewhere, but it was the revelation of Paleolithic pictorial talent that has since captured our imagination.

The discovery of the caves of Altamira, in northern Spain, was due more to luck than to rigorous scientific investigation. In 1869, a hunter was looking for his dog, whose barks had unexpectedly quieted, and suddenly found himself inside the previously unknown cave complex. The importance of Altamira was not recognized until six years later, when a local amateur archaeologist, Marcelino

de Sautuola, heard the story and began his own investigation. It took him four years to locate the site. In 1879, he was exploring the caves with his twelve-year old daughter, who suddenly exclaimed, "Papa, look at the painted bulls." Sautuola published his discovery the following year, convinced of both the authenticity and age of the paintings. The report was greeted with skepticism, however, and he died without proving his theories. Only twenty-three years later, in 1902, did they find acceptance.

THE ORIGINS OF ART

5. Deer. *Altamira (Santander), Spain. Rock painting. Ca. 12,000 B.C.E. Interpretations of the function of these murals vary considerably. Modern visitors prefer to think of them as part of some magico-religious experience, but there is little evidence to confirm this.*

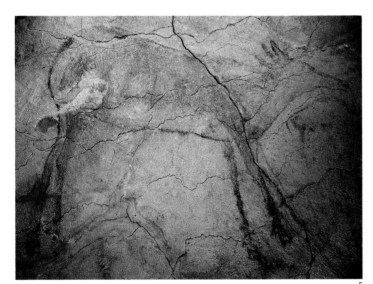

5

6. Bison. *Altamira (Santander). Rock painting. Ca. 12,000 B.C.E. Deep inside the cave complex, these murals were painted—and seen—only by the light of simple oil lamps, which reinforced their power.*

6

of horses, bison, wild cattle, deer, bears, and occasionally fish. Not restricted to Europe, Stone Age cave paintings have also been found in Mesoamerica, Australia, and Africa; the paintings in Africa include representations of rhinoceroses and zebras. The most commonly depicted animals were generally the largest in the area, perhaps indicating that the images were expressions of physical power. When the human figure appeared, it was usually represented schematically. Women were rarely depicted in cave paintings, but natural rock formations were often sculpted into female forms—further examples of the tactile representation of the woman's body.

The pigments used for prehistoric cave paintings were invariably local metal ores, pounded on site and mixed with some medium. At Lascaux the medium was water; elsewhere resins, albumen, and other substances were used. Yet neither the graphic content nor the composition of the pigment tells us very much about the purpose of the paintings, and interpretations vary. Some people have suggested that they are meaningless decorations inspired by visual experience. To others, the location provides a clue. Contrary to the popular misconception that prehistoric humans lived inside the caves, they actually lived in tents made from animal skins. The paintings are frequently located deep within the cave complexes, leading some theorists to suggest a magico-religious interpretation of either hunting or fertility or both. There is little evidence, however, to confirm this view with any certainty.

From Nomad to Farmer

The end of the Ice Age (ca. 10,000 years ago) had a radical effect on the climate of Europe. The growth of woodlands marked

a   b   c

7

8

7. Stonehenge. *Salisbury, England. Ca. 2000 B.C.E. The focus of a ritual cult in ancient Britain, its real meaning remains obscure. The huge stones were deliberately aligned to relate to sunrise on a midsummer day and sunset on a midwinter day.*

8. *Map of Paleolithic Europe:*
   a) Principal areas of mural art;
   b) Principal areas of portable art;
   c) Maximum extent of glaciation during the Ice Age.

Check Out Receipt

Shorewood - Troy Public Library

Friday, February 19, 2016 12:22:17 PM
93441

Item: 31560001259783
Title: Art in world history
Due: 03/11/2016

Item: 31560001746110
Title: Kung fu panda 2
Due: 02/26/2016

Item: 31560002010300
Title: Jurassic world
Due: 02/26/2016

Item: 31560002006779
Title: Marvel Avengers, age of Ultron
Due: 02/26/2016

Item: 31560001751904
Title: Mr. Popper's penguins
Due: 02/26/2016

We have new hours!
Mon-Thurs 9am - 9pm
Fri & Sat 9am-6pm and
Sun 1pm-6pm!

the end of Paleolithic human dependence on hunting and gathering as the means of subsistence. The transition to agriculture was slow and gradual, but the results were revolutionary. Starting in the Middle East and spreading gradually into Europe through Greece, Neolithic humans abandoned their nomadic existence and settled down to farming. Temporary tents were replaced by permanent dwellings.

Larger communities were established, with more organized forms of religion and ritual. Excavations at Catal Hüyük (ca. 6000 B.C.E.) in southern Turkey have provided firm evidence of religious ritual, in this case associated with aurochs (extinct wild cattle), whose long horns were used to decorate shrines. Other areas of Europe developed different divinities and rituals. The importance of light and heat to crop production was reflected in the number of communities that worshipped sun deities.

At a practical level, the technique of making and firing pottery developed in response to the functional needs of agricultural production and storage.

Abstract patterns were used to decorate plates, cups, and other implements. These objects were used for both household and ritual purposes, with greater elaboration suggesting the latter function.

The Spread of Agriculture

Agriculture spread very slowly across Europe. By the time it reached the British Isles (ca. 2500 B.C.E.), further developments had taken place in the Middle East. Successful farming was creating enough wealth to to support a class of nonproducers, who had established literate civilizations in Mesopotamia (see chapter 2) and Egypt (see chapter 3). They had also discovered

9. Graffiti. *Grotta dell'Addaura, Montepellegrino, Sicily. Upper Paleolithic. This series of figures was not composed as a unified scene. But the emphasis on form and movement suggests a new approach to the depiction of human figures.*

10. Vase in human form. *National Museum, Belgrade. Terracotta. Third millennium B.C.E. This vase, with distinctive human features, was found at Vinca, a Neolithic site southeast of Belgrade. It is typical of the pottery produced in the Neolithic villages of southeastern Europe.*

11. and 12. Two cups. *Istituto di Antropologia, Pisa. From the Grotta del Leone, Agnano. Terracotta. Ca. 3000 B.C.E. The development of pottery to make ritual objects and household implements reflected the increasing stability of an agricultural lifestyle.*

10

11

9

12

that the high-temperature kilns developed for pottery could be used for smelting copper and other metals. Knowledge of metalworking slowly filtered into northern Europe in the wake of agriculture, and it was followed by another Mesopotamian invention: bronze (ca. 3000 B.C.E.). Metals soon replaced pottery in the production of the most valued items, such as religious objects and jewelry. The Celtic cultures, which dominated northern Europe until conquest by the Romans, made extensive use of bronze and other metals, developing distinctive decorative traditions. Unlike the Mediterranean cultures, however, the Celts left no evidence of a written language. Their graves have yielded large quantities of objects whose military, religious, and decorative functions provide only clues regarding their attitude toward art.

The origins of art are irrevocably linked to the development of human life and society. Why art should have begun, and why it took the forms it did, are questions for which we have no real answers. Why we need to know is part of a deep-rooted desire to understand our origins, which has proved one of the most potent forces in the development of civilization.

13

13. Necklace. *National Museum, Belgrade. Gold. Second millennium B.C.E. Decorative jewelry, such as this necklace, reflects the increasing technical skill, artistry, and wealth in Bronze Age Europe.*

14. Ritual crowns. *Museo Civico, Riva del Garda. Bronze. Ca. 1600 B.C.E. These crowns were found with ceramic, wood, and other bronze objects* *in the remains of a lakeside settlement. Their incised abstract patterns reflected a desire to embellish precious objects.*

14

M ESOPOTAMIA, NAMED BY THE GREEKS as the "land between the rivers," is justifiably called "the cradle of civilization." Yet it was hardly an ideal location for such a momentous development. The vast plain formed by the Tigris and the Euphrates rivers was a hostile environment, with extreme seasonal variations in temperature and frequent, often destructive flooding. The area was settled in about 5000 B.C.E. by farmers from the surrounding hills who had discovered that this inhospitable land could be made astonishingly fertile by irrigation. Their technical inventions

CHAPTER 2

KINGDOMS OF MESOPOTAMIA

Land Between the Rivers

included the potter's wheel (ca. 3500 B.C.E.) and wheeled carts (ca. 3250 B.C.E.). Successful farming generated surplus wealth that was used to support a nonagricultural class of priests, scribes, traders, and artisans. By 3000 B.C.E., a series of separate city-kingdoms had emerged from the prehistoric village cultures—the first vital steps in the development of urban society.

Early Sumerian Culture

Sumerian culture developed in cities such as Ur, Lagash, Kish, and Uruk (biblical Erech), whose territories included

1

agricultural land. From the start, life in these new communities was dominated by religion. The gods of Mesopotamia were far from kind. Like the hostile environment they represented, their power was awesome and demanded placating. The Sumerians placed statues of worshippers in shrines so that prayer could continue on their behalf during their absence.

The accumulation of religious wealth stimulated the development of cylinder seals to identify personal possessions. It also led to writing, in about 3000 B.C.E. Using local materials, scribes recorded information on clay tablets with a reed, which made distinctive wedge-shaped signs known collectively as cuneiform. Schools were set up to teach writing. The need to keep accounts and measure land led to a counting system. We still use Sumerian numeration, based on sixty, in our calculation of time and degrees.

The gods invested earthly authority in kings, whose power was initially symbolized by a residence within the temple complex. As royal power grew, a separate palace structure evolved, attached to the temple. Sumerian temples were raised on platforms to reinforce their heavenly context. A lack of abundant stone for building led the Sumerians to experiment with the structural potential of brick, developing the arch and barrel vault, both found in the Royal Cemetery at Ur. These tombs also provide evidence of the extravagance of court life. They were filled with objects of religious significance, such as musical instruments decorated with scenes of banquets and military campaigns, reflecting the preoccupations of the Sumerian dynasties. Wealth was expressed through the use of precious stones and metals in such objects, which show considerable technical expertise.

2. Lion-headed eagle. *Treasury of Ur, Mari. Lapis lazuli, gold, bitumen, and copper. Ca. 2500 B.C.E. In ancient Sumerian mythology, this eagle with a head of a lion was the symbol of the deity Ningirsu.*

1. and 4. Statuettes of worshippers. *Iraq Museum, Baghdad. Stone. Ca. 2700 B.C.E. These roughly carved figures were images of worshippers from the temple of Abu at Tell Asmar. All attention focused on the enormous eyes through which they could visualize their awesome gods.*

2

3. Pre-Sargonic seals. *Iraq Museum, Baghdad. Ca. 2300 B.C.E. Cylinder seals were developed to record property; their intaglio designs left a distinctive pattern when rolled over clay.*

3

4

Sargon of Akkad

The Mesopotamian plain was linked with Asia Minor, the Mediterranean, and Iran by mountain passes that provided routes for traders, migrant peoples, and invading tribes. Mercantile, racial, and military movements all played a part in the highly complex history of Mesopotamia. The drift of tribes from the Arabian and Syrian deserts established a Semitic influence to the north of Sumer. Adapting Sumerian culture to suit their own traditions, these northern peoples used cuneiform to establish a distinctive written language, Akkadian (ca. 2500 B.C.E.). The conquest of Sumeria by Sargon of Akkad in about 2300 B.C.E. had important consequences. The Sumerian cities gave their allegiance to individual divinities within a national pantheon, but the Semitic tribes were organized by family loyalties.

The position of Sargon of Akkad at the head of a unified kingdom introduced a new style of leadership, which was reflected in a new approach to art. Images of royal power began to increase, and statues of worshippers became rare. The victory stele of Sargon's grandson, Naram-sin, expressed the new idea of kingship. The old Sumerian concept of temporal power invested by the gods disappeared. Naram-sin was represented both as a leader of soldiers and as a god himself, his spiritual as well as temporal authority symbolized by the horned crown of divinity.

Ur and Lagash

The Old Akkadian Empire fell under pressure from belligerent northern tribes, and the Sumerian cities seized the opportunity to reassert their independence. Gudea, the ruler of Lagash (ruled 2143–2124 B.C.E.) restored the image of his city with new temples and other civic improvements.

KINGDOMS OF MESOPOTAMIA

5. Musical instrument. *Iraq Museum, Baghdad. Inlaid wood. Ca. 2450 B.C.E. Found in the royal tombs at Ur, this elaborately inlaid object displays high-quality craftsmanship. The bull's head on the sound box reflects the Sumerian belief in the divine power of animals.*

6. Helmet. *Iraq Museum, Baghdad. Gold. Ca. 2450 B.C.E. The elaborate headdress, with its stylized detail and use of gold, conveys a conspicuous image of power.*

6

7

8

8. Victory stele of Naram-sin. *Louvre, Paris. Pink sandstone. Ca. 2300 B.C.E. Carved to celebrate his expanding empire, this image shows Naram-sin ascending the mountain of divinity. Not only was he positioned above his soldiers, but he was presented as being notably larger.*

9. Head of an Akkadian ruler. *Iraq Museum, Baghdad. Bronze. Ca. 2350 B.C.E. Grand and imposing, the stylized features of this head represents Sargon of Akkad or one of his successors.*

7. Prism. *Iraq Museum, Baghdad. Ca. 710 B.C.E. The distinctive wedge-shaped signs of cuneiform evolved from simplified pictograms into a complex abstract language.*

5

9

The enduring influence of the Akkadian style of leadership, however, was reflected in the twenty or more statues of himself placed in the city's shrines. Lagash was captured by the ruler of Ur, Ur-Nammu, whose conquest of Mesopotamia consolidated the concept of divine kingship. Ur-Nammu's ziggurat was one of many architectural projects commissioned throughout his empire, including other temples, a palace, and a vaulted burial chamber. The collapse of Ur marked the end of Sumerian civilization. Semitic Akkadian became the dominant language of Mesopotamia, and the focus of political power shifted north to Babylon.

Hammurabi, King of Babylon

Hammurabi's reign as king of Babylon (ca. 1792-1749 B.C.E.) saw a gradual extension of his control over Mesopotamia. As part of the effort to impose order on his empire, Hammurabi introduced a new code of law, representing an important extension of royal power. His commemorative stele was crowned by a representation of Hammurabi receiving the laws from the Sun God, thereby imbuing them with divine authority.

Concerned with individual rights over possessions, the laws regulated mercantile exchange and included the concept of professional responsibility for doctors, builders, and others. Once again the personality of an individual ruler played an important part in the survival of an empire. After Hammurabi's death, the kingdom fell apart.

The Assyrians

The far-flung conquests of the Assyrian army, vividly described in the Hebrew Bible, were the result of a skilled and well-

10. Gudea. *Louvre, Paris. Stone. Ca. 2150 B.C.E. The ruler of Lagash holds the divine waters, symbolizing the powers given him by the gods. His stylized facial features contrast with the realistic musculature of his arms and shoulders, reinforcing both his physical and spiritual strength.*

11. Stele of Hammurabi. *Louvre, Paris. From Susa. Black basalt. Ca. 1750 B.C.E.*

12. Ziggurat. *Ur. 2100 B.C.E. Like the Egyptians, the Sumerians constructed mountains to their gods. On top of the ziggurat was the temple, a visual expression of the physical and spiritual superiority of the deity.*

10

11

12

organized fighting force with strong leadership. Its mastery of the siege and other military tactics made it almost invincible. By 800 B.C.E. it had carved out a substantial empire. Assyrian rulers were warriors, not lawgivers. It was war, not peace, that guaranteed their power, and their victories brought enormous wealth in the form of tributes. The Hebrew Bible relates how Hezekiah was obliged to give the Assyrians gold from the Temple of Jerusalem; the Assyrians also removed obelisks from Egypt as symbols of their conquest.

Assyrian art and architecture were important propaganda vehicles for military power. The capitals at Nimrud (founded by Assurnasirpal II), Khorsabad (by Sargon II), and Nineveh (by Assurbanipal) were dominated by royal palaces. Built on an unprecedented scale, the palaces nevertheless illustrate how much the Assyrians adopted from the old Sumerian style. Sargon II's palace at Khorsabad (see box, page 32) was typical. Although the old ziggurat form was used for the temple, it was a subsidary part of the palace complex; this was a direct reversal of the early Sumerian plan, in which the ruler was housed within the religious buildings themselves.

Guarded by *lamassu*, or human-headed winged bulls, the palace was approached by a processional corridor. Visitors proceeded up a staircase and through a series of courts into the presence of the king. The brick structure was faced with limestone reliefs depicting Assyrian military ascendancy, including battle scenes, the sacking of cities, and the payment of tributes. Other images reinforced the image of Assyrian strength and breadth of power. These reliefs are some of the earliest examples of narrative art and denote the tendency in Assyrian art to depict

KINGDOMS OF MESOPOTAMIA

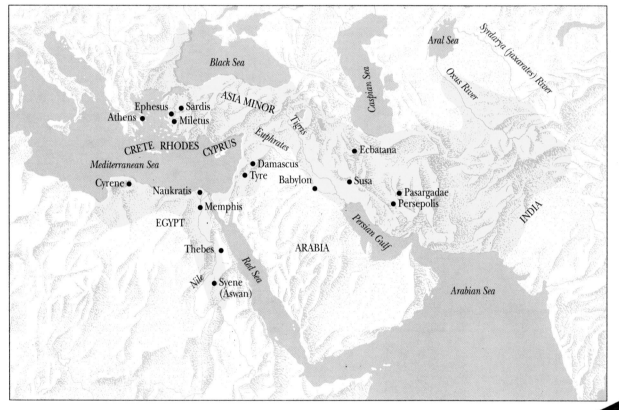

13. Map of the Persian Empire at its greatest extent.

14. Assurnasirpal II. *British Museum, London. From Nimrud. Stone. Ninth century* B.C.E.

14

15. Lamassu. *Louvre, Paris. From Khorsabad. Limestone. Ca. 720* B.C.E. *This human-headed winged bull combined the physical strength of the animal with the intellect of a human. Its five legs allowed it to be viewed realistically from both the front and the side.*

15

SARGON'S PALACE AT KHORSABAD

The Assyrians were the dominant power in the Middle East for nearly 300 years (ca. 900–612 B.C.E.). The palace of Sargon II (ruled 721–705 B.C.E.) at Khorsabad was excavated in the nineteenth century and has provided important insights into Assyrian palace design. The vast and imposing structure, set on a citadel on the perimeter of a huge walled city, was carefully planned for maximum effect. The inner sanctum, the throne room, was approached through a series of courtyards and halls positioned deliberately to require numerous changes of direction.

Lumber was imported from Lebanon, but the basic structure of the palace was mud brick. Stone facing was ideally suited for propagating the image of power. Essentially militaristic, Sargon's choice of subject matter for the reliefs reinforced this theme. Religious images were rare, and the narrative reliefs recorded Assyrian conquests with scenes of slaughter or the paying of tribute. Assyrian power was presented as an inexorable military machine, resistance to which was futile. Other reliefs reflected Assyrian leisure activities, notably the hunting and slaying of lions, which reinforced the image of physical strength. This was given further visual expression in the contrast between the stylized faces and hair of the human figures and the careful attention paid to musculature. Scenes of banquets, so popular with the early Sumerians, were of little interest here.

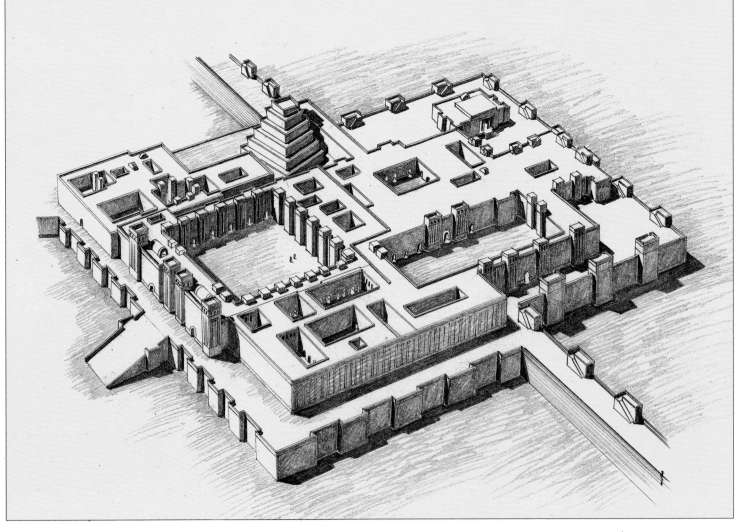

the achievement of its people in a realistic and factual manner.

Nebuchadnezzar and the Neo-Babylonian Empire

Success led to overextension, and Assyrian forces fell to the Medes and Babylonians, who split the empire between them. Nebuchadnezzar, the son of the Babylonian leader, consolidated his father's conquests and created what has been called the Neo-Babylonian Empire. The fame of Nebuchadnezzar's new palace in Babylon —with its ziggurat (the Tower of Babel) and Hanging Gardens—has come down to us through the Hebrew Bible. The image is one of unprecedented material wealth and the potency of money. The Babylonians were primarily traders, not fighters. As an expression of the power of money, Nebuchadnezzar imitated the grandeur of Assyrian royal architecture but avoided representations of military strength. His chief concern was a revival of the culture of old Babylon. This was the message of decorations on the Ishtar Gate that combined the bull, which was sacred to the Sumerians, with the dragon, symbol of the Babylonian god Marduk.

The Rise of Persia

Babylon fell to the Persians in 539 B.C.E. The Persian invasion introduced yet another racial group into Mesopotamia: descendants of Aryan tribes from the Caucasus Mountains who had migrated to Persia in about 1000 B.C.E. A powerful military force, the Persians established their Achaemenid Empire on an unprecedented scale. By 480 B.C.E., it stretched from India to the Mediterranean (see Figure 13). It was divided into provinces under the local authority of satraps, whose powers were both administrative and judiciary. The highly organized Persians

16. Ishtar Gate (restored). Vorderasiatisches Museum, Pergamon Museum, Berlin. From Babylon. Glazed brick. Ca. 575 B.C.E. A ceremonial gateway at Nebuchadnezzar's palace in Babylon. Other features included his famous Hanging Gardens and 295-ft (95-m) ziggurat, believed to be the biblical Tower of Babel.

17. Dragon, from the Ishtar Gate (restored). Iraq Museum, Baghdad. From Babylon. Glazed brick. Ca. 575 B.C.E. With little available local stone, the architects of Mesopotamia developed the potential of brick as a building material, decorating it with glazed tiles.

16

17

took full advantage of the enormous wealth of Mesopotamia, uniting the empire through coinage, taxes, laws, and an efficient road system.

Before establishing an empire, the Persians had shown little interest in monumental architecture. In conquering Babylon and the old Assyrian Empire, however, they apparently recognized its value as a symbol of imperial power. So the Babylonians developed monumental architecture of their own, constructing palaces at Pasargadae, Susa, and Persepolis. Often described as eclectic, Achaemenian architecture consciously adopted features from conquered lands—Assyrian relief sculptures with human-headed winged bulls, glazed brick decorations from Babylon, and fluted columns from the Ionian city-states. In his lavish palace at Persepolis, Darius I (ruled 522–486 B.C.E.) elaborated on Assyrian palace design and reinforced the image of Persian wealth and power with a series of intricately sculpted staircases decorated with statues of tribute-bearers. In his inscription on the palace at Susa, Darius listed the precious materials used in its construction and the countries of origin of the workers. Clearly he took pride in the fact that the stonecutters were Ionian, that the brickworkers were Babylonian, and that the silver and copper were from Egypt, all attesting to the breadth and power of the new empire. The building thus reflects the unification of all these cultures under Persian rule.

The kingdoms of Mesopotamia developed a series of original forms and styles to depict royal authority, culminating in the architecture of the Achaemenid Empire and having a powerful impact on later civilizations.

18. Archers of the Royal Guard. *Louvre, Paris. From Darius's palace at Susa. Enameled brick. Sixth century B.C.E. Stylized figures of archers, the foundation of Persian military success, provided fitting images for the decoration of royal palaces.*

18

19. Stairway to the Royal Audience Hall. *Persepolis. Sixth century B.C.E. A symbol of the magnitude of Persian power, the palace at Persepolis included two enormous hypostyle halls. The audience hall, or apadana, was 250 ft (76 m) square.*

20

19

21

20. Capital. *From Persepolis. Sixth century B.C.E. Reinforcing Persian power, the capitals in the palace at Persepolis were decorated with symbols of their subject nations: bulls and lions from Mesopotamia, Ionic capitals from Greece, and foliage ornamentation from Egypt.*

21. Tomb of Darius II, *Naksh-i-Rustan.*

NCIENT EGYPT WAS THE NILE VALLEY. Cultivation of this thin strip of arid land relied entirely on the annual floodwaters of the Nile, which covered the valley floor with a fertile layer of rich silt. Protected by the natural barriers of mountain and desert, Egypt's agricultural system provided enough wealth to support a remarkably stable civilization. Evidence suggests that farming began there in about 5000 B.C.E., creating small rural communities that gradually amalgamated into two separate kingdoms, Upper and Lower Egypt. By 3200 B.C.E., according to tradition, the two realms were united

CHAPTER 3

ANCIENT EGYPT AND THE EASTERN MEDITERRANEAN

The Nile Valley, Crete, and Mycenae

under a single ruler, King Menes. His successors, the pharaohs, are grouped into a series of thirty-one dynasties, divided by historians into the Old Kingdom (ca. 2700–2280 B.C.E.), the Middle Kingdom (ca. 2050–1800 B.C.E.), and the New Kingdom (ca. 1550–1200 B.C.E.). These corresponded to long periods of strong centralized government, with intermediate phases in which the authority broke down.

Unlike the civilizations of Mesopotamia, which faced an unreliable climate, Egypt could count on the regularity of the annual Nile flood. This rhythm

1

had a profound effect on the development of Egyptian civilization. From June on, water levels in the south began to rise, reaching their full height at Memphis in September. Crops were planted after the floods receded and were harvested in early May. The reliability of this pattern allowed the Egyptians to reject the problems inherent in lunar cycles and adopt a calendar year of 365 days. The Nile provided an efficient communication system that allowed the development of an effective centralized government. It also facilitated the transport of goods, especially heavy building stone from quarries in the surrounding mountains.

Egyptian Society

Egyptian society was based on stability and security. At its head was the pharaoh, whose power was exercised through a highly structured tier of bureaucrats, ranging from the vizier, a sort of chief administrator, to the scribes. Inspired by the Mesopotamian model, Egypt developed a distinctive system of writing, which combined ideograms and phonetic symbols. The complexity of the writing system and its importance in Egyptian life were reflected in the official status accorded to scribes. The scribes constituted the supervisory class of Egyptian society, recording a wide variety of vital information, from the expected crop yields, on which taxes were assessed, to the punishments meted out to lawbreakers.

The stability of Egyptian civilization is partly explained by the absolute power of the pharaoh, whose position as a god-incarnate united spiritual and temporal power. The pharaoh ruled as the god Horus and became Osiris upon his death. According to Egyptian mythology,

1. Great Sphinx. *Giza. Dynasty IV, ca. 2600 B.C.E. This head of a pharaoh attached to the body of a lion, symbolizing both intellectual and physical supremacy, was part of the large complex of buildings and monuments originally attached to the Pyramid of Khafre.*

2. *Map of Ancient Egypt and the Nile Valley.*

3. Isis suckling Horus. *Museo Egiziano, Vatican. Stone. First century B.C.E. Isis, wearing a horned headdress that symbolized her divinity, was often portrayed suckling her son, Horus. These images established precedents for the development of Christian iconography.*

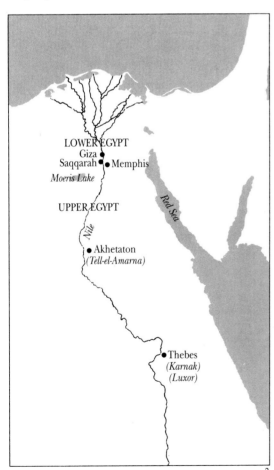

2

3

4

4. Stele of the Treasurer. *Museo Archeologico, Florence. Stone. Dynasty XII (1991–1786 B.C.E.). The prime function of the complex hieroglyphics found in Egyptian tombs was to ensure survival for eternity, communicating prayers to the deities through a combination of pictorial and phonetic symbols.*

Horus was the son of Osiris and his sister-spouse Isis. He was conceived after Osiris had been killed by his uncle Seth, the embodiment of evil. Osiris's body was torn up and scattered by Seth, but found and reunited by Isis, who then miraculously conceived Horus. Egyptian deities embodied the powers of nature. In another aspect, Horus was the sky god and often identified with Re, the great sun god. Other deities were also identified with Re, notably Amun; the cult of Amun-Re became an important part of the state religion during the New Kingdom. The complex relationship between Horus and

Osiris was typical of Egyptian mythology, and the multiple interpretations of the myth indicate that consistency was not essential in reinforcing religious belief. The pharaoh's identification with Horus, the protagonist of the central myth of Egyptian religion, established a direct link between his subjects and divinity.

The Pyramids

The unification of temporal and spiritual power in the figure of the pharaoh gave religious significance to the royal buildings

of Ancient Egypt. The tombs of the early pharaohs were subterranean burial chambers covered by a mound of rubble, an evocation of the primeval hill created by an all-powerful god out of the waters of chaos. The idea was common to both Mesopotamian and Egyptian mythologies and given visual expression in their architecture. The pyramid of King Zoser (ca. 2600 B.C.E.) was an extension of this concept, its stepped surface suggesting that the pharaoh ascended a staircase to heaven. Later pyramids, which incorporated the burial chamber within the structure, purified this image and abandoned the physical steps

5. Pyramids of Giza. *Dynasty IV. The earlier stepped exteriors were replaced by smooth facings, still visible at the top of the Pyramid of Khafre (left).*

6. Anubis. *Museo Egiziano, Vatican. Painted stone. Dynasty XXI (1085–950 B.C.E.). The Egyptian god of the dead, Anubis was a common image in tomb decoration.*

7. Step pyramid of Zoser. *Saqqara. Dynasty III, ca. 2700 B.C.E. Intended to mark the site of Zoser's underground tomb, as well as to protect it, this man-made mountain created an image of power to reflect the divinity of the pharaoh and to symbolize the hill of creation out of the chaos of water.*

5

6

7

in preference to a smoother, more divine surface. These royal tombs were originally surrounded by smaller imitations, commissioned by members of the royal family and court officials who were granted permission as a sign of favor.

The pyramid was standard for royal tombs throughout the Old and Middle Kingdoms. The pharaohs of the New Kingdom made a decisive break with tradition, choosing to hide their tombs in the hills around Thebes, the so-called Valley of the Kings. These tombs featured a complex system of anterooms and corridors that ultimately led to the burial chamber. The allusion

to ceremonial procession was also a key element in the design of the temples and palaces of the New Kingdom, reflecting the increasing elaboration of court ritual. The modest core of the Temple of Amun at Karnak was expanded with a succession of pylons and courts to create a deliberately impressive approach to the shrine.

Survival in the Afterlife

Much of our knowledge of ancient Egyptian life comes from objects preserved in the tombs. For the Egyptians, however, these objects represented much more than

the status and lifestyle of the deceased. They were believed to be imbued with magical properties that would ensure the eternal survival of the owner. The tombs of the pharaohs provided models for those of court officials, who decorated their burial chambers with scenes of life on their estates. Statues of the dead were inscribed with words that would vouchsafe survival. Stelae often depicted offerings to the gods to perpetuate worship in the afterlife. Models, reliefs, and wall decorations ensured continuation of everyday pursuits, from agricultural production and administration to leisure

8

8. Stele fragment. *Museo Egiziano, Vatican. Limestone. Dynasty XVIII, ca. 1300 B.C.E. Details on inscribed reliefs were originally brightly colored and followed the same formulas as those of painted decoration.*

9. Temple of Amun. *Karnak. Dynasty XIX (1314–1197 B.C.E.). The scale of Egyptian temple complexes and the precision of their designs testify to the technical skill of the Egyptians and the efficiency with which they were organized.*

10. Plan of the Temple of Amun. *Karnak. Dynasty XIX (1314-1197 B.C.E.): a) Temple of Seti II; b) Temple of Ramses III; c) Hypostyle Hall.*

9

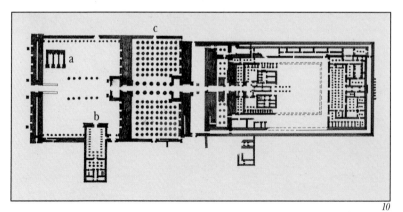

10

The obelisk, a four-sided pillar topped by a pyramid, was an important symbol of Egyptian power. Its form evolved from the cone-topped stones used as cult images in early Egyptian history. By the New Kingdom (ca. 1550–1200 B.C.E.), obelisks, erected in pairs, were standard commemorative structures at the entrances to Egyptian temples. Decorated with hieroglyphics that referred to religious protocol and edicts, they were dedicated to the divinity of the temple they served.

Obelisks were carved on three sides while still attached to the rock face; the last side was finished after the entire pillar was extracted. Transported on specially constructed boats down the Nile, they were laid on the ground and erected by means of ropes and pulleys. The tallest known Egyptian obelisk —about 137 feet (42 m)— is still in its quarry at Aswan.

Obelisks have long exerted a powerful fascination over foreigners. As images of Egyptian power, they also testify to the considerable technical abilities of native craftsmen. The Assyrian King Assurbanipal looted an obelisk from Thebes as a symbol of his military success in the seventh century B.C.E., and Roman conquerors also carried away a considerable number. Two of the latter, known as Cleopatra's Needles, now stand in New York City and London.

ANCIENT EGYPT AND THE EASTERN MEDITERRANEAN

11. Cattle Census. *Egyptian Museum, Cairo. Wood. Dynasty XI (2134–1991 B.C.E.). From the tomb of the Chancellor Meket-re, who sits under a canopy with his scribes recording the size of his herd.*

12. Rahotep and Nofret. *Egyptian Museum, Cairo. Painted limestone. Dynasty IV, ca. 2600 B.C.E. Rahotep's wealth and Nofret's femininity are indicated by her clothes and jewels, but especially by her pale skin.*

13. Slave making beer. *Museo Archeologico, Florence. Painted stone. Dynasty V, ca. 2400 B.C.E. Images of everyday life were included in Egyptian tombs to ensure continuity after death.*

14. Obelisk. *Piazza Santa Maria del Popolo, Rome. This obelisk, approximately 79 feet (24 m) high, was taken from the Temple of the Sun at Heliopolis. Brought to Rome by Emperor Augustus, it was given a place of honor in the Circus Maximus. It owes its present site to Pope Sixtus V.*

12

13

11

14

activities. The wealth and status of the pharaohs were expressed in the lavish decoration and complex structure of their coffins. Immortality was not only embodied in the contents but also in the elaborate ritual of mummification and the use of the hardest stone available, granite, for the floors of the burial chambers. But for grave robbers, these tombs would survive intact today.

Convention and Style

Egyptian art conformed to established conventions. Its sense of order and lack of stylistic development reflected the stable and conservative nature of Egyptian society. Representations of the human form were based on a geometric grid to ensure consistent proportional relationships between body parts. Two-dimensional images of people were presented in a distinctive way: the head and legs appear in profile; the eye and upper body are viewed frontally. Seated figures were typically represented with their hands on their knees.

Given the function of these images, completeness was more important than reality. Social status was invariably reinforced through relative size, perhaps the most effective way of conveying this attribute. Thus, men were often shown larger than their wives and children. In many images of royal couples, however, the husband and wife are depicted as equal in size, indicating the important role of women in pharaonic succession: the throne passed to the eldest daughter, who conferred the right to rule on her husband.

The divine status of the pharaohs is reflected in their idealized portraits and poses. Their subjects were not bound by the same conventions, however, which allowed for a more realistic approach to portraiture. Men were often depicted with darker

15

16

15. Tutankhamen hunting wild fowl. *Egyptian Museum, Cairo. Dynasty XVIII, ca. 1340 B.C.E. From Tutankhamen's tomb, this ivory panel was part of an elaborately ornamented chest and illustrated royal leisure pursuits.*

16. *Grid showing proportions and pose typical of Egyptian figure representation.*

17. Goddess Hathor and Pharaoh Seti I. *Museo Archeologico, Florence. Painted stone. Dynasty XIX, ca. 1292 B.C.E.*

17

18. Couple. *Louvre, Paris. Wood. 2500–2200 B.C.E.*

18

complexions than their wives, contrasting his life of outdoor work and her life of comfort and leisure; similar themes appear throughout the history of art. The increasing elaboration of court life during the New Kingdom was evidenced by changing styles of dress. Simple, white fabrics were replaced by colored materials that were cut in more sensual styles and worn with exceptionally large earrings.

Building Materials

Egypt was rich in natural resources. Gold was available in large quantities in the eastern deserts. Limestone and sandstone were extensively quarried to provide the building materials for royal tombs, temples, and palaces. Stone replaced traditional mud-brick for important architectural monuments, primarily because of its durability. The Egyptians were innovators in the use of stone and pioneers in techniques of quarrying. The stone was transported by barge on the Nile, taking full advantage of the floodwaters to minimize the distance of overland transport. The Egyptians did not immediately develop such labor-saving devices as the pulley or cart, preferring to rely on the abundant supply of physical human strength. Accommodations were set up alongside the quarries and building sites to house the masses of workers required for the construction and embellishment of the monuments. Other materials, particularly wood, were imported by the state. Copper and turquoise were mined in Syria under royal protection, and African tribesmen in the south traded ivory and ebony for Egyptian goods. The number and size of building projects gave rise to a new class of craft specialists. Like the resident laborers, these craftsmen were paid in kind, typically in grain and other foodstuffs.

19. Sarcophagus of Tutankhamen. *Egyptian Museum, Cairo. Dynasty XVIII, ca. 1340 B.C.E. Solid gold decorated with enamel and precious stones expressed the wealth and power of this pharaoh, who died at age 19. His mummified body was placed inside the coffin, itself enclosed in two larger ones before being encased in a stone sarcophagus.*

20. Seated scribe. *Louvre, Paris. From Saqqara. Painted limestone. Dynasty V, ca. 2490 B.C.E. Having trained hard to master the complexities of hieroglyphics, the scribe was accorded exceptionally high status in Ancient Egypt.*

19

20

The Reign of Akhenaten

Egyptian art was produced primarily in a religious context. The decisive role of the pharaoh in the determination of artistic ideals is best illustrated by the reign of Amenhotep IV (1379–1362 B.C.E.). Under his predecessor, Amenhotep III, court life achieved unprecedented levels of luxury. With the increasing power of the priests of Amun, however, the state religion posed a threat to the position of the pharaoh. In reaction to this, Amenhotep IV changed the state religion to the worship of a single supreme being, the Sun Disk (Aten). He changed his name to Akhenaten and moved the capital from Thebes to Akhentaten (now Tell el-Amarna), removing all inscriptions from statues of Amun. The new way of thinking was deliberately reflected in a more liberal approach to the arts. Angularity was rejected in favor of more rounded forms. Rigidity and formality gave way to looser, more formal images. Akhenaten and his wife were depicted at play with their family, a marked contrast to the omnipotent impersonality of traditional pharaonic representations. But Akhenaten's religious revolution, which established the world's first major monotheistic cult, did not last. His successor, Tutankhamen, restored the traditional religion, destroyed the temples honoring Aten, and revived old artistic styles.

21. Bust of Nefertiti. *Ägyptisches Museum, Berlin. Painted limestone. Dynasty XVIII, ca. 1360 B.C.E. Carefully balanced and exquisitely finished, this sophisticated image of female beauty was unusual in Egyptian art.*

22. Amenhotep IV (Akhenaten). *Egyptian Museum, Cairo. Stone. Dynasty XVIII, ca. 1365 B.C.E. From the temple erected by Akhenaten and dedicated to the sun god, the elongated features of this head reflect the breakdown of tradition while maintaining an image of authority.*

22

23. Akhenaten and his family. *Egyptian Museum, Cairo. From Tell el-Amarna. Painted limestone. Dynasty XVIII, ca. 1360 B.C.E. Akhenaten's religious revolution had a dramatic effect on the portrayal of human figures. The rigid earlier formulas were replaced by a more fluid approach to form and more intimate images of the divine ruling family.*

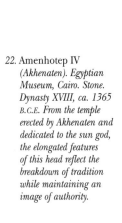

23

21

Crete

Egypt established contacts with the other civilizations in the eastern Mediterranean. Archaeological evidence, a large quantity of Cretan and Mycenaean pottery found in Egypt, testifies to the strong trade links between these cultures, but surprisingly little is known about either Crete or Mycenae. Although Homer immortalized Mycenaean culture in his epic poems, the *Iliad* and the *Odyssey*, and later Greek sources refer to a King Minos of Crete, the physical remains of Minoan Crete and Mycenaean Greece were not discovered until the nineteenth century, when archaeologists successfully followed the trail indicated in classic literary texts.

At the center of Cretan power was the palace at Knossos. Its intricate plan, most likely the basis of the mythical labyrinth of Daedalus, was the result of repeated additions and ongoing repairs. The palace's scale and decoration, much of it restored, provides evidence of an advanced civilization. Clay tablets inscribed with two different syllabic scripts (Linear A and B) testify to the literacy of Minoan Crete. Linear A has not yet been deciphered, which has hampered our understanding of the culture. Statues like the goddess holding sacred snakes (see Figure 25) or the vase in the form of a bull (see Figure 24) are generally assumed to have a religious association. Minoan civilization came to an abrupt end in about 1450 B.C.E. The theory that its demise resulted from a volcanic eruption on nearby Santorini, while attractive, is probably false. The more likely explanation was the rise of a warlike and expansionist culture on the Greek mainland, centered in Mycenae. The latter theory is substantiated by the existence in Knossos of Linear B, which has been deciphered and found to be a form of Greek.

24. Rhyton (drinking vessel) in the form of a bull's head. *Archaeological Museum, Heraklion. Steatite. Ca. 1500 B.C.E. The proliferation of bulls in Cretan art and the labyrinthine plan of the palace at Knossos have reinforced its association with the ancient Greek myth of Theseus and the Minotaur.*

25. Snake Goddess. *Archaeological Museum, Heraklion. Glazed terracotta. Ca. 1550 B.C.E. Elegant and feminine, this small statue of a religious figure holding snakes has little in common with the stylized images of Egyptian religious art.*

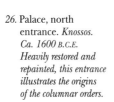

26. Palace, north entrance. *Knossos. Ca. 1600 B.C.E. Heavily restored and repainted, this entrance illustrates the origins of the columnar orders.*

Mycenae

The Mycenaeans arrived in Greece at about 2000 B.C.E., absorbing elements of the indigenous culture. Mycenae itself dominated a number of quasi-independent centers, including Athens. Early Mycenaean culture owes much to the Minoans, but later evolved its own forms and styles.

The Mycenaeans developed a distinctive circular structure, or *tholos*, for their royal tombs; they filled the tombs with objects of considerable value but whose significance remains obscure. Royal palaces were built as fortresses, reflecting the importance of military strength in their acquisition of land and wealth. The Mycenaean civilization collapsed in the twelfth century B.C.E., during a period of general unrest in the eastern Mediterranean that included the Trojan War. The Mycenaean dominion in Greece was replaced by that of the Dorians, an invading tribe from the north whose development set the scene for the emergence of classical Greece.

27

28

27. Funeral mask. *National Archaeological Museum, Athens. Gold. Ca. 1500 B.C.E. Found in the royal tomb, this solid funeral mask belonged to a king, often identified as Agamemnon, immortalized by Homer in the Iliad.*

28. Lion Gate. *Mycenae. Ca. 1250 B.C.E. The massive, defensive entrance to Mycenae reflected the military culture of these early Greeks.*

THE FERTILE, WELL-DRAINED VALLEY of the Yellow River provided an ideal climate for the development of primitive agricultural communities in China around 5000 B.C.E. Excavations at Neolithic sites have yielded large quantities of stone tools and elaborately decorated pottery. Evidence suggests that the silkworm and jade, both distinctive features of later Chinese culture, date as far back as 2000 B.C.E. With the emergence of the Shang Dynasty (ca. 1550–1030 B.C.E.), Chinese civilization began to take on a more definitive character.

CHAPTER 4

CIVILIZATION AND EMPIRE IN CHINA

Early Chinese Art

The Shang Dynasty

Ancient literary references to the Shang Dynasty have only recently been supported by archaeological evidence. Oracle bones with distinct inscriptions indicate that a written language, using symbols that were the ancestors of modern Chinese characters, had developed by that time. Excavations at Anyang (Honan Province) and other sites provide evidence of established urban communities. The most spectacular Shang remains, however, are its tombs. Shang rulers were buried with all of their personal possessions, and the tradition included

1

human sacrifice on a large scale. Among the objects found in the Shang tombs are a number of elaborately decorated bronzes, which demonstrate considerable technical ability. These ritual vessels were made for offering food and wine to ancestral spirits, the central feature of ancient Chinese religious practice. The importance of these objects is reflected in the distinctive shapes that evolved for separate stages of the ritual. The *ding* was used for cooking food over an open fire, its legs functioning as heat conductors. The *chia* performed a similar function for wine. And the *zun*, whose shape derived from older ceramic traditions, was used for libations.

The Chou Dynasty

The Shang Dynasty declined and was finally overthrown by a seminomadic people called the Chou. Under the Chou Dynasty (1027–256 B.C.E.), the kingdom was divided into feudal states. Shang traditions continued, and the increasingly ornate forms and decoration of bronze vessels reflected the growing elaboration of court ritual. In turn, the power of the Chou Dynasty declined. Although the Chou court remained the focus of cultural unity within the kingdom, the feudal states struggled among themselves for control. This period of political chaos and social instability was also one of major importance in the development of intellectual thought. Many schools of philosophy flourished, all attempting to find a remedy for moral and political decline. The parallel with contemporaneous developments in the Greek city-states is striking. Unlike the Greeks, however, the Chinese did not question the propriety of monarchic rule, an essential element of their ancestor worship. Confucius, who died in 479 B.C.E., ten years before Socrates was

1. Yang-shao pottery. *Terracotta. Neolithic. Contemporaneous with the ancient civilizations in Mesopotamia, Egypt, and the Indus valley, neolithic pottery in China was produced on a wheel and elaborately decorated with abstract designs.*

2. Ding. *From Zhengzhou, Henan province. Bronze. Shang Dynasty. Discovered only in the twentieth century, the Shang Dynasty tombs have revealed a wealth of objects, ranging from bronze ritual vessels, jade, weapons, and chariots to the bones of humans slaughtered in sacrifice.*

3. Tripod cooking jar. *Terracotta. Late Neolithic. The tripod form of this vessel was designed to sit over a fire.*

2

3

born, introduced the concept that the right to high office should be based on merit, not birth. He taught that a political system based on loyalty and respect for authority was a guarantee of peace and order. Other schools differed. The Legalist philosophers believed that the authority of the state should be enforced by a rigid code of laws. The Taoists developed a more mystical philosophy based on submission to the universal principle, or Tao, and emphasized the pursuit of harmony with nature. This had an important effect on the development of poetry and painting in Chinese culture.

The First Emperor of the Ch'in

At the same time that the Romans were fighting for supremacy in the Mediterranean, a similar contest was taking place in China, as the most powerful states struggled for control of the old Chou kingdom. The resulting Ch'in Dynasty (221–207 B.C.E.) united the country under a single king, who named himself Ch'in Shih Huang-ti ("First Emperor of the Ch'in"), a choice deliberately recalling one of the semidivine heroic rulers of Chinese myth.

The reign of Shih Huang-ti marked a major revolution in Chinese society. All traces of the old Chou Dynasty were destroyed,

and the old feudal rulers were dispossessed. The empire was organized under a single language and code of law, with law enforcement and tax collection handled by government officials in separate administrative districts. Under the influence of the Legalist philosopher Han Fei Zi, occupations that did not contribute directly to the military success of the state were reviled and many scholars were put to death. Many books, especially historical and philosophical works, were burned; texts on medicine and agriculture were generally spared. Weights, measures, and axle widths were standardized. Goods were stamped

5

6

4. *Zun. From Lingbao, Henan province. Bronze. Shang Dynasty. The molds for Chinese bronzes were made of terracotta and assembled into a whole before being filled with the molten alloy.*

5. Chia. *From Hejia, Sha'anxi province. Bronze. Shang Dynasty. The form of Shang bronzes derived from earlier terracotta vessels, but the new material allowed for the development of more elegant tripods, decorated here with phoenix uprights.*

6. Painting on silk. *Excavated from a Chou tomb, Changsha, Hunan province. Late Warring States. Silk is thought to have existed in Neolithic China, but this painting on silk of a dragon lifting a man to heaven is one of the earliest examples found to date.*

4

7

7. Zun. *Bronze. Late Shang or early Chou Dynasty. Later bronze vessels became more ambitious in style, imitating animals and birds.*

with a symbol to identify their maker, in an effort to ensure quality.

The emperor's architectural patronage was prodigious. His vast palaces included a series of apartments modeled on those of each of the feudal rulers he had conquered. The supreme symbol of his imperial power, however, was the Great Wall (later faced in stone), built by convicts; countless lives were lost during its construction. Shih Huang-ti's fear of death was well documented, and a workforce of 700,000 men began building his tomb, designed to ensure his immortality, soon after he became emperor. The now famous army of terracotta warriors, which guarded him in death, was found approximately one mile from the tomb itself beginning in 1974. The figures were carefully buried under a wooden roof waterproofed by woven matting and clay; the efforts at preservation underscored the importance of their function. The three pits in which they were found contained more than 7,300 life-size soldiers, including both infantry and crossbowmen, as well as horses and chariots. The careful rendering of detail, such as protective iron-mail coats and studs on the soles of boots, makes every soldier authentic and formidable. The human figures are similar in size and bulk, but their facial features differ considerably, reinforcing the idea that this was a real army of individual soldiers. The wooden vehicles have disintegrated into dust, but the bronze chariots found near the tomb itself have survived. They probably belonged to the imperial household, their greater status indicated by the use of more expensive and durable materials.

Shih Huang-ti died in 210 B.C.E. and was succeeded by his son, who was assassinated four years later. The Ch'in Dynasty, albeit brief, was among the most important in Chinese history. The unification of China

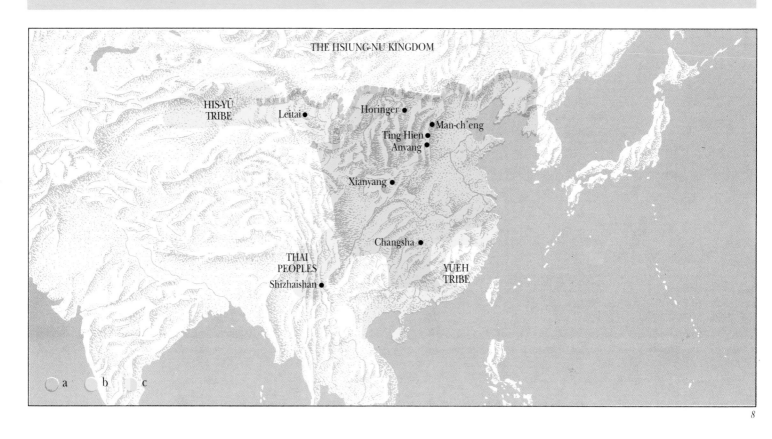

THE HSIUNG-NU KINGDOM

HIS-YÜ TRIBE

Leitai ●

Horinger ●

● Man-ch'eng
Ting Hien ●
Anyang ●

Xianyang ●

Changsha ●

THAI PEOPLES

YÜEH TRIBE

Shizhaishan ●

● a   ● b   ● c

8

8. *Map of ancient China:*
   a) The Great Wall,
      which was rebuilt
      and refaced many times
      after its inception
      in ca. 220 B.C.E.;
   b) early kingdoms;
   c) Han Empire in
      221 C.E.

9. Terracotta army. *Xianyang. Terracotta. Ch'in Dynasty. Discovered in 1974 by farmers digging a well, the terracotta army was made to guard the first emperor of China, Shih Huang-ti, after his death. It included 7,300 life-size figures and took thirty-eight years to complete.*

10. Soldier. *Xianyang. Terracotta. Ch'in Dynasty. Precise attention to detail and form, as well as to individualized facial characteristics, reflected the importance of the project to the emperor.*

11. State coach. *Xianyang. Bronze. Ch'in Dynasty. From the wheel hubs to the details of the harness and the forms of the horses, no effort was spared to create lifelike images.*

12. Soldier. *Xianyang. Terracotta. Ch'in Dynasty.*

under a single emperor, who exercised power through a highly organized bureaucracy, provided an important model for later dynasties.

The Han Dynasty

The establishment of the Han Dynasty (206 B.C.E.–220 C.E.) consolidated the revolutionary changes made by the Ch'in, but the Legalist domination of the bureaucracy was replaced by Confucianism. The Han emperors were of humble origin and favored the new educated classes. The empire was now administered by a meritocratic elite, chosen through examination. The Ch'in ban on books was lifted, and Emperor Wu-ti founded the Imperial Academy (136 B.C.E.) for the education of government officials, who prided themselves on their loyalty to the emperor and their respect for scholarship and the past. The historian Ssu-ma Ch'ien standardized the imperial ancestry and the lines of descent from divine rulers of the Chinese past. His history of China formed the basis of the Standard Histories that documented subsequent dynasties and provided a systematic historical record unrivaled in the world. The power of the centralized imperial authority was reinforced by elaborate ritual and ceremony.

The enormous imperial palaces of the Han emperors, made of wood and lavishly decorated with rich colors and wall paintings, have survived only in literary descriptions. The use of more permanent materials was reserved for the imperial tombs, which included vaulted brick structures and stone statues and reliefs. One of the few imperial Han tombs to have been discovered (1968) was that of Emperor Wu Ti's brother, Liu Sheng (died 113 B.C.E.), and his wife, Princess Tou Wan.

9

10

11

12

Both bodies were clad in extravagant burial suits made from jade plaques sewn with gold thread. Jade was not only extremely hard to carve and therefore expensive, but also erroneously thought to have the power of preserving bodies from decay. The development of iron-cutting tools at the end of the Chou Dynasty encouraged more elaborate designs and made jade objects more widely available. Originally restricted to religious and funerary use, jade items such as the *pi*, a flat disc symbolizing heaven, eventually lost their ritual meaning and were regarded as objects of beauty, collected by the new scholarly classes.

The increasing prosperity of China under the Han Dynasty owed much to the expansion of trade. Chinese silk was sold in markets throughout the Roman Empire. The wealth acquired by bureaucrats and court officials allowed them to become patrons of the arts, widening a field traditionally reserved for emperors and nobles. The rigid hierarchy of court life inevitably led to a correspondence between formal status and personal expenditures; indications of rank were duly recorded in tombs. One particular official could boast the use of a parasol, fourteen carriages, twenty-eight servants, and thirty-nine horses.

Such tombs were often decorated with processions of carriages carrying the official and his staff on an inspection tour, the size of the retinue indicating his rank. Following the pattern established under the Shang and Chou Dynasties, the dead were buried with objects of value, especially bronzes. The contents of Han tombs also included terracotta models of buildings, ranging from pigsties to grand houses, and other objects of everyday life. This move away from the inclusion of material wealth in tombs reflected the increasingly symbolic nature of the ritual, with important implications for later dynasties.

13

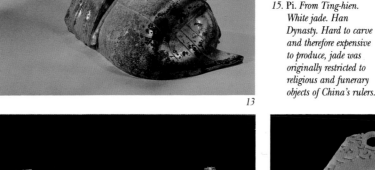

13. Lamp. *From Man-ch'eng, Hebei province. Bronze. Han Dynasty. This lamp in the shape of a girl was one of the many possessions buried with Princess Tou Wan.*

14. Burial suit of Princess Tou Wan. *From Man-ch'eng, Hebei province. Han Dynasty. Made from 2,160 jade plaques stitched together with gold thread, this extravagant burial vestment illustrated the wealth of the Han Dynasty.*

15. Pi. *From Ting-hien. White jade. Han Dynasty. Hard to carve and therefore expensive to produce, jade was originally restricted to religious and funerary objects of China's rulers.*

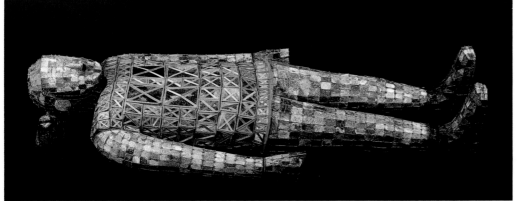

14

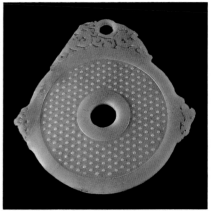

15

The Han Dynasty went into decline, and the Chinese institutionalized a new concept of imperial mandate: that the rise and fall of dynasties was a reflection of the passage from morality to decadence. As one dynasty lost its ability to rule justly, the Mandate of Heaven was withdrawn and passed to another. The Han Dynasty fell in 220 C.E. and was followed by a long period of disorder. It would be nearly four centuries before another strong ruler would impose his rule throughout China, by which time the Han Dynasty had become known as the Golden Age of Chinese culture.

The emergence of Confucianism as a dominant current in Chinese culture reflected the importance of ancestor worship in Chinese tradition. Not a religion in any formal sense, Confucianism was essentially a moral code governing social and political behavior. Confucius (ca. 551–479 B.C.E.) was considered neither a prophet nor divine, but he was respected as a philosopher. His writings stressed the importance of duty and respect from a son to his father,

ANCESTOR WORSHIP AND THE ARTS

both literally in the family unit and metaphorically in the social context, i.e., the unquestioning loyalty to the emperor. Emphasizing conformity and tradition, the Confucian system was regulated by a set of correct, as opposed to unacceptable, modes of behavior. Ancestor worship was not, strictly speaking, a religious act but expressed the continuity of

loyalty due to the deceased by their successors. Pious descendants made offerings to their ancestors in rooms attached to burial chambers, and the great Shang bronzes were designed as part of these ceremonies. The contents of Han tombs reinforced the importance of ancestral influence after death. Family burial mounds included a wide range of objects, from bamboo cooking utensils and lacquered toilet sets to books and silk clothes.

CIVILIZATION AND EMPIRE IN CHINA

16. Flying Horse. *From Leitai, Gansu province. Bronze. Western Han Dynasty, late second century or early third century C.E. The horse was a symbol of Han power, but the grace of this animal, with its hoof resting on a swallow, suggests elegance rather than brute strength.*

17. Han official in his chariot. *From the tomb of a Han general in Leitai, Gansu province. Bronze. Western Han Dynasty, late second century or early third century C.E. Lacking a parasol of high rank, this official was a member of a large procession of dignitaries.*

16

18. Model of house. *From Shizhaishan, Yunnan province. Bronze. Han Dynasty. Most ancient Chinese buildings were made of wood and have long since disappeared. These tomb sculptures give some idea of the style of Han buildings.*

19. Wall Painting. *From Horinger tombs, Inner Mongolia. Han Dynasty. Early wall paintings in Chinese tombs typically depict the rank of their owners in official processions.*

17

18

19

GREECE AND ROME

If the "fertile crescent" was the cradle of the earliest civilizations in the Middle East, Greece can justly be defined as the "birthplace" of the Western world. The two great powers on the Mediterranean, the Greeks and later the Romans, sprang from those cultures that had flourished during the Aegean era around the second millennium B.C.E. Crete, as well as Egypt and the Middle East, provided the cultural foundations for the new ideas.

After the Dorian invasion, Greece reorganized into city-states: the polis.

A new impulse sprang from the unequalled cultural, political, and religious unity and blossomed in an outstanding urban organization that had the acropolis and agora as its focal points.

Even Homer's epic poems served as an important tool for unification. A new artistic language was born (one that was of "human dimension") and it spread through the Ancient Greek settlements in Southern Italy. Even the Etruscans, whose trade and contacts with the Hellenic world

are well documented, were inspired by Greek art. But, without a doubt, the greatest heir to their civilization was Rome.

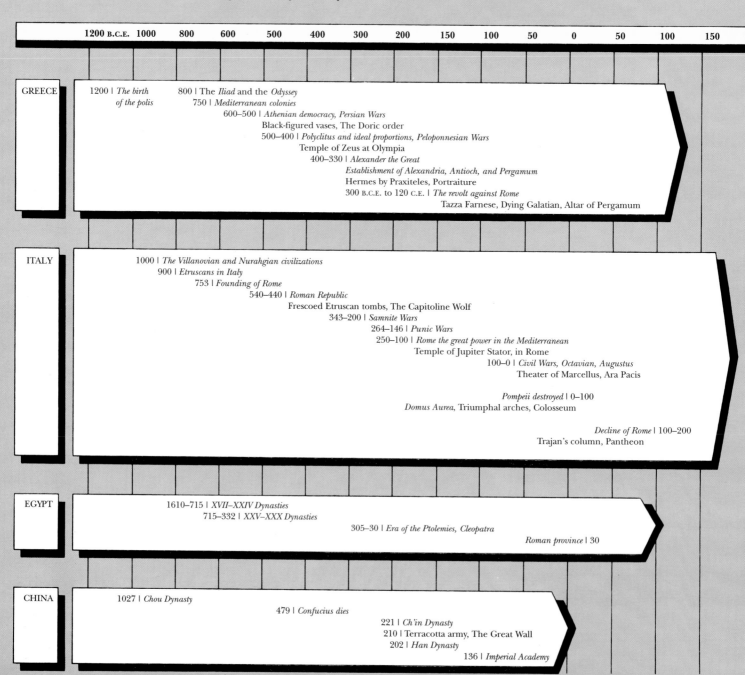

| 1200 B.C.E. | 1000 | 800 | 600 | 500 | 400 | 300 | 200 | 150 | 100 | 50 | 0 | 50 | 100 | 150 |

GREECE

1200 | *The birth of the polis*
800 | The *Iliad* and the *Odyssey*
750 | *Mediterranean colonies*
600–500 | *Athenian democracy, Persian Wars*
Black-figured vases, The Doric order
500–400 | *Polyclitus and ideal proportions, Peloponnesian Wars*
Temple of Zeus at Olympia
400–330 | *Alexander the Great*
Establishment of Alexandria, Antioch, and Pergamum
Hermes by Praxiteles, Portraiture
300 B.C.E. to 120 C.E. | *The revolt against Rome*
Tazza Farnese, Dying Galatian, Altar of Pergamum

ITALY

1000 | *The Villanovian and Nurahgian civilizations*
900 | *Etruscans in Italy*
753 | *Founding of Rome*
540–440 | *Roman Republic*
Frescoed Etruscan tombs, The Capitoline Wolf
343–200 | *Samnite Wars*
264–146 | *Punic Wars*
250–100 | *Rome the great power in the Mediterranean*
Temple of Jupiter Stator, in Rome
100–0 | *Civil Wars, Octavian, Augustus*
Theater of Marcellus, Ara Pacis
Pompeii destroyed | 0–100
Domus Aurea, Triumphal arches, Colosseum
Decline of Rome | 100–200
Trajan's column, Pantheon

EGYPT

1610–715 | *XVII–XXIV Dynasties*
715–332 | *XXV–XXX Dynasties*
305–30 | *Era of the Ptolemies, Cleopatra*
Roman province | 30

CHINA

1027 | *Chou Dynasty*
479 | *Confucius dies*
221 | *Ch'in Dynasty*
210 | Terracotta army, The Great Wall
202 | *Han Dynasty*
136 | *Imperial Academy*

THE EMERGENCE OF THE GREEK
city-state, or *polis*, has proved to be
of profound importance to the
history of civilization. The fall of Mycenae
during the twelfth century B.C.E. was
followed by the migration of various Greek
tribes, notably the Dorians from the north,
who moved into Greece and forced
the indigenous Ionians into Asia Minor.
Geographical barriers and a sense
of independence encouraged the
development of separate city-states,
each with its own ruling authority, army,
and coinage. Conflicts inevitably
resulted, but competition was partially

CHAPTER 5

CLASSICAL
GREECE

Art in the Greek City-States

institutionalized in events such as the
Olympic Games, founded in 776 B.C.E.
This month-long festival, staged every four
years, was held to honor the god Zeus,
but it stressed the cultural unity of the
Greek states. It was open to all and
preceded by a declaration of truce.
The states shared a common language
—Doric and Ionic were Greek dialects—
and the same pantheon of gods.

In about 750 B.C.E., population growth
led to the founding of Greek colonies
throughout the Mediterranean, especially
in southern Italy and Sicily. These followed
the established pattern of independent

1

city-states, growing in number as trade increased; by 600 B.C.E. they totaled nearly 1,500. With a sense of superiority over non-Greek-speaking peoples, whom they regarded as barbarians, and intent on spreading Hellenic influence, the new city-states maintained strong cultural links with Greece.

Vase Decoration

Trade continued to expand, and the Greeks prospered. Their elaborately painted pottery containers were decorated with scenes depicting religious, cultural, and economic aspects of Greek life. The main export was olive oil, and the importance of agriculture was stressed in the decoration of storage jars and other pottery. Stories from Greek history and mythology were another frequent subject. The *François Vase*, for example, portrayed scenes from the lives of Achilles and Theseus. This krater, or wine-mixing jar, was made in Athens, exported to Italy, and found in an Etruscan grave, indicating the extent of Greek trade. The black-figure technique of painting was developed in Corinth and taken up in Athens before 600 B.C.E.

The style owes much to earlier Mycenaean and Egyptian representations, which was also true of early, or Archaic, Greek sculpture.

Archaic Figure Sculpture

Greek figure sculpture developed in a religious context. Male and female figures, the *kouros* and *kore*, were made as dedications to a god or as memorials over graves. The kouros shown below (see Figure 5), from a cemetery in Attica, was never intended as a true portrait yet represents the young Kroisos, who died

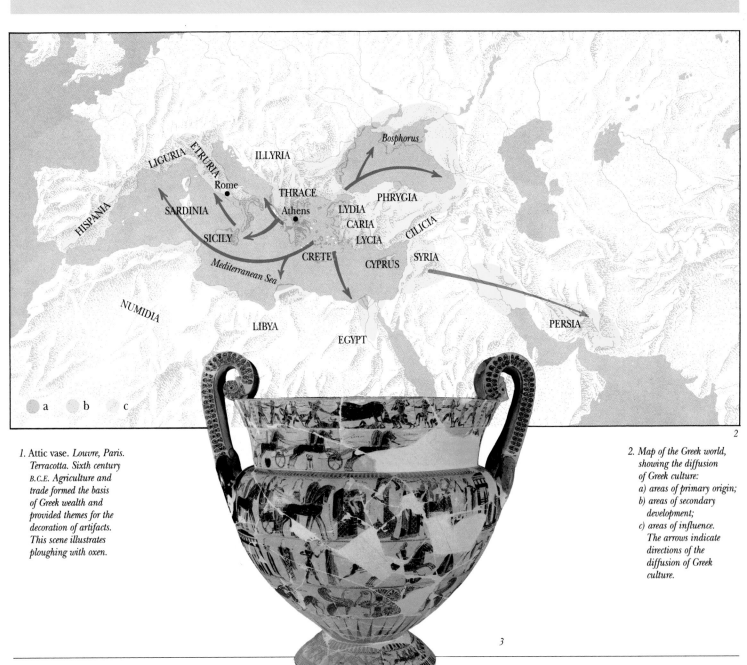

1. Attic vase. Louvre, Paris. Terracotta. Sixth century B.C.E. Agriculture and trade formed the basis of Greek wealth and provided themes for the decoration of artifacts. This scene illustrates ploughing with oxen.

2. Map of the Greek world, showing the diffusion of Greek culture: a) areas of primary origin; b) areas of secondary development; c) areas of influence. The arrows indicate directions of the diffusion of Greek culture.

in battle. The male kouros, typically a nude, stressed physical attributes and reflected the importance of athletics and other tests of strength in a society whose survival depended on superior physical power. The kore, by contrast, was inevitably clothed (see Figure 4). Although her breasts are visible beneath the stylized drapery, her face is almost indistinguishable from that of the kouros. The kore was intended as a status symbol, her femininity —and the wealth of her male patron— embodied in her clothes, elaborate hairstyle, and jewelry.

The Spirit of Inquiry

The Greeks revolutionized thinking about the physical world and the individual's relation to it. Up to that time, explanations generally had been based on myth; supernatural events provided simple explanations for otherwise incomprehensible phenomena. Greek philosophers tried to *understand*. Through observation and analysis, they sought rational explanations and provable theories about the world around them. Thales of Miletus (ca. 636–546 B.C.E.) predicted a solar eclipse, and Pythagoras

of Samos (ca. 560–480 B.C.E.) established basic principles of mathematics and astronomy.

By the fifth century B.C.E., interest had shifted to "man" and human experience. Hippocrates (ca. 460–377 B.C.E.) applied the scientific method to the study of human diseases with a rigorous observation of symptoms, and Herodotus (ca. 485–430 B.C.E.) wrote a systematic account of the Persian Wars. Plato (ca. 428–347 B.C.E.) developed theories of social and political relationships, education, and aesthetics in pursuit of an ideal world. The new spirit of inquiry challenged traditional beliefs.

4. Kore. *National Archaeological Museum, Athens. Marble. Ca. 520 B.C.E. The ornamentation and contrivances of the kore were a marked contrast to the natural physicality of the kouros, a telling comment on the relative status of male and female in Greek society.*

5. Kouros. *National Archaeological Museum, Athens. Marble. Ca. 530 B.C.E. From a cemetery in Attica, this statue was never intended as a portrait but as a representation of Kroisos, who had died in battle.*

3. The François Vase. *Museo Archeologico, Florence. Terracotta. Ca. 560 B.C.E. This Attic krater from the Etruscan city of Vulci is an early example of a signed work. It includes the signatures of both its painter, Clitias, and its potter, Ergotimos. Pride in creativity and awareness of individual style were among the major Greek contributions to the history of art.*

4

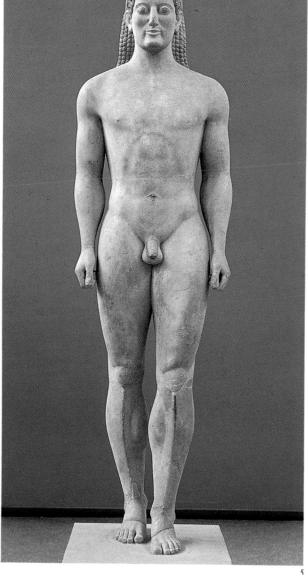

5

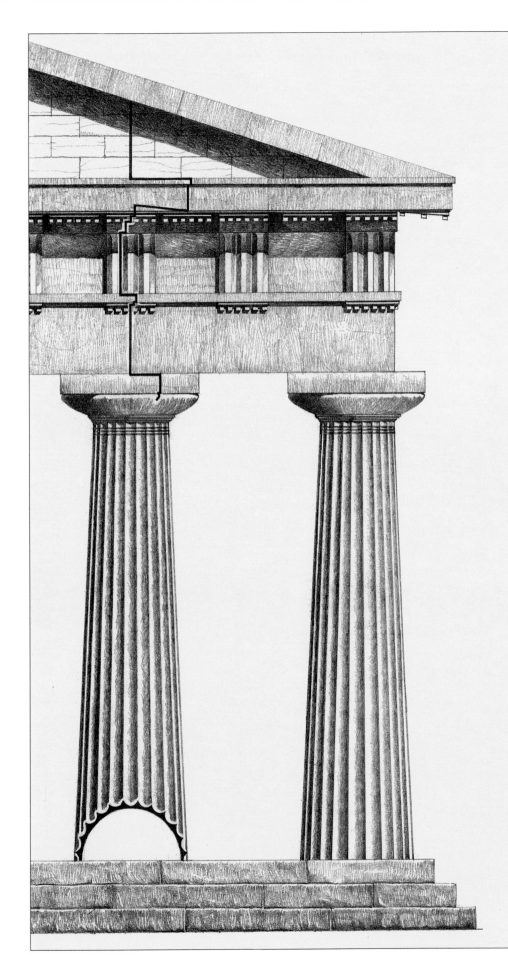

The Doric order was developed by the Greeks as a visual expression of cultural unity. From its origins in Greece during the mid sixth century B.C.E., the style was soon adopted in the Greek city-states of southern Italy and Sicily. Its basic characteristics were established by 600 B.C.E., and later changes amounted to refinements.

Reflecting increasing Greek prosperity, the development of Doric style coincided with the transition from timber to stone in the construction of monumental architecture. Tapered columns sitting directly on the stylobate without bases supported a distinctive capital, composed of two sections: the rounded *echinus* and the square *abacus*. The function of the capital was to hold up the rectangular blocks forming the architrave; its relative size decreased as Greek builders became more competent with new construction methods. Above the architrave were the frieze and cornice, the three elements combining to form the entablature.

The Doric frieze reflected the style of earlier wood buildings. The grooved slabs, known as *triglyphs,* recalled the ends of wooden rafters. Their translation into a decorative context was reinforced by the *guttae* below, derived from the earlier wood pegs. The spaces between them, *metopes,* were usually decorated with sculpted reliefs that related to the function or dedication of the building.

All three Greek orders (Doric, Ionic, and Corinthian) were adopted by the Romans for the articulation of their buildings. Vitruvius, a Roman architectural theorist, set rules for their relative proportions and other prescriptions for their use. His recommendation that the Doric be used for masculine deities was not consistent with its application in classical Greece, where it had stronger political and cultural overtones. Never popular in imperial Rome, the Doric order reappeared during the Renaissance when, following Vitruvian thinking, it was associated with morality. A true revival came with the advent of neoclassicism during the nineteenth century.

In many city-states, oligarchies (rule by the few) replaced the old monarchies. At the same time, the freedom of the individual was enshrined in constitutions. By 500 B.C.E., the Athenians had broadened the ruling class to include all free male citizens, a political system they called democracy (from *demos,* "people," and *kratia,* "power").

A New Architectural Language

The desire to impose mathematical order on the natural world found expression in the development of a formal architectural language, which emphasized Greek cultural unity. As wealth increased, stone replaced wood in the construction of important buildings, notably temples. The new stone temples imitated their wooden predecessors as closely as possible. The ends of the transverse wood beams that had supported the roof and the pegs that had held them in place were translated into *triglyphs* and *guttae,* separated by *metopes,* or spaces, that decorated stone friezes. A distinctive capital developed at the top of the column, with a rounded *echinus* (so called because of its similarity to a sea urchin) topped by an angular *abacus,* supporting the stone blocks of the entablature. These features defined what was later called the Doric order, an architectural counterpart to the Dorian dialect. Plain, sturdy, and conservative, the Doric order was characterized by its simple capital, distinctive frieze, and squat columns. As builders became more confident and proficient, the capital and abacus became lighter. This trend toward the decorative was developed in the Treasury of the Athenians at Delphi, with its elegantly proportioned columns and sculpted metopes, where the Athenians housed their dedications to Apollo.

6. Treasury of the Athenians. *Delphi. Soon after 490 B.C.E. (rebuilt 1906). A desire for elegance and technical precision led to a slimmer, lighter interpretation of the Doric order.*

7. Temple. *Segesta, Sicily. Late fifth century B.C.E. Massive and imposing, this Doric temple in Sicily illustrates the spread of Greek influence in the Mediterranean.*

6

8. Temple of Hera (Basilica) and Temple of Neptune. *Paestum. The capitals of the Basilica (ca. 550 B.C.E.) in the foreground are considerably heavier than those of the rear Temple of Neptune (ca. 450 B.C.E.), illustrating the refinement of the Doric order.*

7

8

Greek Temples

Except in states ruled by tyrants, art was not used as propaganda for individual rulers. The civic temple, not the royal palace, was the image of the Greek city-state. Despite their omnipotence, the Greek gods are remarkable in religious history for their human weaknesses: they are quarrelsome, greedy, emotional, lustful, and sometimes even deceitful. This is less surprising in a culture that valued individual freedom; the reciprocal nature of the Greek relationship with their gods was more open than most. As a result, the classic Greek temple lacked hierarchical elements, such as a grand entrance, and was surrounded by a uniform colonnade. The inner sanctuary housed a statue of the relevant deity but was not used for services; these typically took place outside. The emphasis on exterior design also reflected the civic function of the building. Sculptural decoration was typically limited to the two pediments and the metopes in the frieze. At the Temple of Zeus in Olympia, completed about 460 B.C.E., contemporary interest in the human form is reflected in the emerging realism of sculptural elements. The trend is most noticeable in the figure of Apollo on the west pediment, whose facial features show a marked change from the kouroi of the preceding century. The metopes of the temple depict the mythical labors of Hercules, demonstrating the same concern for realistic portrayal. The severity of style is typical of the Dorian preference for simplicity and moderation.

Analysis of the Human Form

The philosophical interest in "man" was clearly reflected in Greek sculpture, which displayed a growing fascination with the human

9. Athena, Hercules, and Atlas. *Olympia, Museum. Marble. Ca. 460 B.C.E. A metope from the Temple of Zeus at Olympia, this relief depicts the story of the golden apples of the Hesperides, one of the seven Labors of Hercules. With the help of Athena, Hercules is holding up the world for Atlas, who has just returned with the apples and offers them to Hercules.*

9

10. Apollo and a centaur. *Olympia, Museum. Marble. Ca. 460 B.C.E. Part of the relief of the west pediment at the Temple of Zeus, Olympia. The figure of Apollo illustrates a growing interest in realistic portrayal, in contrast to the earlier stylization of the kouroi.*

10

11

form. Facial features were based increasingly on the observation of real models, although statues like the *Charioteer* (Figure 13) were by no means portraits. The use of bronze allowed for the development of poses that would have been impossible in marble. The statue of Poseidon (or Zeus?) with his right arm stretched back to throw a spear (Figure 14) is clearly based on first-hand observation and analysis of an actual pose. The same is true of the *Discobolos* (Figure 12). Despite the innovations in style, however, the function of these statues changed little. Statues of athletes were generally religious offerings, symbolizing excellence in human achievement. The distinctive pose of the *Doryphorus*, or spear bearer (Figure 11), was especially influential. The statue was carved by Polyclitus to illustrate his treatise on proportion. His emphasis on mathematical relationships to explain and codify the natural world typified the Greek intellectual revolution and led to other treatises on perspective and foreshortening. The ideal form, according to classic Greek thought, was to be found in mathematical proportions. The Greek words for order, moderation, arrangement, embellishment, and ornamentation all had the same root: *kosmos.* The Greeks were highly conscious of style and made qualitative judgments about art in much the same way that they recognized and assessed differences between their political leaders. Their minds were trained to do so. This insight is important in considering the great landmark of Greek architecture, the Athenian Acropolis.

Pericles and the Acropolis

At the beginning of the fifth century B.C.E., the Persian King Darius I led an invasion of Greece but was held off at the Battle of Marathon in 490 B.C.E. His successor,

11. Doryphorus (spear bearer). *Museo Nazionale, Naples. Marble. Roman copy of a Greek original by Polyclitus dating to ca. 450 B.C.E. The statue was originally carved to illustrate his treatise on the proportions of the human figure.*

12. Discobolos (discus thrower). *Museo delle Terme, Rome. Marble. Roman copy of a Greek bronze original dating to ca. 450 B.C.E. In their pursuit of realism, Greek sculptors became increasingly attentive to form and pose.*

13. Charioteer. *Delphi Museum. From the Sanctuary of Apollo. Bronze. Ca. 470 B.C.E. Simplicity and moderation were the hallmarks of classical Greek style.*

14. Poseidon (or Zeus?). *National Archeological Museum, Athens. Bronze. Ca. 460 B.C.E. The use of bronze allowed Greek sculptors to experiment with a wider variety of poses than those allowed by the more restrictive medium of marble.*

12

13

14

Xerxes I, mounted another invasion ten years later and overcame the combined armies of Sparta and Athens. The Persians marched into Athens, whose citizens fled to nearby islands, and burned the city. The tide finally turned with the defeat of the Persian fleet at Salamis in 480 B.C.E. The Greeks had emerged victorious, but the destruction of the buildings on the Athenian acropolis had been a severe blow to civic pride.

An acropolis, or upper city, was a common feature of Greek cities. It was the site of their most important buildings and the most visible symbol of civic power.

Rebuilding the Athenian acropolis was a celebration of the Greek victory but also a statement of the city's prestige. Pericles, the political leader of Athens from about 460 to 429 B.C.E., recognized the power of architecture as visual propaganda: it could be used to proclaim the Greek victory over Persia and to declare Athenian supremacy in the Greek world. Work on the Acropolis was paid for by funds contributed in the interest of defending Greek liberty from further Achaemenid (Persian) threats.

Pericles's first project was the largest and most important structure on the site, the Parthenon, begun in 447 B.C.E.

Built in honor of the city's patron goddess, Athena Parthenos (Athena the Virgin), the temple was dedicated in 438 B.C.E. with the installation of a giant gold and ivory statue of Athena by the sculptor Phidias, a friend of Pericles. The structure itself followed the standard design of a Doric temple, but it was conspicuously grander and more refined than the Temple of Zeus at Olympia. In both temples, the number of columns on each side was one more than double the number at each end, but the Parthenon was two columns wider than the Temple of Zeus. The Parthenon was made entirely of marble,

15

15. Parthenon. *Athens. 447–432 B.C.E. The Temple of Athena was Pericles's first project on the Acropolis, and it housed a colossal statue of the goddess by Phidias. Grander than any earlier Doric temple, it provided an important symbol of Athenian authority in the Greek world.*

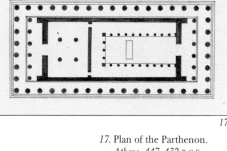

17

17. Plan of the Parthenon. *Athens. 447–432 B.C.E. Following Greek custom, the columns on each side totaled one more than double the number at each end.*

16

16. View of the Acropolis. *Athens. The Acropolis, or upper city, was the prime symbol of Athenian power and prestige. Its rebuilding after the destruction of the Persian wars was a major priority.*

whereas the Temple of Zeus restricted the use of marble to the roof and sculptural decoration. The sculpture on the Parthenon, designed and supervised by Phidias, gave expression to the Athenian victory. The two pediments were decorated with stories of Athena, paying tribute to her ultimate role in the campaign. Other sculpted images celebrated the power of the gods over their enemies, symbolizing both Greek and Athenian prestige. The Battle of Gods and Giants, or *Gigantomachy*, commemorated victory over the powerful Persians: brain outwitting brawn. Images depicting the mythical struggle between Lapiths and centaurs suggested the physical and cultural superiority of Greeks over barbarians: man against beast.

The Ionic Order

Athens was unwilling to give up its leadership position among the Greek city-states. Ultimately this led to conflict with its major rival, Sparta. Fighting broke out in 431 B.C.E. and split the Greek states along political lines: the democracies supported Athens; the monarchies and oligarchies joined with Sparta. Sparta, a Dorian Greek monarchy, was noted for athletic and military prowess, distrusting the intellectual and artistic achievements of Athens. In its struggle against Sparta, Athens sought the support of the Ionian city-states of Asia Minor.

It was at this point that the Ionic order was introduced on the Acropolis, first in the Temple of Athena Nike ("Bringer of Victory") and then in the Erechtheion. The latter was built in honor of the legendary king Erechtheus, purported to be an ancestor of both Athenians and Ionians, and reinforced the political theme. The Ionic order is proportionally slimmer than Doric and is further distinguished

18. *Detail of the Ionic order and decorative frieze taken from the Temple of Athena Nike.*

19

19. Horsemen. *British Museum, London. Marble. Ca. 440 B.C.E. Part of the Panathaenic procession carved in the frieze of the Parthenon. Phidias's exploitation of relief techniques was a major inspiration to later sculptors.*

20. Temple of Athena Nike. *Athens. Ca. 425 B.C.E. This small temple on the Acropolis marked the earliest use of the Ionic order in Athens.*

18

20

by a decorative capital. In contrast to the masculine severity of Doric design, the Ionian order has a distinctly feminine aspect. The Erechtheion, for example, features a portico supported by six elaborately dressed female figures, called caryatids. The introduction of the Ionic order in the prestigious buildings of the Athenian Acropolis again reflected the role of architecture in the pursuit of Athenian political aims.

As recounted in Thucydides's *History of the Peloponnesian War,* Athens finally fell to Sparta after a disastrous battle in Sicily (415–413 B.C.E.) and political turmoil erupted at home. Yet the intellectual and artistic achievements of Athens and other city-states secured a timeless legacy. The influence of classical Greece in the development of Western civilization cannot be overstated.

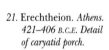

21. Erechtheion. *Athens. 421–406 B.C.E. Detail of caryatid porch.*

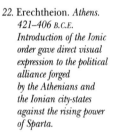

22. Erechtheion. *Athens. 421–406 B.C.E. Introduction of the Ionic order gave direct visual expression to the political alliance forged by the Athenians and the Ionian city-states against the rising power of Sparta.*

21

22

THE DEFEAT OF ATHENS BY SPARTA in the Peloponnesian war (431–404 B.C.E.) marked the end of an era. Democracy was restored in 403 B.C.E., but disillusionment with politics showed in the decline of popular Athenian involvement in government. Intellectual and cultural achievements gained in prestige. Not confined to Athens, this pattern inevitably weakened the confederacy of Greek city-states, creating a prime target for conquest. The opportunity was seized by King Philip II of Macedonia, whose highly trained army easily overcame the disorganized and dispirited Greeks.

CHAPTER 6

THE HELLENISTIC AGE

Art in the Empire of Alexander the Great

Despite the warnings of the Athenian orator Demosthenes, Athens was taken by Philip in 338 B.C.E. Upon Philip's death in 336 B.C.E., his son, Alexander, ruled a united Greek empire.

Cultural Change

The early fourth century B.C.E. was a period of social and political uncertainty in Athens, a fact reflected in sweeping cultural changes. State-commissioned comedy in fifth-century Athens had poked fun at government institutions, an approach that would have been unthinkable if these institutions had

1   2   3

in fact been threatened. Dramatists in the fourth century, by contrast, favored more contrived stories of private life. Attitudes also changed regarding depiction of the human body. Praxiteles's statue *Hermes* struck the traditional pose of classical male nudes, bearing his weight on one leg, but the figure was distinctly more idle than relaxed. Sensuality replaced the severe masculinity of earlier works, a trend reinforced by the growing preference for highly polished finishes. Frequent depictions of Dionysius, the god of wine, further reflected a turning away from the manly virtues of pre-war Athens. Concern with the beauty, rather than the strength, of the human body was also evidenced in female statuary. Praxiteles's *Aphrodite of Cnidos*, the first known female nude in classical Greek sculpture, stressed the sexual desirability of her physical form, an interpretation that had been ignored by earlier sculptors. Another distinct trend was an elongation of the human body. According to the classic prescription of Polyclitus (ca. 450 B.C.E.), the ideal ratio between the male head and total height was 1:8. Lysippus, however, preferred a ratio of 1:10 for his *Apoxyómenos*, or scraper, in about 330 B.C.E. By lengthening the arms and legs, he achieved a more graceful image.

Plato and Aristotle

Intellectual and cultural life in Athens during the early fourth century was perceived as morally degenerate by many Athenians. Prominent among them was the philosopher Plato (ca. 428–347 B.C.E.), who idealized the morality and austerity of the Athenian past. Plato's aesthetic theories have been immensely influential. He connected

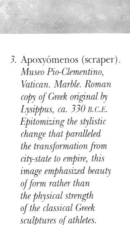

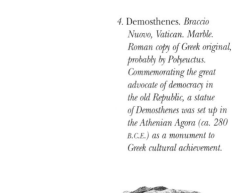

4. Demosthenes. *Braccio Nuovo, Vatican. Marble. Roman copy of Greek original, probably by Polyeuctus. Commemorating the great advocate of democracy in the old Republic, a statue of Demosthenes was set up in the Athenian Agora (ca. 280 B.C.E.) as a monument to Greek cultural achievement.*

4

5

1. *Praxiteles,* Hermes with young Dionysius. *Olympia, Museum. Marble. Ca. 350 B.C.E. Sensual and idle, the elongated proportions of this and similar statues were connected in Plato's mind with the decline of the Republic.*

2. Aphrodite. *Museo Pio-Clementino, Gabinetto delle Maschere, Vatican. Marble. Roman copy of Praxiteles's Aphrodite of Cnidos, ca. 350 B.C.E. The first female nude in Greek sculpture; the gesture of the right arm suggests a degree of modesty.*

3. Apoxyómenos (scraper). *Museo Pio-Clementino, Vatican. Marble. Roman copy of Greek original by Lysippus, ca. 330 B.C.E. Epitomizing the stylistic change that paralleled the transformation from city-state to empire, this image emphasized beauty of form rather than the physical strength of the classical Greek sculptures of athletes.*

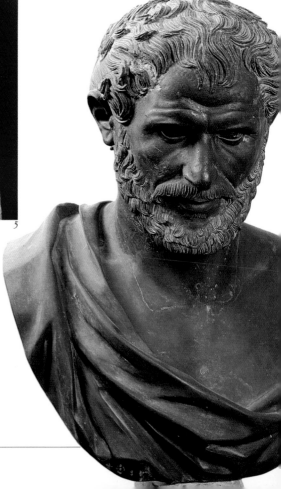

the stylistic changes that took place after 400 B.C.E. with more fundamental developments in Athenian society. Art was an expression of the culture in which it was produced, he maintained. Plato's criticism of contemporary extravagance and praise for the simplicity of the Greek past suggested a reluctance to accept change. King Philip, however, took a very different view of contemporary Athens. His high regard for its intellectual and cultural life had led him to appoint Aristotle (383–322 B.C.E.) as tutor to his son, Alexander. Aristotle had trained in Athens under Plato, but he had been born

in Macedonia. His interest in the real world stood in marked contrast to Plato's idealism. Aristotle understood how style could be manipulated to create a specific effect, an idea that would have important implications for the art of Alexander's empire.

Alexander the Great

Alexander the Great (356–323 B.C.E.) was aptly named. His reign lasted less than thirteen years, but his skills as a general and personal charisma created one of the great empires of the ancient world. Aristotle had

advised Alexander to treat the Greeks as equals and the barbarians as slaves. Believing in the innate superiority of his people, Alexander imposed Greek culture and political authority throughout the empire, appointing his own generals as provincial governors. When he died, the empire split into three kingdoms ruled by the descendants of these governors.

Imperial power creates splendor, and new cities grew up to rival Athens. Among these new centers of Greek culture were Pergamum, Antioch, and Alexandria. Conquests of the Persian and Egyptian empires gave Alexander and his successors

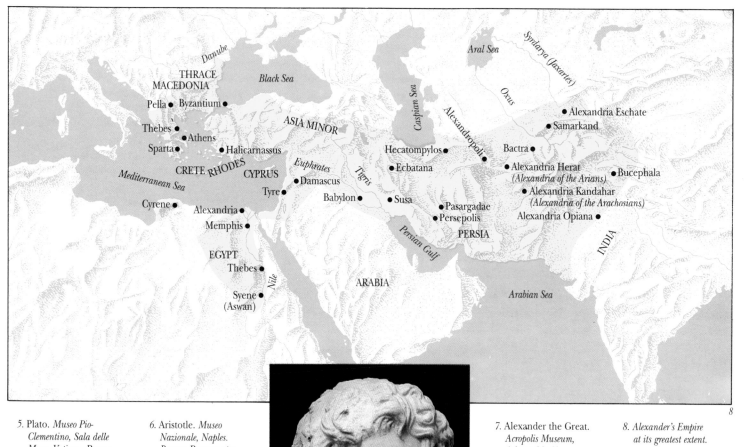

8

5. Plato. *Museo Pio-Clementino, Sala delle Muse, Vatican. Roman copy of a Greek original, ca. 330 B.C.E. Plato's contribution to the development of aesthetics was considerable. His belief that moderation, conservatism, and order were the product of a moral society influenced later developments in European art.*

6. Aristotle. *Museo Nazionale, Naples. Bronze. Roman copy of a Greek original from the fourth century B.C.E. The commemoration of individuals was unacceptable in democratic Athens. With the rise to power of Alexander the Great, images of personal achievement became more common.*

7. Alexander the Great. *Acropolis Museum, Athens. Marble. Ca. 340–330 B.C.E. One of the many statues commissioned by Alexander to reinforce his position. His employment of Apelles and Lysippus to create painted and sculpted portraits set a standard for imperial patronage.*

8. *Alexander's Empire at its greatest extent.*

7

a taste for imperial ostentation. Wealth and grandeur became essential elements of an art that gave visual expression of Greek ascendancy. Reflecting that purpose, painting and sculpture in Athens followed new directions in style and content. Among these trends was the derivation of an image for an absolute ruler, common in the art of Egypt and Persia but not in Athens. Alexander's triumph over King Darius III of Persia in 333 B.C.E. was commemorated in a painting that survives as a mosaic copy from Pompeii (Figure 9). The Parthenon sculptures of the previous century, which commemorated the Greek triumph over Persian invaders, had used mythological battles to represent the victory. Now, by commissioning a painting of the actual event, Alexander rejected the anonymous imagery of democratic Athens and directly emphasized his personal achievement. Still, the picture relies on a classic Greek device, expressing innate superiority through nudity and lack of artificial aids. The victorious Alexander is portrayed bareheaded on a horse, while the defeated Darius is protected by a helmet and chariot.

The Development of Portraiture

Portraiture was rare before 350 B.C.E., and its development in the Hellenistic empire illustrates the growing importance of the individual. The anonymous athletes that graced the old Greek temples were images of human excellence, not recognizable figures. The worship of physical prowess now gave way to public adulation of intellect, with statuary portraits honoring Plato, Aristotle, the orator Demosthenes, and others. Although relatively few images of Alexander remain, he is known to have been painted by Apelles and to have

9. Battle of Darius and Alexander. *Museo Nazionale, Naples. From the House of the Faun, Pompeii. Mosaic. Second century B.C.E., copied from Greek painting of ca. 300 B.C.E. The image of Alexander, bareheaded on his horse, reinforced the Greek victory over Darius, despite his helmet and protective chariot.*

commissioned sculptural portraits by Lysippus. The great rulers of Egypt and Persia had competed with gods, not other mortals, and the Hellenistic rulers adopted the same idea. Royal dynastic portraits replaced anonymous athletes in the temples. Mausolus, the king of Halicarnassus, stressed his equality with the gods by commissioning a giant statue of himself, a type previously associated with religion, to sit on top of his vast tomb. Other rulers were even more explicit in their expressions of power. The *Tazza Farnese*, for example, glorifies Queen Cleopatra of Egypt and her son,

10. Statue of Mausolus. *British Museum, London. From the Mausoleum of Halicarnassus. Marble. 359 B.C.E.*

10

THE MAUSOLEUM OF HALICARNASSUS

One of the Seven Wonders of the ancient world, the tomb to Mausolus, ruler of the state of Caria in Asia Minor during the fourth century B.C.E., has given us the word "mausoleum" for a sepulchral monument. Work on the tomb began while Mausolus was still alive and was finished by his wife, Artemisia, after his death in 353 B.C.E. According to legend, Artemisia drank her husband's ashes mixed with wine, making herself a living tomb for his remains. The marble monument was built on a truly grand scale. The main body of the tomb stood on a high block base, fronted by pillars and surmounted by a stepped pyramid approximately 23 feet (7 m) high. A statue of Mausolus crowned the structure. The Mausoleum was destroyed by earthquake sometime before 1400 C.E. Reconstructions are based on a description in Pliny's *Natural History* and on archaeological evidence at the site.

Monumental tombs for the rulers of a state were by no means a new development. The ancient Egyptians, most notably, had built the pyramids to mark the graves of the early pharaohs. This degree of self-glorification was unheard of in democratic Athens, where the commemoration of individual achievement was seen as inappropriate. But the Mausoleum of Halicarnassus was a foretaste of developments that were to take place in Greek culture with the rise of Alexander the Great. The Mausoleum exemplified the growth in extravagance and scale that Plato associated with the rise of monarchic power.

Ptolomy VI. In the company of the Nile, who holds a cornucopia, they are personified as Isis, the wife of the Nile, and her son Horus.

Alexandria

Alexander the Great founded many cities, designating sixteen of them Alexandria. Following the old Greek practice of naming cities after gods (such as Athens and Poseidonia, now Paestum), this came as another expression of the emperor's divine aspirations. Foremost among the sixteen cities was the new capital of Egypt, laid out in the classic grid pattern devised by Hippodamus of Miletus in the fifth century B.C.E. The orderly, rectilinear plan, exploited on a grand scale in Alexandria, was perfectly suited to the expression of imperial power. Order in the city mirrored order throughout the empire. The urban plan also allowed for grand vistas and broad avenues; the city's main street measured 108 feet (33 m) wide and more than 4.3 miles (6.9 km) long.

Alexandria was the intellectual center of the Hellenistic world. Alexander's belief in the superiority of Greek culture led to the opening of libraries and teaching institutions for the dissemination of knowledge, an integral part of the Greek imperial image. The great library of Alexandria possessed 700,000 volumes at its peak, and some of the greatest minds of the ancient world pursued their studies and taught in the Egyptian capital. Euclid developed his geometrical theorems, Archimedes discovered specific gravity, and Heron experimented with the power of steam. And while it had been established as early as 400 B.C.E. that the Earth is a sphere, it was in Alexandria that Eratosthenes first calculated its circumference; he was only 49.7 miles (53.1 km) off.

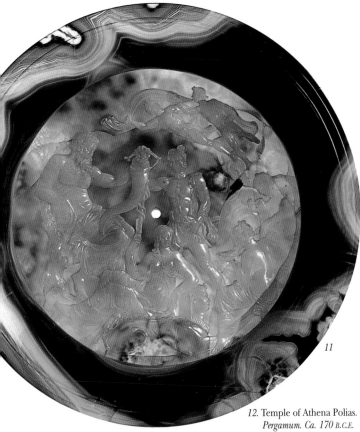

11

12

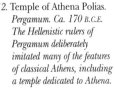

13

12. Temple of Athena Polias. *Pergamum. Ca. 170 B.C.E. The Hellenistic rulers of Pergamum deliberately imitated many of the features of classical Athens, including a temple dedicated to Athena.*

11. Tazza Farnese. *Museo Nazionale, Naples. Ca. 200 B.C.E. This sardonyx cameo, intricately carved with an allegory of the power of Cleopatra I, was typical of the luxurious and extravagant tastes of the Hellenistic age.*

13. Dying Galatian. *Musei Capitolini, Rome. Marble. Roman copy of a Greek original, ca. 200 B.C.E. In a dignified posture of defeat, the physical pose of this statue illustrates careful analysis of the human form.*

Images of Power

The absolute rulers of the Hellenistic empire placed new demands on the designers and craftsmen who carried out their artistic and architectural commissions. The extent of Greek control opened up new opportunities for trade, and the appearance of new materials led to the development of new skills. The use of expensive stones, such as the sardonyx of the *Tazza Farnese*, enhanced the imperial theme. The vast wealth of the empire paid for the construction of new cities, rivaling each other for splendor. Like Athens,

Pergamum (located on the Aegean coast of Anatolia), was built around an acropolis. Other features of the city suggested a deliberate adoption of the Athenian image, including dedication of the main temple to Athena and a copy of her Parthenon statue in the library. Even Pergamum's disorganized layout was reminiscent of the old Greek city. Imperial power was expressed in the location

of the royal palace on the Acropolis and was reinforced by the use of a dedicatory inscription on the propylon of the temple, recording its commission by Eumenes II. A visual expression of wealth and power, the use of inscriptions to record patronage became an important means of conveying authority.

During the turbulent period following the death of Alexander, Attalus I had secured Pergamum with his victory over the Gauls (Galatians) and established the city as a major center of Hellenistic culture. Attalus commissioned statues to memorialize his victory, including the *Dying Galatian*.

14. Altar of Zeus. *Pergamum. Staatliche Museen, Berlin. Marble. Ca. 170 B.C.E. This imposing image of royal power reinforced the Pergamene victory with mythological allegories.*

15. Gigantomachy (Battle between Gods and Giants). *Staatliche Museen, Berlin. From the Altar of Zeus. Pergamum. Marble. Ca. 170 B.C.E.*

16. Plan of the Acropolis, Pergamum:
a) Arsenal;
b) Temple of Trajan;
c) Temple of Athena;
d) Theater;
e) Altar;
f) Agora.

14

15

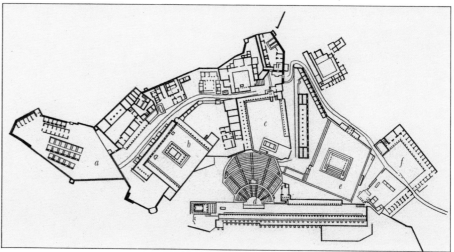

16

Use of the Doric order, the hallmark of democratic Athens, declined during the Hellenistic age. Simplicity and solidity were replaced by ornamentation and elegance, giving visual expression to imperial wealth and power. The Doric and Ionic were combined on the propylon of the Temple of Athena in Pergamum. But the new taste was reflected above all in the growing popularity of the Corinthian order for grand temples, such as the Temple of Olympian Zeus in Athens.

The Corinthian order is distinguished by its ornate and decorative capital, with small volutes springing out from carved acanthus leaves. Placed on a column of Ionic proportions, the added height of the capital makes the whole appear more slender. Corinthian columns had been used in the interiors of Greek temples, frequently to designate the site of the cult statue. The association between elaboration and prestige undoubtedly enhanced the appeal of the Corinthian order in the Hellenistic age. The Roman architectural theorist Vitruvius gave an account of its supposed origins in his treatise. After the funeral of a young Corinthian virgin, her nurse put a basket containing her treasured possessions on top of the monument, covering it with a tile. The following spring, an acanthus plant grew around the basket, the weight of the tile forming volutes at each corner.

Eumenes, his son, erected a more prestigious monument, the Altar of Zeus. The subject matter of the decorative friezes clearly derives from the Parthenon, with images such as the *Gigantomachy* (Battle of Gods and Giants). Their treatment, however, is deliberately different. The images on the Parthenon, all but hidden from human view, had paid homage to the role of the gods in military victory. The figures on the Altar of Zeus, carved in high relief and outlined with a drill, were meant to be seen, even from a distance, and suggest a more secular understanding.

They emphasize the magnitude of Attalus's own achievement and imply, by analogy, his godlike status.

To reinforce the real rather than the symbolic nature of an event, Hellenistic sculptors depicted exaggerated physical and emotional responses, enhancing reality with an emphasis on drama and dynamism. The pose and drapery of the *Winged Victory of Samothrace*, for example, suggest that she has just landed on the prow of a ship. The horror on the face of Laocoön and his contrived pose emphasize the terrible death he is to suffer.

18

17. Temple of Olympian Zeus. *Athens. Begun 174 B.C.E. The columns were composed of a series of blocks held together with pins; the quality of the joints depended on the skill of the craftsmen.*

18. Laocoön and His Sons. *Museo Pio-Clementino, Vatican. Marble. Ca. 50 B.C.E. Human agony, expressed in physical contortion and drama, reinforced the power of the gods. Laocoön had advised the Trojans against accepting the wooden horse left by the Greeks as a gift, which was actually filled with soldiers.*

19. Winged Victory (Nike) of Samothrace. *Louvre, Paris. Marble. Early second century B.C.E. Fluttering drapery clinging to the female body emphasized movement and reinforced the reality of this image of victory.*

17

19

Private Patronage

Private wealth increased as trade expanded, and the rich imitated patterns of imperial grandeur. Art was no longer restricted to the service of the gods or the state. The wealthy decorated their houses with wall frescoes and elaborate floor mosaics depicting a wide variety of scenes, ranging in subject matter from the mythological and exotic to the trivial (see Figure 22). Like democratic Athens, the Hellenistic empire succumbed to superior military strength. Roman expansion in the Mediterranean led to the conquest of Greece in 146 B.C.E. and of Egypt in 31 B.C.E. Yet the idea of Greek intellectual and cultural superiority, pervasive throughout the Hellenistic empire, did not die with the Romans. The absorption of Greek culture in the Roman Empire ensured its survival.

21

22

20. Flora. *Museo Nazionale, Naples. Wall painting from Stabiae. First century B.C.E. Delicately portrayed and viewed from behind, this image of the goddess of spring was intended as decoration, not an object of veneration.*

21. Nilotic scene. *Museo Nazionale, Naples. Mosaic. First century C.E. The diversity and richness of animal and plant life in the fertile Nile Valley provided the inspiration for this Hellenistic mosaic.*

22. Floor mosaic. *Museo Gregoriano Profano, Vatican. Based on an original by Sosus, Pergamum. Second century B.C.E. The ultimate in Hellenistic style: an expensive floor mosaic designed to show the discarded remains of the previous night's banquet.*

ITALY IN 800 B.C.E. WAS A LAND OF MANY small tribes—the Umbrians, Ligurians, Veneti, Latins, and others—whose names are still used to describe their locations in modern Italy. During the eighth century B.C.E., two cultures developed that were to have a decisive influence on Rome's rise to imperial power. The first signs of Etruscan civilization in central Italy date from ca. 800 B.C.E., and the earliest Greek colonies in southern Italy were founded ca. 750 B.C.E. (see chapter 5).

CHAPTER 7

THE RISE OF ROME

From Etruscan Civilization to Republican Rome

The Etruscans

Although there is some debate as to whether the Etruscans were indigenous or invaders from the eastern Mediterranean, by 600 B.C.E. they had established an aristocratic urban culture. This was supported by a successful agricultural hinterland and a prosperous trade in metals, for which the Greeks were major customers. Like the Greek city-states, Etruscans cities were independent but organized in a loose confederacy, united by religious beliefs and culture. The Etruscans borrowed much from the Greeks in the elaboration of their own,

1

distinct culture. They adapted the Greek alphabet to write down their language, which is not of Indo-European origin and still not fully understood. They also adopted Greek figure styles, seen on imported vases, for the decoration of their tombs.

Unlike the Greeks, but like the Egyptians, the Etruscans believed in the continuity between life and death. Their tombs were vast, underground masonry structures, often built in streetlike rows of uniform houses —images of a well-organized society. The tombs were individualized by their interior decorations, the choice of theme often reflecting a love of luxury and leisure, such as hunting and fishing. According to the Greeks, the Etruscans were great drinkers, which explains their fondness for banquet scenes in wall decoration and sculpture. Although the figure style owes much to Greek influence, the subject matter is entirely Etruscan. Unlike the Greeks, for example, the Etruscans often included women.

The Etruscans did borrow the rectangular plan and columnar style of Greek temple design, adapting these features to their unique religious practices. Whereas Greek observances were generally held outdoors and their temples reserved for cult statues and offerings, the Etruscan temple was the place where priests interpreted divine will, manifested through nature—including animal livers (haruspicy). Their temples followed a more hierarchic plan, raised on a podium with steps leading to a colonnaded entrance; the frontal emphasis of the design was reinforced by a closed back wall. Large statues decorated the roofline; the example of *Apollo* (Figure 8) reflects not only the stylistic influence of Greek art but the incorporation of Greek deities and myths into the Etruscan religion.

An Etruscan monarchy was established in Rome in the late seventh century B.C.E.

1. Sarcophagus. *Museo Nazionale di Villa Giulia, Rome. From Cerveteri. Terracotta. Late sixth century B.C.E. This reclining couple rested on top of a sarcophagus in an informal and affectionate image of individuals enjoying their banquet.*

2. Tablet inscribed in Etruscan. *Museo Nazionale di Villa Giulia, Rome. From a sanctuary at Pyrgi. Gold. Ca. 500 B.C.E.*

3. The principal centers of Etruscan civilization in northern Italy.

Mantua
Adria [Atria]
Bologna
Volterra
Arezzo
Cortona
Vetulonia
Perugia
Roselle
Volsinii
Vulci
Tarquinii
Cerveteri
Veii
Rome

3

5. Model of a sheep's liver. *Museo Civico, Piacenza. Bronze. Second century B.C.E. Haruspicy, or divination through the observation of animal livers, was an important feature of Etruscan religion. Bronze diagrams such as this were an aid to interpretation.*

4. Cemetery of Crocefisso del Tufo. *Orvieto. Begun sixth century B.C.E. What appears to us as a row of terraced houses is, in fact, a series of tombs. Their rich decoration illustrates the Etruscan belief in the continuity of life after death.*

4

5

This served to unify and urbanize the small agricultural hill settlements, founded by the Latins, around a convenient crossing point on the Tiber. The marshes between the Capitoline and Palatine hills were drained, creating a political center (forum) separate from the religious buildings on the Capitoline. The Etruscans also introduced efficient farming methods, land surveying, and military conscription, as well as new religious beliefs and an architectural style. Growing wealth and prosperity led to the overthrow of the Etruscan monarchy in about 510 B.C.E. and its replacement by an oligarchic republic. Rome retained many elements of Etruscan culture, which assisted its expansion in Italy from from the fifth century B.C.E. on. Efficient and eminently practical, the early Republic found its best expression in the construction of a road network, emphasizing domination through centralized control.

Development of Roman Culture

As Rome expanded, a mythology developed to explain its importance. Eschewing the pantheon of Greek gods, the Romans adopted the Trojan prince Aeneas (immortalized in Virgil's national epic poem, the *Aeneid*) as their common ancestor. The twins Romulus and Remus, suckled by a she-wolf, were the mythical founders of Rome. All three heroes were mortal and embodied the traits admired by the Romans: military skill, perseverance, and loyalty. The popular interest in national origins was reinforced by the assigning of a specific date for the founding of Rome (April 21,

6. Fishermen and birds. *Tarquinia, Tomba della Caccia e della Pesca. Fresco. 540–530 B.C.E. The tombs of Etruscans were decorated with scenes depicting their leisure pursuits.*

7. Banquet scene. *Tomba dei Leopardi, Tarquinia. Fresco. Ca. 480 B.C.E. Representations of the human figure in Etruscan wall paintings show the influence of archaic Greek vase decoration, especially in the treatment of the face.*

8. Apollo. *Museo Nazionale di Villa Giulia, Rome. Terracotta. Ca. 515–490 B.C.E. From the Portonaccio Temple at Veio, this image of Apollo has strong visual links with the kouros of archaic Greek sculpture, indicating trade links between the two cultures.*

9. *Reconstruction of an Etruscan temple: a) façade; b) side elevation.*

8

a

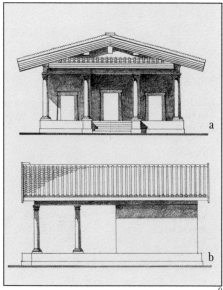

b

6

7

9

753 B.C.E.), thereby emphasizing the values and standards of its founders.

Ancestor worship was a vital part of Roman life. The statue of a Roman patrician holding his ancestral busts (Figure 14) recalled the old Roman tradition of carrying wax death masks of ancestors at funerals.

It is not surprising that a tradition of realistic portraiture developed in Republican Rome. Intended as private images, they were often intimate portraits notable for their lack of idealism. Political life was an extension of the family unit. It depended on the relationships between patricians and their *clientes*, men of humbler rank under their protection. A patrician looked after the interests of his *clientes*, who gave their protector political support in return, thus reinforcing patrician rule.

Greek Influence

Expansion continued inexorably, and by 133 B.C.E. Rome was the dominant power in the Mediterranean. Direct contact with Greek culture and its carefully cultivated image of artistic and intellectual superiority was so intimidating that the victorious Romans did not attempt to impose their own culture in the Hellenic world. On the contrary, the Romans were profoundly influenced by it. Like their Etruscan predecessors, they borrowed elements of Greek culture and adapted them. Greek gods were adopted into the Roman pantheon; the Greek Zeus was identified with the Roman Jupiter, Aphrodite with Venus, and Dionysius with Bacchus. Greek words were Latinized, sometimes with subtle changes of meaning; the Greek word *architekton*, designating the chief worker on a building site, became the Latin word *architectus*, a designer of buildings. Respect for the Greek intellectual achievement led to the employment of Greek tutors in Rome

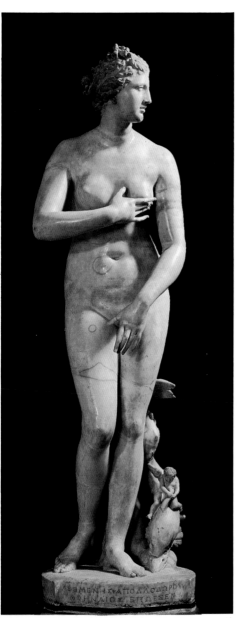

10. Medici Venus. *Uffizi, Florence. Marble copy of an original perhaps by Praxiteles. First century B.C.E. Profoundly influenced by the cultural achievement of the Greeks, the Romans employed Hellenistic sculptors to copy the masterpieces of the earlier civilization.*

11. Bust of an old man. *Museo, Ostia. Marble. First century B.C.E. Patrons in Republican Rome preferred verisimilitude to idealized portraits.*

12. Bust of Cato and Portia. *Museo Pio-Clementino, Sala dei Busti, Vatican. Marble. First century B.C.E. Affectionate and intimate, this double portrait bust reflects the virtues of family life in Republican Rome.*

10

11

and inspired Roman theorists, who applied their analytical skills to more practical subjects, such as agriculture and public service. The spoils of conquest stimulated a taste for luxury. Knowledge of Greek art led to the development of connoisseurship. Wealthy Romans, such as Cicero, amassed collections of Greek sculpture. As originals became rare, the demand for copies increased. (These copies provide a major source of contemporary knowledge about Greek art.)

Inevitably, Roman art and architecture also responded to the fashion for Greek culture. The Romans exploited the potential of images of wealth and power as propaganda for their growing empire. They used the Greek orders as decoration for their own architectural structures. The Temple of Fortuna Virilis in the Forum Boarium (Cattle Market) is Ionic, but its plan derives directly from Etruscan prototypes. The structure of the Tabularium (State Archive) was Roman, but the Doric order that decorated it was deliberately Greek. The decorative use of Doric and Ionic orders directly contravened Greek practice, in which the columns played an essential structural role. The Roman application, while declaring conquest over the Greek world, thus stood as an eloquent symbol of Greek cultural supremacy. The Roman taste for opulence found expression in the increasing use of marble. One of the earliest marble buildings in Rome was the Temple of Jupiter Stator, commissioned by the conqueror of Macedonia, Quinto Caecilius Metellus, in 146 B.C.E.

Luxury and Civil War

Roman conquest led to an enormous increase in prosperity and encouraged private patronage on a scale previously

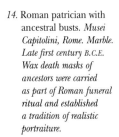

13

13. Capitoline Wolf. *Musei Capitolini, Rome. Bronze. Ca. 500 B.C.E., twins added between 1471 and 1509. For centuries the image of the wolf symbolized Roman power. The realism of this skilled piece of bronze-casting had no precedents in Greek culture.*

14. Roman patrician with ancestral busts. *Musei Capitolini, Rome. Marble. Late first century B.C.E. Wax death masks of ancestors were carried as part of Roman funeral ritual and established a tradition of realistic portraiture.*

12

14

unknown. Inspired by Hellenistic examples, Roman patricians began to build palaces of unprecedented luxury and grandeur. Pliny described how marble columns for these private palaces were dragged past the terracotta ornaments of the old temples, observing that the sumptuary laws that had previously restrained private patronage were being flouted in the face of the new taste for opulence. Early interiors, painted to resemble marble paneling, were replaced during the first century B.C.E. by the imitation of more elaborate architecture, complete with trompe l'oeil pictures and sculpture, reflecting the increasingly grandiose tastes of the Roman patriciate. Victorious commanders amassed vast personal fortunes and consummate power as provincial governors. This encouraged higher political ambitions, which the Republican system, based on moral obligation and personal restraint, was unable to contain.

The civil war that began in 49 B.C.E. was the result of a power struggle between Pompey, loyal to the Republic, and Julius Caesar, the conqueror and governor of Gaul, who wanted supreme power. Caesar won and was appointed dictator for ten years. His acceptance of the role of emperor for life in February 44 B.C.E. led to his murder the following month—and another civil war.

Caesar recognized the power of architecture as political propaganda and drew up grandiose plans for the imperial capital, the centerpiece of which was a redesign of the Forum Romanum (Roman Forum). Although little was work done before his death, the scale and grandeur of the project deliberately reflected both the new imperial status of Rome and his own position. The Basilica Julia was conspicuously larger than the nearby Tabularium (see plan, page 81). The Forum Romanum had been established by the

15. Wall decoration from House of the Farnesina. *Museo delle Terme, Rome. Late second style, first century B.C.E. The Roman architectural theorist Vitruvius described how wall decorations evolved. The earlier preference for realistic representation was replaced by fantasy.*

16. Wall decoration from the Casa dei Grifi. *Antiquarium Palatino, Rome. First style, late second century B.C.E. Brightly colored walls painted with realistic architecture contrasted with black and white mosaic floors.*

15

16

17

18

19

Etruscans as Rome's political center, and Caesar's own new forum, the Forum Julium, was a deliberate statement of his lineage and ambitions. It enclosed a temple dedicated to Venus Genetrix, the mother of Aeneas, providing an image of both state and personal propaganda: Caesar was a member of the Julian family, which traced its ancestry back to Iulus, the son of Aeneas.

The Age of Augustus

The civil war that followed Caesar's assassination was finally settled with Octavian's defeat of Mark Anthony and Cleopatra at the Battle of Actium in 31 B.C.E. Peace and stability were restored. Octavian was now the supreme leader of the Roman Empire and supported by the Senate, which granted him the title Augustus in 27 B.C.E. Augustus ruled the empire until his death in 14 C.E. at age 77. During his forty-five years in power, he reformed the Roman state machinery, establishing a basis for imperial government that lasted for more than two centuries.

Personal ambition had been the downfall of Julius Caesar, so Augustus sought to restore public confidence by stressing the Republican virtues of moderation and respect for Roman traditions. Recognizing the importance of art as propaganda, he encouraged such works as Virgil's *Aeneid*, whose central theme was the origin and destiny of Rome. The unprecedented opulence of pre-Augustan Rome had been criticized by staunch Republicans, notably Cicero, and such thinking became central to the Augustan image. The historian Livy commented that luxury was of foreign origin, introduced by the Roman conquest of Asia. Roman morality was shown to have triumphed over foreign decadence. In the same spirit, Vitruvius lent a moral framework to Greek architecture. His concept of architectural

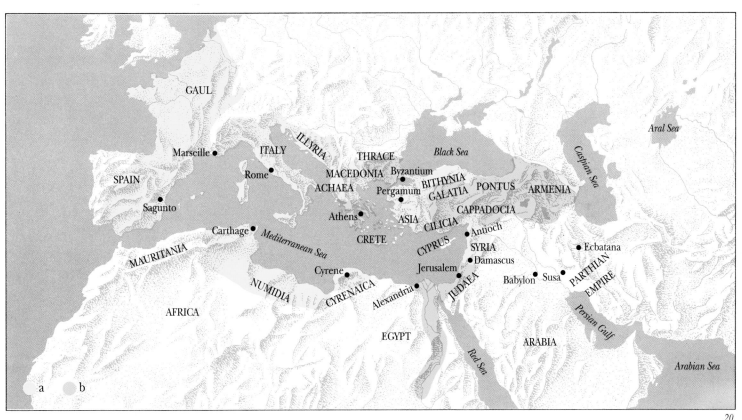

20

17. Temple of Fortuna Virilis. *Forum Boarium, Rome. Early first century B.C.E. An early example of a Roman temple, deriving its form from Etruscan architecture and its use of column orders from Greece, this format became standard in imperial Rome.*

18. Tabularium. *Rome. Ca. 80 B.C.E. Roman exploitation of the arch, already common in Middle Eastern architecture, was a significant improvement over the post-and-lintel method used by the Greeks.*

19. Temple of Vesta. *Forum Boarium, Rome. Early first century B.C.E. Distinctly Hellenistic in style, this early marble building was an example of the developing taste for luxury in Republican Rome.*

20. *The Roman Empire at the death of Augustus in 14 C.E.:*
a) *limits of the empire;*
b) *vassal states.*

decorum established rules for the use of the orders: Doric for male and warlike deities (e.g., Hercules and Minerva), Corinthian for feminine goddesses (e.g., Venus), and Ionic for those in between (e.g., Bacchus and Diana). He encouraged architectural expenditure as means of conferring dignity on the patron, who, by following Vitruvius's rules, would avoid the decadence intrinsic in the arbitrary use of decoration and splendor.

Augustan Rome

The Emperor Augustus imposed order on Rome. He divided the city into administrative districts, repaired the drainage system and bridges, and built new roads and aqueducts. His numerous projects included new temples and, as part of his restoration of traditional values, the renovation of older ones. He also encouraged private citizens to contribute to public works projects. Notable among those who did was his trusted friend and general, Agrippa, who realized Caesar's projects in the Campus Martius. Like Caesar, Augustus recognized the importance of creating a visual image for Rome's imperial power. Although his architecture owed much to the cities of the Hellenistic world, its message was distinctively Roman. Under the cloak of Republican respectability, Augustus was able to realize Caesar's grandiose projects for the Forum Romanum, completing the Basilicas Julia and Aemilia, the Senate House, and the Rostrum (orator's platform). Formality replaced informality, reflecting the institutionalization of Roman governmental machinery.

Julius Caesar's role in the foundation of the new Rome was acknowledged by the Temple of Divus Julius in the Forum Romanum, located on the site of his cremation. A society that worshiped its

21. Cicero. *Uffizi, Florence. Marble. Copy from original, ca. 43 B.C.E.* An orator, political leader, and writer, Cicero (106–43 B.C.E.) was an ardent supporter of the Republic.

22. Theater of Marcellus. *Rome. Dedicated 13–11 B.C.E.* Use of the arch enabled the Romans to build vaulted structures that supported tiers of seats, rather than relying on natural hillsides for seating, as the Greeks had.

23. Temple of Mars Ultor. *Rome. Dedicated 2 B.C.E.* Grand and imposing, this temple to Mars the Avenger in the Forum of Augustus reinforced the restoration of peace and Roman control of the Mediterranean.

24. Augustus as Pontifex Maximus. *Museo delle Terme, Rome. Marble. Ca. 10 C.E.* Augustus's institution of imperial rule was not accompanied by major stylistic change. On the contrary, he reinforced continuity by upholding Republican traditions.

21

22

23

24

THE FORUM ROMANUM

The Forum Romanum was the administrative heart and preeminent symbol of Roman power. Even before the arrival of the Etruscans, the area between the Capitoline and Palatine hills had been the center of ancient Latin settlements on the seven hills. The site developed as a marketplace under the Etruscans, but it was only with the establishment of the Republic that the forum developed its distinctive political character. After rebuilding the Etruscan temple of Castor and Pollux in the new Hellenistic fashion, Republican patrons constructed the new Basilica Aemilia (law court) and Tabularium (state archives) and paved the area with travertine marble.

A major reorganization of the Forum, planned by Julius Caesar and undertaken by Augustus, imposed order on the haphazard complex of buildings that had been erected in response to changing demands. Imitating the formal layouts of colonnaded public spaces in the cities of the Hellenistic world, the new plan introduced axiality and institutionalized the informal layout of the old Republican forum. New temples and basilicas proclaimed the prestige of the empire. A marble Rostrum (orator's platform) and a new Curia (senate house) deliberately reinforced the Republican tradition within the context of imperial rule.

Later emperors continued to embellish the Forum Romanum. The Arch of Septimius Severus (203 C.E.) occupied a prominent position below the Tabularium, and the Emperor Diocletian rebuilt the Curia after it had been destroyed by fire (283 C.E.). The Forum fell into decay after the demise of the empire and was used as a marble quarry by medieval and Renaissance popes, yet it has exerted a powerful fascination over later European powers and modern-day visitors.

Planimetry of the Roman Forums. The buildings from the Republican Period are shown in gray and those from the Imperial Period in black:

a) Basilica Aemilia;
b) Arch of Septimius Severus;
c) Temple of Concord;
d) Temple of Vespasian;
e) Basilica Julia;
f) The Forum;
g) Temple of Vesta;
h) Temple of Faustina and Antoninus;
i) Basilica of Constantine;
l) Temple of Venus and Rome;
m) Temple of Castor;
n) Curia (Senate House);
o) Temple of the Divine Julius Caesar;
p) House of the Vestals;
q) Temple of Saturn;
r) Arch of Titus.

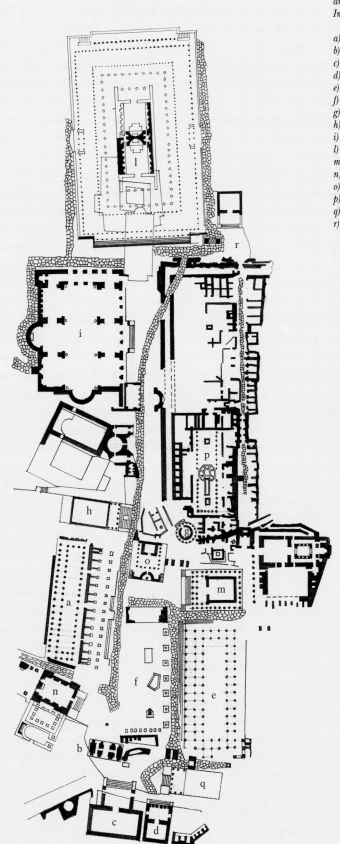

mortal founders had no problem deifying its contemporary heroes, and Caesar's deification set a precedent for the future. If the scale and scope of Augustus's plans were innovative, the style was emphatically not. His emphasis on the continuity of the Republic was visually expressed by the combination of Greek decorative orders with Roman structures, as in the Theater of Marcellus. Here, the system of arches used in building the Tabularium was applied to the construction of sloping terraces on flat land. This was another example of Roman technical superiority over the Greeks, who had relied on natural hills for tiered theater seating.

Like Caesar, Augustus built his own forum, the Forum Augustum. Decorated with Greek caryatids, it was filled with statues of Roman heroes accompanied by inscriptions detailing their fame. The Forum Augustum enclosed a temple to Mars Ultor (the Avenger), derived from earlier Republican temples. The style reinforced Roman links with Augustus's new colonies in France and Italy, populated with troops demobilized after the civil wars.

Augustus said that he had found Rome brick and left it marble. Newly opened quarries at Luni, in Tuscany, allowed marble to be imported more cheaply,

making it less of a luxury. One of the first Roman buildings to use this marble was Augustus's Temple to Apollo. This combination of temple and library was inspired by Hellenistic examples, but Augustus built *two* libraries on the site, one Greek and one Latin, to stress Roman parity with Greek achievement.

The *Ara Pacis* ("Altar of Peace")

The restoration of political order and the ability of Rome to maintain peace through superior strength were key themes in the propaganda of the *Pax Augusta* ("Augustan

25. Maison Carrée. *Nîmes.*
   Ca. 16 B.C.E.
   The format established
   with the Temple
   of Fortuna Virilis
   in Republican Rome
   was imitated throughout
   the empire as a symbol
   of power.

25

26. Emperor Augustus.
   Braccio Nuovo, Vatican.
   From Primaporta.
   Marble. Ca. 20 B.C.E.
   Inspired by Polyclitus's
   Doryphorus, this statue
   extolled the moral aspect
   of Augustan rule.
   His bare feet indicate
   that the statue
   was posthumous.

26

Peace"). The emperor commissioned an altar dedicated to peace, the *Ara Pacis Augustae*, completed in the year 9 B.C.E. The ornate marble structure, with extensive relief, combined past and present in an original and typically Roman way. The origins of Rome are depicted in such scenes as the Sacrifice of Aeneas, while a procession of the imperial family, senate, and other dignitaries dramatizes the Roman destiny. Although the figure style is clearly influenced by Greek prototypes, the message is quite different. The latter scene records an actual procession, which took place on July 4, 13 B.C.E., in stark contrast to the mythological imagery that decorated Greek commemorative altars. The imagery of the Ara Pacis evokes little sense of awe. The children, symbols of imperial continuity, seem more concerned with not getting lost than with religious ceremony.

Augustus himself is depicted as *princeps*, or first among equals, on the same level as the other dignitaries. Presented in this way, the image of Augustus emphasized the power of Rome to maintain peace. His military breastplate (see Figure 26) is decorated with symbols of peace.

Despite the grandeur of his public architecture, Augustus was reputed to have simple tastes and to have lived modestly. Livia, his wife, decorated the walls of her villa with garden scenes. The theme of gardens was not based on Greek precedent but reflected, in an aristocratic context, the agricultural origins of Roman religion and political power.

If the grand and public images of Augustus needed to reinforce the Republican foundation of his position, smaller works were less restricted. The *Gemma Augustea* cameo (Figure 30), cut in the state workshops, depicts Augustus as a companion of the gods. His adopted heir, Tiberius, stepping off

27. Ara Pacis Augustae. *Rome. Dedicated 9 B.C.E. The Ara Pacis, or altar of peace, was built as a propagandist monument to the Augustan regime.*

28. The Imperial family. *Ara Pacis Augustae, Rome. Marble. Dedicated 9 B.C.E. Recording a procession that took place on July 4, 13 B.C.E., this relief emphasizes the reality of the event in its informal details and contrasting, naturalistic poses.*

29. Sacrifice of Aeneas. *Ara Pacis Augustae, Rome. Marble. Dedicated 9 B.C.E. Like Virgil's epic poem* The Aeneid, *which charted the voyage of the Trojan prince Aeneas to Rome, this image gave official expression to the origins of the Roman people.*

his chariot, emphasized the continuity of the imperial tradition, its strength reflected in the conquered barbarians beneath. The piece is more explicit in its expression of imperial propaganda and more overt in its development of Hellenistic images of wealth. Augustus's successors, less concerned with their Republican roots, placed greater emphasis on such imperial themes. Yet the republican image that Augustus created for Rome retained its power for centuries, providing a standard and a propaganda message that later emperors would revive.

31. Wall painting from the Villa of Livia. *Museo delle Terme, Rome. Fresco. Ca. 25 B.C.E. This naturalistic ornament was not inspired by Greek precedent, as so much was in Ancient Rome, but illustrates the emergence of a distinctive Roman style of wall decoration.*

30. Gemma Augustea. *Kunsthistorisches Museum, Vienna. Sardonyx cameo. 12 C.E. The taste for luxury in Ancient Rome developed as a result of contact with the extravagant arts of the Hellenistic world. Wealthy Roman patrons employed its gem cutters, stone carvers, and mosaicists to create works that reinforced their rise to power in the Mediterranean.*

30

31

THE ROMAN EMPIRE WAS AN extraordinary military and administrative achievement. Roman legions conquered land from Spain east to the Persian Gulf and from the Scottish borders south to Egypt and North Africa. Roman administration was imposed on the cities of the old Hellenistic empires; elsewhere conquest was followed by colonization and civilization. Schools were set up throughout the empire to teach Latin, while Roman technology exploited local resources and improved agriculture. Trade flourished as markets grew. Italian wine was exported as far as India, and trade

CHAPTER 8

THE IMPERIAL IDEAL

Art in the Roman Empire

missions were sent to China. Rome imported luxury goods on a massive scale. Gold and silver were mined in Spain. France was famous for its cheese. In Egypt, known as the granary of Rome, the imperial army safeguarded wheat production. African marbles enlarged the choice of prestigious building materials. The power of the empire was reinforced by a massive program of harbor, road, and bridge construction. In less developed Western Europe, where the essential tool of the civilizing process was urbanization, the systematic construction of aqueducts ensured the survival of new cities.

1

The Romans were above all practical, and it was in the field of structural technique that they made their major contribution to architectural history. Concrete had been developed during the Republic with the discovery that lime mixed with volcanic sand, *pozzolana*, would harden in contact with water. Concrete was versatile. It could be faced with brick and embellished with marble or stucco. It also simplified the construction of arches and vaults, and it was in the exploitation of this potential that the Romans excelled. Arches and vaults had long been used in the Middle East, but they assumed prime importance in Roman architecture. Huge vaulted platforms freed buildings from the restrictions of site. Such structures provided physical proof of Roman technical superiority, creating images that satisfied their lofty aims.

The Influence of Greece

Rome may have conquered the old Hellenistic empires, but it was profoundly influenced by Greek achievements. Latin was established as the language of government, but Greek remained the language of culture. To decorate their most innovative and distinctive structures, the Romans adapted the columnar orders and other motifs from Hellenistic art. Roman art and architecture is often dismissed as derivative, which is unfortunate. Yet it is crucial to the understanding of Roman culture to recognize that it consciously owed this debt. The stylistic language of classical Greece was applied as a decorative veneer over structures that symbolized the new imperial power. Showing a preference for richer ornamentation and variety, the Romans copied the late Hellenistic practice of combining orders

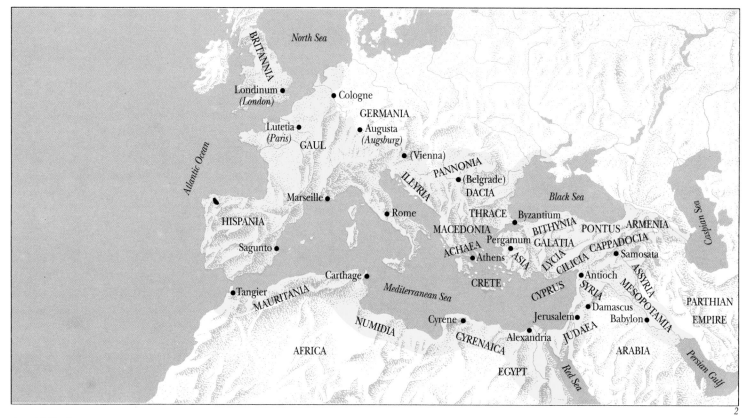

1. and 3. Pantheon (interior). *Rome. 118–125 C.E. restored. Construction of the massive hemispherical dome testified to the enormous advances made by Roman engineers.*

4. Pantheon. *Rome. 118–125 C.E. The façade was commissioned by Emperor Hadrian to replace the one*

by Domitian. The original façade was commissioned during the reign of Augustus by Agrippa, whose name was recorded on the frieze.

2. The Roman Empire at its greatest extent, ca. 400 C.E.

on their façades. They also adapted features of the Greek orders to create a fourth, the Composite order, identified by its Ionic volutes placed on top of Corinthian acanthus leaves (see Figure 7).

Nero and Extravagance

The Roman emperors patronized art and architecture in grand style. Augustus had established an ideal for imperial rule, disguising his position of supreme power behind the moral virtues of old Republican Rome. By concentrating on public monuments, he deliberately avoided expressions of personal power. But the absolute authority of the emperor inevitably encouraged self-glorification and a pattern of increasing grandeur, as successive emperors added to the scale and opulence of their predecessors. Nero (r. 54–68 C.E.) was explicit in his expression of supremacy. His use of gold to reinforce the image of wealth and power was legendary. According to Pliny, he covered an entire Roman theater in gold to impress the visiting king of Armenia. Nero's palace earned its name, *Domus Aurea* ("Golden House"), for the extravagance of its decoration. Centered on an artificial lake, the palace structure achieved unmatched spatial complexity by exploiting the structural potential of concrete.

Inevitably, perhaps, Nero's excesses were followed by a period of restraint. He was the last of the aristocratic Julio-Claudian dynasty, and the extravagances of his reign—as well as his personal artistic diversions—led to political chaos. Order was restored by the Emperor Vespasian (r. 69–79 C.E.), a solid bourgeois soldier who revived the Republican ideals of Augustus and sought to erase the memory of Nero. The most overt architectural statement of the time

5. Aqueduct. *Segovia. First century C.E. The proliferation of aqueducts throughout the empire gave visual expression to Roman technical skill and mastery over nature.*

6. Opus reticulatum. *Villa dei Volusii, Rome. The Romans developed brick facings for their concrete structures, which enhanced both the strength of the walls and their decorative potential.*

7. Composite capital. *Arch of Septimius Severus, Rome. 80–85 C.E. Combining Ionic volutes with Corinthian acanthus leaves, the Roman capital was more decorative than its component Greek parts.*

8. Trojans dragging the wooden horse into their city. *Museo Nazionale, Naples. From the House of the Menander, Pompeii. Panel. Fourth style, ca. 70 C.E. Contemporary with Nero's Domus Aurea, this elaborate painting, depicting a scene from Greek literature, was a typical choice for wealthy patrician interiors.*

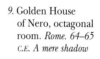

9. Golden House of Nero, octagonal room. *Rome. 64–65 C.E. A mere shadow of its former glory, the remains of this room suggest Emperor Nero's taste for grandeur.*

was the Colosseum, begun in 69 C.E. and inaugurated eleven years later. This massive oval amphitheater was built directly on the site of the Domus Aurea, and the artificial lake was drained. Vespasian also appropriated the massive bronze portrait statue that Nero had commissioned for the entrance of his palace and had it converted into a statue of the Sun.

The Roman Senate rejected dynastic succession after Vespasian's second son, Domitian (ruled 81–96 C.E.), repeated the excesses of Nero, and restored the old Republican system of imperial adoption. This produced a line of rulers, from Nerva

(96–98 C.E.) to Marcus Aurelius (161–180 C.E.), who largely conformed to the Augustan ideal that the emperor is the servant of his people and who concentrated on the patronage of public architecture.

The Imperial Forums

The most potent image of Roman power was the Forum Romanum. Established as the political center of Rome by the Etruscans and systematized by Julius Caesar and Augustus, it had also inspired both these patrons to build their own forums (see chapter 7). Later emperors revived this

practice, eager both to emulate their illustrious predecessors and to record their own achievements in the permanence of architecture. The Templum Pacis in Vespasian's Forum commemorated the suppression of the Jewish rebellion in Palestine. On display inside were symbols of Vespasian's reign: spoils from the Temple in Jerusalem and masterpieces of Greek sculpture from Nero's Domus Aurea.

The Forum of Trajan was the grandest, and the last, of the imperial forums in Rome. It coincided, significantly, with the greatest extent of the empire and the largest

10

12

10. Colosseum. *Rome. Inaugurated 80 C.E. Built on the site of a lake, which formed part of Nero's Domus Aurea, the Colosseum combined the Doric, Ionic, Corinthian, and Composite orders, setting an important precedent for later designers.*

12. Remains of the Tabularium and the Forum Romanum. *Rome. Despite its ruined state, the Forum Romanum still evokes the grandeur of Ancient Rome.*

11. Reconstruction of the Tabularium and the Forum Romanum. *Soprintendenza alle Antichità, Rome. Watercolor by Becchetti. This imaginative view gives some idea of the original appearance of the major buildings in the Forum Romanum, from left to right: Temple of Saturn, Temple of Vespasian, Temple of Concord, and the Arch of Septimius Severus, with the Tabularium behind.*

13. Trajan's column. *Rome. 110–113 C.E. A symbol of imperial military achievement, reinforced by the subject matter of the spiral reliefs, the column also marked Trajan's tomb.*

14. Trajan's market, interior hall. *Rome. Ca. 100–112 C.E. Built of concrete and faced with brick, the scale and grandeur of Trajan's market complex underlined the importance of trade in the growth of Roman prosperity.*

11

population of Rome (1.5 million). It was financed by the spoils of Trajan's Dacian campaign, commemorated in the reliefs on Trajan's column and the figures of Dacian captives supporting the attic story of the forum. The use of caryatids above the colonnades recalled the Forum Augustum, but whereas the focus of the Forum Augustum had been the Temple of Mars Ultor, Trajan's Forum centered on the Basilica Ulpia. The basilica was a specifically Roman building type and destined to be enormously influential through its adoption by Constantine for Christian worship (see chapter 9).

In the pre-Christian empire, it functioned both as a law court and as a center for commercial transactions. A rectangular building whose roof was supported by columns, its form had been standardized by Julius Caesar in the Basilica Julia in the Forum Romanum.

Trajan's more secular interpretation of imperial power was not only expressed in the prominent position of the Basilica Ulpia but also in his construction of an adjacent market complex and his equestrian monument at the center of the piazza, or square. This emphasis on the military, legal, and commercial elements of his power

contrasted with the small colonnaded courtyard at the back of the Basilica Ulpia, which contained a temple dedicated to the deified Trajan by his successor, Hadrian.

Imperial Propaganda

The tradition of deifying emperors after their death had started with Augustus's temple to Divus Julius in the Forum Romanum, and it soon took on an important role in the propagation of the imperial image. Significantly, neither Nero nor Domitian was deified. Roman religion was based on veneration of the memory

15. *Reconstruction of the imperial forums:*
    a) Forum of Vespasian with the Templum Pacis;
    b) Forum of Nerva (Forum Transitorium);
    c) Forum of Augustus with Temple of Mars Ultor;
    d) Forum of Caesar (Forum Iulium);
    e) Forum of Trajan;
    f) Basilica Ulpia;
    g) Trajan Markets.

13

14

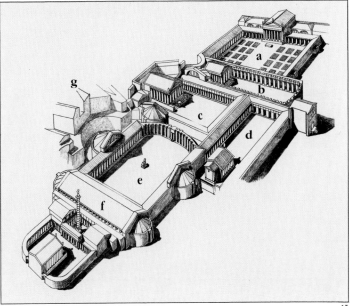

15

of ancestors, and imperial deification had more to do with the institution of the emperor than with his possession of divine power. State religion was thus an expression of loyalty to Rome and a civic obligation. In private, citizens could worship a deity of their own choice. This allowed for the continuation of local cults throughout the empire, which proved a successful method of ensuring Roman domination.

Another form of imperial propaganda was the triumphal arch. Originally temporary structures, they were soon built in stone as permanent reminders of the glory of Rome. It had been a Republican tradition that wealth gained by conquest should be used to commission public works, and triumphal arches illustrate the extent to which this concept had been adapted to the purposes of imperial power. Decorated with reliefs that commemorated a particular achievement, they provide an important insight into the Roman preference for factual imagery, rather than allegory, to reinforce their power. This is reflected in the naturalistic representation of figures and the illusion of depth in arch reliefs.

The standards of any culture may be judged by its largest buildings. Those of imperial Rome were dedicated to leisure and popular entertainment. The Republican tradition of wooing supporters by staging elaborate shows as part of an election campaign was institutionalized by the emperors. Enormous amphitheaters, theaters, circuses (race courses), and public baths were commissioned as part of their public monument programs. Baths were such an important part of Roman life that the early Christian fathers condemned bathing as a time-wasting luxury. Roman bath complexes included a series of vast vaulted rooms of varying temperatures and provided an ideal opportunity for Roman architects and engineers to exploit their technical skills.

16. Apotheosis of Antoninus Pius and his wife, Faustina. *Cortile delle Corazze, Vatican. Marble. Ca. 165 C.E. This relief from the base of the column of Antoninus Pius, erected by his successor, Marcus Aurelius, depicts the process of imperial deification.*

17. Arch of Titus. *Rome. 80–85 C.E. Originally temporary structures that celebrated the return to Rome of victorious generals, triumphal arches were soon built in stone as permanent symbols of Roman glory. The inscription, which begins with the traditional Republican formula, "The Senate and People of Rome," reinforced the image of the emperor as servant of the people.*

18. Triumphal procession of Titus. *Arch of Titus, Rome. Marble. 80–85 C.E.*

As Vespasian's son and general, Titus was responsible for suppressing the Jewish rebellion in Palestine. The sculptural decoration of this arch faithfully recorded the events of the war, which included the destruction of Jerusalem and Titus's triumphal return to Rome. The seven-branched candlestick from the Temple in Jerusalem was subsequently placed in the Templum Pacis in Vespasian's Forum.

17

16

18

Imperial Rome was the heir to two distinctive cultural traditions. The morality and virtue stressed by the old Republic provided a marked contrast to the tastes for extravagance and luxury inherent in the supreme power of the Hellenistic emperors. Republican portraiture had concentrated on realistic representations; Hellenistic rulers, following traditions established by Alexander the Great, had preferred idealized images as expressions of supreme authority. Private portraiture

IMPERIAL PORTRAITURE

sustained the Republican tradition of realism, while official imperial images generally took on a more grandiose aspect. Above all, the portraits of individual emperors reflected the images they desired to present. Vespasian's deliberately unflattering marble bust, executed in classic Republican style, is perhaps best understood in the context of his predecessor, Nero, whose

excesses were legendary and who commissioned a colossal bronze image for his Domus Aurea. Commodus, who like Nero suffered a *damnatio memoriae* after his death, adopted the divine attributes of Hercules—an approach reflected in statues and temples throughout the empire. Another common imperial image was the equestrian monument, chosen by Trajan, Marcus Aurelius, and others as a visual expression of the military power of Rome.

Images of Power in the Empire

Architecture was a vital part of imperial propaganda throughout the empire. As a vehicle for the benefits of Roman civilization, it also proclaimed the wealth and power of the new administration through the use of lavish materials and a consistent language of decoration and inscription. It was the provincial governor's job to allocate public funds for building projects and to ensure that they conformed with Roman practice. The old cities of the Hellenistic empires were embellished with Roman temples, basilicas, and other images

THE IMPERIAL IDEAL

19. Equestrian monument of Marcus Aurelius. *Piazza del Campidoglio, Rome. 166–180* C.E.

20. Emperor Commodus as Hercules. *Musei Capitolini, Rome. Marble. 180–193* C.E.

21. Vespasian. *Museo delle Terme, Rome. Marble. 69–79* C.E.

19

20

21

of victory. New cities were laid out on a grid plan whose focal point was a civic center, containing a forum, basilicas, administrative buildings, public baths, amphitheater, temples (for both Roman and local cults), triumphal arches, equestrian and other monuments, schools, and colonnaded "streets" for shelter from the weather. The layout deliberately recalled that of Rome itself.

The Decline of Rome

Conquest brought staggering wealth to Rome, and provided many with the opportunity to amass vast fortunes through speculation.

Merchants grew rich through trade and invested in land. As in so many other cultures, the new monied class developed a taste for extravagance. The craftsmen of the empire fashioned rich jewelry and other luxury items from precious gems and glass to gold and silver. The old Republican values of moderation and virtue declined in the face of increasing wealth. According to Pliny, money was the reason for the decline in the Republican tradition of portraiture; he described how Romans during Vespasian's reign collected portraits of strangers for their value rather than

for their artistic merit or subject matter. As luxury increased, so did decorative complexity.

The power of Rome began to wane after the death of Marcus Aurelius in 180 C.E. His successor, Commodus, was judged unfit to rule and strangled in his bath. Attacks by barbarian tribes on the northern frontiers added to worsening monetary problems at home. Instability was reflected in the growing popularity of the mystical religions of the East, such as Mithraism and the Egyptian cult of Isis and Osiris. It also encouraged the spread of Christianity. Civil wars led to the rise of a series

22. Baths of Caracalla. *Rome. 212–216 C.E. The largest buildings in imperial Rome were neither temples nor palaces but baths. By 400 C.E., there were eleven in Rome, and they were a key feature in towns throughout the empire. According to Tacitus, baths encouraged a love of pleasure and ease, a subtle method of destroying the will to resist Roman domination.*

23. Triumph of Neptune. *Baths of Neptune, Ostia. Mosaic. Ca. 139 C.E. Elaborate mosaic floors, decorated with appropriate imagery, were an essential feature of Roman interiors.*

24. The small hunt. *Piazza Armerina, Sicily. Mosaic. 310–330 C.E. Illustrating the leisure pursuits of the wealthy, this magnificently detailed mosaic demonstrates the high degree of skill attained by craftsmen throughout the empire.*

22

23

24

of military emperors who exercised supreme power, and the image of the old Republic became increasingly remote.

Diocletian (ruled 285–305) attempted to solve the problems by reorganizing the imperial administration, dividing control among four emperors, each with his own courts and army, in separate cities (Milan, Nicomedia, Trier, and Sirmium). Now the figure of the emperor himself grew more remote, reflected in a decline in naturalistic portraiture, a preference for frontal representation, and an emphasis on themes of power and ritual.

Imperial Rome provided a vast array of images to express wealth and power. Its emperors used architecture to convey morality or extravagance, military strength, and the rule of law. Its basilicas, temples with their explicit inscriptions, vast palaces with their fresco and mosaic decorations, colossal statues, intimate portraits, equestrian monuments, triumphal arches, and columns with their reliefs depicting actual events have all had a potent effect on later cultures. Above all, the scale and grandeur of the Roman achievement inspired emulation in rulers from Charlemagne to Napoleon and Hitler.

25. Parabiago plate. *Museo Civico Archeologico, Milan. Silver. Fourth century C.E. The great fortunes amassed by speculators were reflected in the acquisition of extravagance and luxury.*

26. Temple of Bacchus. *Baalbek, Lebanon. Mid-second century C.E. Later Roman architecture was characterized by increasingly elaborate architectural details.*

27. Basilica of Maxentius. *Rome. Begun ca. 307. Initiated by the last pagan emperor, Maxentius, and completed by his Christian successor, Constantine, the scale and grandeur of this building made it one of the major achievements of imperial Rome.*

25

26

27

RELIGIONS AND CONQUESTS BETWEEN EAST AND WEST

The spread of Christianity marked a decisive turning point in the development of the cultures linked to the Roman world. In 313, Constantine officially embraced Christianity (Edict of Milan) and the religion became the basis of the imperial government. Art and architecture also took on new forms and symbols.

After the outstanding accomplishments of Imperial Rome, the Eternal City remained a fundamental point of reference for both spiritual and artistic matters. St. Peter's, in particular, became the model for many later buildings, such as the Hagia Sophia in Constantinople, the city that became the imperial residence in 330.

This period also marked the beginnings of the art of mosaics in both East and West. But, the West was invaded by the barbarians and Ravenna replaced Rome as the artistic leader.

The great political and cultural rebirth of the West, still inspired by the imperial ideal, came under the Carolingian Empire.

However, the rise of Islam also played an important role. The Arabs' conquests carried their great philosophical and scientific achievements to the West. In the meantime, the very different cultures of Africa, China, and India —the last two intimately bound to the spread of Eastern philosophies— continued to advance.

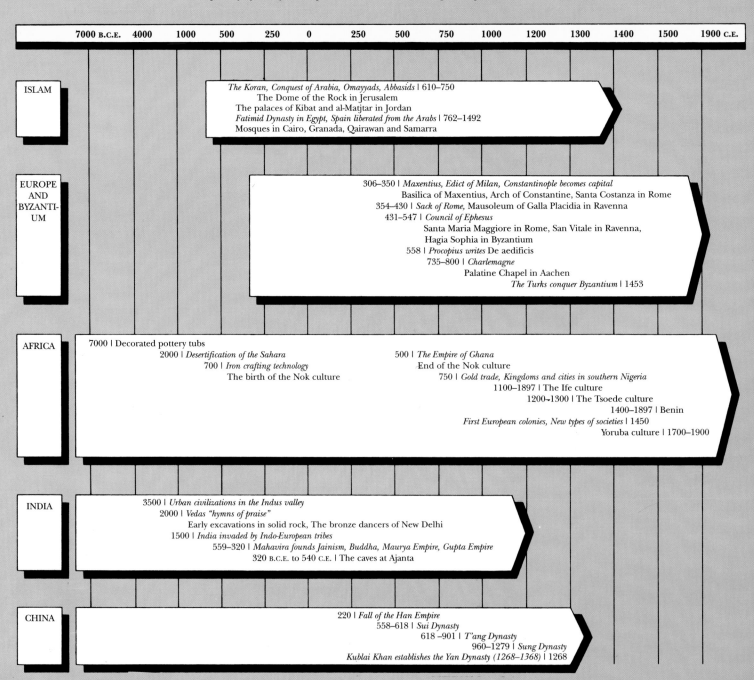

	7000 B.C.E.	4000	1000	500	250	0	250	500	750	1000	1200	1300	1400	1500	1900 C.E.

ISLAM

The Koran, Conquest of Arabia, Omayyads, Abbasids | 610–750
The Dome of the Rock in Jerusalem
The palaces of Kibat and al-Matjtar in Jordan
Fatimid Dynasty in Egypt, Spain liberated from the Arabs | 762–1492
Mosques in Cairo, Granada, Qairawan and Samarra

EUROPE AND BYZANTI-UM

306–350 | *Maxentius, Edict of Milan, Constantinople becomes capital*
Basilica of Maxentius, Arch of Constantine, Santa Costanza in Rome
354–430 | *Sack of Rome,* Mausoleum of Galla Placidia in Ravenna
431–547 | *Council of Ephesus*
Santa Maria Maggiore in Rome, San Vitale in Ravenna,
Hagia Sophia in Byzantium
558 | *Procopius writes* De aedificis
735–800 | *Charlemagne*
Palatine Chapel in Aachen
The Turks conquer Byzantium | 1453

AFRICA

7000 | Decorated pottery tubs
2000 | *Desertification of the Sahara*
700 | *Iron crafting technology*
The birth of the Nok culture
500 | *The Empire of Ghana*
End of the Nok culture
750 | *Gold trade, Kingdoms and cities in southern Nigeria*
1100–1897 | The Ife culture
1200–1300 | The Tsoede culture
1400–1897 | Benin
First European colonies, New types of societies | 1450
Yoruba culture | 1700–1900

INDIA

3500 | *Urban civilizations in the Indus valley*
2000 | *Vedas "hymns of praise"*
Early excavations in solid rock, The bronze dancers of New Delhi
1500 | *India invaded by Indo-European tribes*
559–320 | *Mahavira founds Jainism, Buddha, Maurya Empire, Gupta Empire*
320 B.C.E. to 540 C.E. | The caves at Ajanta

CHINA

220 | *Fall of the Han Empire*
558–618 | *Sui Dynasty*
618–901 | *T'ang Dynasty*
960–1279 | *Sung Dynasty*
Kublai Khan establishes the Yan Dynasty (1268–1368) | 1268

CHAPTER 9

CHRISTIANITY AND THE STATE

Late Imperial and Byzantine Art

PAGAN ROME WAS SURPRISINGLY TOLERANT of different religions. Although public religion, notably the worship of deified emperors, was a civic obligation, in private Roman citizens could worship any deities they chose. Christians, however, believed in only one god and refused to worship others. This was both the official reason for their persecution and their ultimate triumph. The Christian message, which promised salvation from oppression and deliverance through suffering, appealed to the poor and racial minorities of the empire. While this posed a threat to Roman authority, it attracted multitudes of followers.

The first Christians were working-class. They worshiped in private houses around a communal meal, which began with the breaking of bread and ended with a blessing over wine, supervised by professional clergy. There were few official buildings and little Christian art. Contrary to popular belief, catacombs were not places of secret worship but burial chambers with space designated for funeral services. Christians objected to cremation, but most were too poor to buy land for their tombs, as wealthy Romans did, so they dug underground passages for communal burial. Modest, simple, and explicitly Christian, their

1

decorative art emphasized salvation through belief.

The Rise of Christianity

Christianity spread rapidly through the empire, encouraged by the missionary work of St. Paul. By the first century, the new religion had gained adherents in Egypt, Syria, Greece, Anatolia, and Italy itself. By 250 C.E., 60 percent of Asia Minor had been converted. The movement survived severe persecution at the hands of the Romans, and by 312 it was one of the most popular religions in the empire. Constantine's embrace of Christianity, both as a matter of faith and as an ideological claim to the throne, proved monumentally important to the future of the religion. His victory over rival Emperor Maxentius in 312 and the Edict of Milan in 313 established Christianity as the official, but not exclusive, religion of the empire. Private religion was still a matter of personal choice, but conversion was encouraged by tax concessions. Christianity was now the state religion and an integral part of the imperial administration. Christian art became state art. The image of Christ was changed from "Savior of the Poor" to "Emperor of Heaven," the latter as the spiritual counterpart to Constantine, the emperor on earth. The new image took on all the trappings of imperial power. The plain table became an elaborate altar and the focus of a long, hierarchical procession separating the imperial family and clergy from the laity. This represented a profound change from the simplicity of early Christianity and one that has been rejected by reformist sects ever since.

2

3

1. Interior of old St. Peter's. *San Martino ai Monti, Rome. Fresco. Sixteenth century. Constantine's adoption of Christianity as the state religion placed Christian art in the context of imperial power. Grand, extravagant, and imposing, old St. Peter's established a precedent for the new religious architecture.*

2. Crypt of the Popes. *Catacombs of San Callisto, Rome. Third century. Roman law required that burials take place outside city walls, and the Christians, whose religious beliefs excluded cremation, preferred underground tombs as a cheaper alternative to purchasing land.*

3. Jonah and the Whale. *Catacombs of Saints Marcellus and Peter, Rome. Wall painting. Late third century. Decorated with scenes from the Bible, these first examples of Christian art reflected the relative poverty of their patrons.*

4. Arch of Constantine. *Rome. Completed 315. Built to commemorate his victory over the pagan Emperor Maxentius, Constantine's arch followed the traditional style. It incorporated roundels from earlier monuments, notably the Arch of Marcus Aurelius.*

Development of a Christian Architectural Style

The first Christians had set a pattern for liturgy but not an architectural framework for its practice. Constantine deliberately avoided classical temple design, with its pagan associations. Instead he chose to adapt the basilica, traditionally the building where imperial justice was dispensed, thus reinforcing the new link between Church and State. His largest church in Rome was St. Peter's, built over the supposed tomb of the first pope.

Its basilican plan was typical, establishing a blueprint for church design in later centuries. It was preceded by an atrium, adapted from the colonnaded settings of important Roman buildings. The interior was also traditional, with heavy entablatures carried on multicolored marble columns with classical capitals. The display of wealth inside contrasted with a plain exterior, emphasizing the interior setting of Christian worship. The axiality of the plan reflected the increasingly hierarchical character of Christian liturgy. The arches in the nave and chancel were symbols of imperial power,

and rich marbles expressed the new material wealth of the Church.

Constantine was an active and ambitious patron of monumental and religious architecture. His architectural projects gave visual proof of Rome's new position as spiritual capital of the Christian world. Many of his churches still stand, if much altered, including Santa Croce in Gerusalemme and St. John Lateran. The Arch of Constantine, erected near the Colosseum in 315, underscored the continuity of the institution of the emperor by following traditional arch design and incorporating panels taken from earlier

5

4

5. Detail of Arch of Constantine. *Rome. Completed 315. These roundels, taken from earlier monuments, show none of the contemporary developments toward a more hierarchical and frontal style.*

6. Sarcophagus of Santa Costanza. *Museo Pio-Clementino, Vatican. Porphyry. Mid fourth century. Originally in Santa Costanza, this elaborately sculpted sarcophagus was made of porphyry, which was not only rare but also hard to carve. Its use was restricted to the imperial family.*

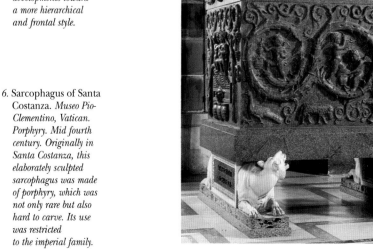

6

arches. The formal style of the panels he commissioned stood in marked contrast to the naturalism of the earlier roundels. Constantinople, which he named after himself in true imperial tradition, became the administrative center of the empire in 330. Little remains of his buildings there, but they were influential prototypes for later patrons. Constantine identified himself as the thirteenth Apostle, and his mausoleum in Constantinople was also a shrine to the Apostles. Its design was an early example of the "Greek cross" (arms of equal length) in Christian architecture.

Orthodoxy and Art

The atmosphere of religious tolerance continued during the fourth century. New Christian and old Roman imagery coexisted. The sarcophagus of Constantia, Constantine's daughter, was consciously imperial in design. It was made of porphyry, an expensive and hard-to-carve material whose use was confined to the imperial family. Its spiral acanthus carvings established a visual link with such pagan monuments as the *Ara Pacis* of Emperor Augustus. The mausoleum in which the sarcophagus was housed, now the Church of Santa

Costanza, featured a dome decorated with saints, testifying to Constantia's faith. But its circular form followed pagan Roman tradition, and the ambulatory vault was decorated with both secular and Christian scenes. Depiction of the wine harvest, for example, carried Christian associations but no specific religious message and more directly imitated secular decoration.

The *Missorium* of Theodosius I (ruled 379–395) makes no overt reference to his Christian belief. The curved architrave and halo both were symbols of imperial power. But the graded sizes of the emperor, co-regents, and soldiers, reflecting their

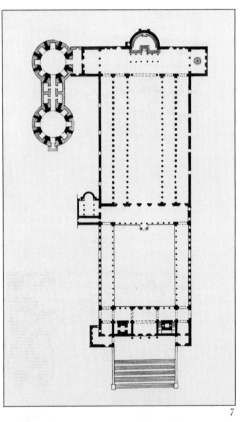

7

7. Plan of the old basilica of St. Peter's, Rome.

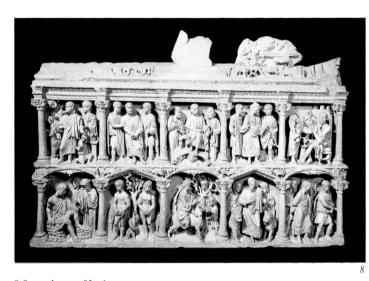

8

8. Sarcophagus of Junius Bassus. *Museo del Tesoro, Vatican. Marble. Fourth century. Traditional in format, this sarcophagus was decorated with Christian imagery to convey the new religious beliefs of its patron.*

9

10

11

relative importance, illustrate the move away from the naturalism of classical art.

During the fifth century, art and architecture increasingly reflected the new Christian perception of the world. The empire had been irrevocably divided after the death of Theodosius in 395. By 400 the western part was under serious threat of invasion, and Rome itself was sacked in 410. Instability led to authoritarian control. The tradition of religious tolerance had ended with Theodosius's ban on pagan practice in 392. Christianity was established as the exclusive state religion, and the church orthodoxy, heavily influenced

by such classical thinkers as Plato and Cicero, became increasingly intolerant of pagan ideas. Scientific advances made by the Greeks, including the observation that the Earth is a sphere, were declared false and heretical. Independent thought was considered dangerous. Power was asserted through adherence to the Bible as the one source of truth in an increasingly unstable world.

The changes were reflected in art and architecture. The lighter arcades characteristic of Santa Sabina gradually replaced the heavy horizontal entablatures used at St. Peter's and Santa Maria Maggiore.

The Romans had supported their arches on piers, and their use of columns, capitals, and entablatures had derived from Greek architecture. The combination of Greek column and Roman arch, a style the Romans deliberately perpetuated, marked a break with classical tradition. Secular decoration in churches, like the vintage scene in Santa Costanza, was condemned as pagan. Art increasingly became a vehicle for Christian dogma. Santa Maria Maggiore was founded by Pope Sixtus III in 432, after the Council of Ephesus declared Mary to be the Mother of God.

9. Santa Sabina, nave. *Rome. Ca. 422–432. Following Greek practice, the early Romans had used columns to support a horizontal entablature. The later combination of arches and columns was a significant step away from the classical language of architecture.*

10. Santa Costanza, interior. *Rome. Ca. 350. The importance of the arch in the articulation of this interior illustrates the beginnings of a rejection of the formal rules of earlier Roman architecture.*

11. Santa Maria Maggiore, nave. *Rome. Ca. 440. One of the major churches in early Christian Rome, Santa Maria Maggiore continued the Roman tradition of using columns to support the entablature, a custom rapidly dying out.*

12

12. Missorium of Theodosius I. *Academia de la Historia, Madrid. Silver. 388. The arch interrupting the architrave above the figure of Theodosius was a symbol of imperial power.*

13. The wine harvest. *Santa Costanza, Rome. Mosaic. Fourth century. Secular in theme and decorative in effect, this mosaic from an ambulatory vault was not specifically Christian.*

13

The tradition of mosaic decoration was popularized by wealthy and extravagant patrons of the Hellenistic empire and adopted by Roman patricians eager to imitate the luxurious standards of their forebears. After the victorious campaigns in the East, the Roman patriciate did not hesitate to imitate the sumptuous lifestyles of their new subjects. Durable and decorative, mosaic was an ideal medium for the decoration of floors but had stylistic limitations.

Small stone cubes, or *tesserae*, were carefully positioned in cement over a cartoon drawing on the surface. No matter the skill of the mosaicist, however, some of the refinement of the drawing was inevitably lost. Republican Romans preferred painted wall frescoes, a better medium for their illusionistic and elegant decorative schemes.

The emergence of Christianity as the state religion of the Roman Empire was expressed in new attitudes toward art. The illusion of reality was no longer a priority, replaced by a growing interest in mystical imagery.

The development of wall mosaics during the Late Empire reflected these changes. Colored tesserae, especially of gilded glass, became more common. They were impractical on floors, but their use on walls was not restricted.

Mosaics had the added advantage of being more expensive than painting and thus a better expression of wealth and prestige.

By deliberately creating an uneven surface, the skilled mosaicist could ensure that his picture caught and reflected light, thereby enhancing the mystical quality of Christian images.

14. Christ enthroned with the Apostles. *Santa Pudenziana, Rome. Apse mosaic. Late fourth century. Books replaced scrolls as a means of recording texts during the late empire. The inscription, "Dominus Conservator Ecclesiae Pudentianae," illustrated the new layout.*

14

15. Adoration of the Magi. *Santa Maria Maggiore, Rome. Mosaic. Ca. 432. This image of the newborn Christ receiving the gifts of the Three Kings from his throne was not intended as a realistic portrayal of the event. On the contrary, it deliberately reinforced both the power of Christianity and its emperor on earth.*

15

A new iconography emerged, which reinforced adherence to the Christian faith. The message was still salvation through belief, but the imagery became more severe. The apse mosaic in Santa Pudenziana depicted a second-century interpretation of the Book of Revelations in which the Four Beasts of the Apocalypse (man, lion, ox, and eagle) were identified with the Four Evangelists (Matthew, Mark, Luke, and John). Apocalyptic imagery deliberately inspired fear of the Day of Judgement and reinforced the need for strict adherence to Church dogma.

At another level, the mosaic can be read as an image of Christ enthroned as Emperor of Heaven, reinforcing imperial power on earth. The same theme is evidenced on the triumphal arch of Santa Maria Maggiore. Its scene of the Adoration of the Magi was clearly not intended as a realistic portrayal, and the newborn Christ personally receives the Kings on an imperial throne. These mosaics illustrate the major stylistic changes that developed in response to Christian belief. Roman gods had been mortal, but the Christian God was emphatically not. Whereas classical art had emphasized the humanity

of their deities in naturalistic figures and poses, Christian art sought another language to convey the supreme power of their incorporeal God. Naturalism was rejected in favor of mystical imagery. The lack of interest in the material world also showed in the development of a two-dimensional figure style, characterized by frontal poses and a lack of physical weight. Without having to make figures look "real," artists could experiment with new ways of representing grace and power. The Romans had used mosaics of durable stones on their floors, preferring paint as a better medium for naturalistic wall

CHRISTIANITY AND THE STATE

16

17

16. Mausoleum of Galla Placidia. *Ravenna. Ca. 425 C.E. Solid and plain on the exterior, the decoration was concentrated on the inside of the building.*

17. Mausoleum of Galla Placidia, interior. *Ravenna. Ca. 425. Expensive and explicitly Christian, this interior provided a fitting context for an imperial tomb.*

18

19

18. Capital. *San Vitale, Ravenna. 526–547. New capital styles developed from the classic orders. Christian details reinforced the change from pagan prototypes.*

19. San Vitale, interior. *Ravenna. 526–547. Exploitation of the patterns in marble slabs was an important element of nonfigurative decoration.*

decoration. The development of glass mosaics on walls, colored with gold and other expensive materials, expressed the new priorities of Christian decoration.

Ravenna

The last emperor in Rome was deposed in 476, and most of the Western Empire was in barbarian hands by 500. Constantinople, meanwhile, the administrative center of the empire, retained its economic power, and the Eastern emperor was now the sole heir to Constantine. This was the inspiration behind Justinian's bid to recreate the grandeur of the early Christian Empire. Soon after his accession to the throne (527), his armies reconquered the Mediterranean, returning Italy to imperial rule. His attempts to impose religious orthodoxy were not successful, but his codification of Roman law based on Christian principles was more effective. The style he created formed the basis of later Byzantine art as well as medieval art in the West. His restoration of order was expressed visually in an ambitious public-works program, including the rebuilding of roads, aqueducts, and churches. The reconquest of Italy was followed by architectural projects in the old imperial capital of Ravenna. San Vitale had been started in the 520s by Theodoric, king of the Ostrogoths, but its plan and interior owed much to Justinian's churches in Constantinople. The columns and capitals were imported from imperial workshops. The capitals marked a decisive break with classical tradition, reinforced by explicit Christian imagery. The chancel mosaics, commissioned by Bishop Maximian, underscored the new power of the emperor in Constantinople; Justinian is shown alongside the patron and a retinue of soldiers and bishops facing the Empress Theodora and her staff.

20. The Emperor Justinian and his retinue. *San Vitale, Ravenna. Mosaic. 548. Not intended as portraits, these stylized figures illustrate the major changes that had taken place since the fall of the Roman Empire.*

20

22. Constantine I. *Hagia Sophia, Istanbul (Constantinople). Mosaic. Late tenth or early eleventh century. This detail of Constantine, from a mosaic of the Virgin and Child enthroned between Constantine and Justinian, emphasized the monetary contribution made by the founder of the city.*

21. Throne of Bishop Maximian. *Museo Arcivescovile, Ravenna. Ivory. Early sixth century. The use of ivory with elaborately carved Christian figures and symbols gave visual expression to the power and prestige of the patron.*

21

Justinian and Constantinople

As an indication of the importance Justinian attached to architecture, one book of his official biography was devoted to his achievements in this area. His greatest projects in Constantinople were conspicuous statements of his power, consolidated after anti-imperial riots (532) destroyed many of Constantine's buildings. Foremost among Justinian's landmarks is the Church of Hagia Sophia ("Holy Wisdom"), constructed at enormous expense in five years (532–537). A monumental architectural achievement and important symbol of imperial prestige, the massive domed structure was built on a scale reminiscent of imperial Rome. Its centralized plan enclosed a vast space reserved for the emperor, his retinue, and clergy. The rest of the audience was kept behind screens in the galleries and aisles, reflecting the rigid hierarchy of Justinian's theocratic rule. Constantine had developed the Roman basilica as an image for his Christian state, but Justinian's Hagia Sophia was inspired by the more overtly imperial buildings of Rome, notably palaces and baths. The architects, Anthemis of Tralles and Isidorus of Miletus, exploited the strength of the pendentive to support an enormous dome, with two half-domes as buttresses. It was a remarkable technical achievement that earned widespread praise from contemporaries. The interior decoration, although much altered today, reflected Justinian's claims to imperial and Christian power. The materials were extravagant. Gold mosaics covered the dome, and multicolored marble slabs with mosaics of crosses, plant forms, and geometric patterns decorated the walls. The capitals, like those at San Vitale, disguised their classical derivation behind vine-tendril decoration;

CHRISTIANITY AND THE STATE

23. Hagia Sophia, interior. *Istanbul (Constantinople). 532–537. The use of pendentives (concave triangular structures) to support the huge dome was an important technical advance, creating an enormous open space for the celebration of Christian ritual. The audience, literally the "hearers," was hidden behind screens.*

25. Hagia Sophia. *Istanbul (Constantinople). 532–537. Described by his biographer Procopius as ugly and married to a beautiful but dissolute dancer, Justinian made considerable efforts to reestablish the power of the Christian Empire, reinforced by the construction of this massive statement of imperial power. The minarets were added later.*

24. Plan of Hagia Sophia. *Istanbul (Constantinople).*

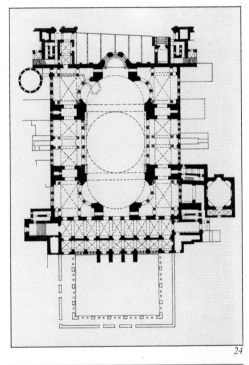

22

23

24

25

their modernity was emphasized by the imperial monograms of Justinian.

Late Byzantine Art

Justinian's reign set a standard for splendor in imperial Byzantine art that was not matched until the tenth century. Further barbarian invasions in the West during the seventh century were followed by the loss of Syria, Palestine, and Egypt to the expanding Muslim Empire in the East. The threat to Constantinople was averted by Emperor Leo III, who held off Muslim Arab forces after a year-long siege (717–718). Leo's belief in the Second Commandment of the Hebrew Bible, forbidding the worship of images, marked the beginning of the so-called Iconoclastic Controversy. Orthodox Byzantine Christians were persecuted for venerating holy images until 1843, when Orthodoxy was restored. The iconoclasts obliterated or destroyed much of the art of the earlier periods, and in the aftermath there was a move to restore figurative mosaics in churches. The Hagia Sophia, whose original ornamentation had been nonfigurative, was now decorated with images. Post-iconoclastic emperors emphasized the Christian basis of imperial power, reviving many earlier traditions. Greek cross plans became the norm for churches, and their domes were decorated with giant images of *Christ Pantocrator*, the heavenly equivalent of the emperor on earth. The wealth of Byzantine art provided a powerful image for Christian rulers in the West, who imitated the style. When Constantinople finally fell to the Turks in 1453, Justinians's churches were converted to Islam and provided models for the construction of new mosques.

26

27

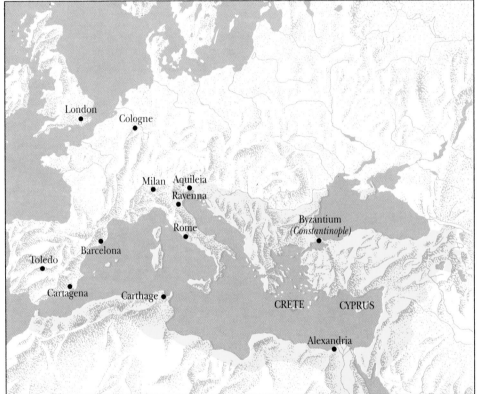

28

26. Christ Pantocrator. *Church of the Dormition, Daphni. Mosaic. Ca. 1100. The powerful image of Christ Pantocrator dominated church interiors, filling domes and apses as a visual expression of the supremacy of the Christian faith.*

27. Christ before Pilate and the Repentance of Judas. *Duomo, Rossano. Codex from Constantinople. Sixth century. Regarding the Bible as the "word of God," Christian patrons commissioned elaborate manuscript copies. Their decorations and illustrations came to be regarded as emblems of prestige.*

28. *Extent of the Byzantine Empire during the reign of Justinian.*

THE DISINTEGRATION OF THE ROMAN Empire in northern Europe during the fifth century was rapid and complete. The vacuum was filled by various tribes, whose power was localized. Angles and Saxons settled in England, Franks and Burgundians in France, and Lombards in Italy, forming the basis for the development of the modern nations of Europe. Generally illiterate and pagan, these tribes had little respect for learning. Portable wealth had greater value than aesthetic beauty or monumental architecture. A gilded copper helmet commissioned by Agilulf, king of the

Lombards (590–616), shows him enthroned with his sword surrounded by armed soldiers. This image of wealth and militancy was typical of the art that dominated Europe after the collapse of the Roman Empire. A purse cover found in the burial mound of an East Anglian king conveyed worldly power through the use of gold, jewels, and high standards of craftsmanship. Elaborate ornamentation took time and skill, adding to the cost of the object. In contrast to the art of pagan and Christian Rome, there was little concern with naturalistic representations of the human form. Yet as new cultures were confronted with the old,

1

the imperial image of Rome continued to exert a strong influence.

Celtic Christianity in Ireland and Northern England

Rome was no longer the capital of an empire, but it was still the spiritual center of Christianity. The papacy wielded considerable influence and exploited it to full potential. By 900, Christianity was enforced as a weapon of state control, and Rome was once again a powerful force in European politics. The process was slow and began with the conversion of pagan

chiefs. Clovis, the leader of the Franks, was baptized in 496, and his successors supported the Church in Gaul.

The situation in the British Isles was more confused. Rome had never conquered the Celtic tribes of Ireland, Scotland, and Wales, and Romano-Christian traditions in England were sharply interrupted by the invasion of pagan Anglo-Saxons in the second half of the fifth century. St. Patrick's evangelical mission to Ireland (ca. 430) had far-reaching ramifications. The new monasteries founded there fulfilled a different function from their prototypes in Egypt and Asia Minor. The latter had been

places of retreat, while the Irish monasteries served as centers of missionary work. Irish monks founded monasteries at Bobbio in Italy and St. Gall in Switzerland, as well as Lindisfarne in England, their center for the conversion of the Anglo-Saxons.

The new mission stations needed clear religious statements communicated in a language that heathens could understand. The stone crosses found in Irish monasteries did just that, their wealth of decorative detail firmly rooted in Celtic tradition. A second function of the missions was to educate converts in the rites of the Christian Church.

1. Purse cover from Sutton Hoo burial. *British Museum, London. Enamel. Before 655. These interlacing patterns and stylized animal forms were typical of the elaborate decoration in the artifacts of the Germanic tribes that swept through Europe after the fall of the Roman Empire.*

2. Muiredach Cross. *Monasterboice, Ireland. Early tenth century. Christian imagery and Celtic style combined to provide comprehensible statements about the new religion.*

3. Triumph of Agilulf. *Museo Nazionale del Bargello, Florence. Gilded copper. Ca. 600. From Agilulf's helmet, this detail illustrates the importance of military skill among the invading barbarian tribes.*

This stimulated the growth of scholarship and the copying of sacred texts, especially the Gospels, which were decorated with ornate Celtic forms. At first only initial letters were elaborated, but soon whole "carpet pages" were ornamented. This decorative emphasis reflected the independence of Celtic Christianity from Rome. Out of touch with the naturalistic tradition of classical art, the monks developed a highly abstract and decorative style, in which drapery folds and even hair conformed to repetitive geometric patterns that reflected the mystical nature of Christianity.

The Influence of Rome

The papacy also founded monasteries as centers of conversion, but these followed the rule established by St. Benedict in Montecassino (ca. 530). The Rule of Benedict eventually replaced Eastern and Celtic rules throughout Europe and became the essential guide for monastic life. Benedictine monasteries maintained close links with the papacy and were a useful tool as Rome attempted to reassert its authority. Gregory the Great, the first monk to be made pope (590–604), sent St. Augustine of Canterbury on a mission from Rome to convert the Anglo-Saxons (597). Roman religious and artistic traditions were introduced into southern England that contrasted with the Irish-Celtic culture in the north. Inevitably this led to conflict. The Council of Whitby (664) formalized papal control in England by imposing Benedictine monasticism at the expense of Irish traditions. Roman culture was introduced into Northumbria by Benedictine monks, notably Benedict Biscop, who founded monasteries at Wearmouth (674) and Jarrow (682).

THE CAROLINGIAN EMPIRE

4

4. Book of Durrow, carpet page. *Trinity College, Dublin. Late Seventh century. These intricate patterns, combining heads of fabulous monsters with interlacing bands, were highly complex and illustrate a love of ornament for its own sake.*

5. Book of Kells, Virgin and Child. *Trinity College, Dublin. Late eighth century. With little interest in realistic images, manuscript illuminators emphasized the decorative potential of the figure, hair, and drapery folds.*

5

Biscop made several trips to Rome and brought back sacred and scholarly texts, which the monks assiduously copied. The *Codex Amiatinus*, for example, is a copy of a sixth-century Italian Bible that he brought to Northumberland. These manuscripts introduced a more naturalistic style and such motifs as the author portrait for each gospel. Biscop's libraries at Jarrow and Wearmouth contained important collections of both religious and secular works. They were an important source for Bede's *History of the English Church* (730) and demonstrate the ongoing Irish-Celtic emphasis on scholarship and education. Literacy was encouraged through monastic schools, considered essential to Christian superiority over the heathens. Alcuin's school at York taught a curriculum that included such classical subjects as grammar, poetry, and astronomy as well as Christian teaching.

The Rise of Charlemagne

With the full support of the papacy and Christian Franks, Anglo-Saxon monks traveled to Germany to convert the Saxons. The new Church established there provided an important base for the growth of the Frankish kingdom under Charlemagne. Baptism became the symbol of acceptance for Frankish overlordship. Charlemagne's grandfather, Charles Martel, had defeated the Muslims at Poitiers in 732. Charlemagne's father, Pepin III, had been crowned king of the Franks after interceding on behalf of the pope with the Lombards in Italy and obtaining territory for the papacy (754); these lands became the foundation of the Papal States and established Rome as a temporal as well as a spiritual power.

Frankish ties with the papacy were further strengthened when, at papal request,

6

6. Lindisfarne Gospels, St. Mark. *British Library, London. MS Cotton. Nero D. IV, f. 93b. Ca. 700. Illuminated by Eadfrith, Bishop of Lindisfarne. The inclusion of author portraits in the Gospels reflected the influence of Roman prototypes, but the style was distinctly Celtic.*

7. Codex Amiatinus, The Prophet Ezra. *Biblioteca Laurenziana, Florence. Ca. 700. Contact between the Celtic Church in northern Europe and the papacy introduced Roman styles of manuscript illumination.*

7

Charlemagne conquered the Lombards and assumed the title of king (774). The strong links between Rome and Charlemagne restored the institution of the Christian State. Charlemagne's military success gave him control of many distinct tribes with no cultural cohesion. Like Constantine more than four centuries earlier, he used Christianity to unify his empire, imposing it under threat of death where necessary. His coronation as Holy Roman Emperor on Christmas Day, 800, marked a historic shift in the balance of European power from Rome to the north. By 1000, the north was not only the political center of Europe but the intellectual center as well.

Revival of Antiquity

Charlemagne imposed a new Christian order on his empire, creating a centralized bureaucracy entrusted to clerical officials. He encouraged uniformity in Christian worship, and the Rule of Benedict was imposed throughout the empire in 816, two years after his death. A plan sent to the Abbot of St. Gall suggested his inclination to standardize monastery design as well. Charlemagne attached great importance to clerical education, insisting that all monasteries and cathedrals have schools. Established under the guidance of Alcuin of York, these schools became centers for the dissemination of standardized texts. Alcuin emphasized the correct use of Latin and encouraged the study of classical works toward that end. His scriptorium in Tours also developed the Carolingian script, which introduced lower-case letters into the print alphabet.

Einhard, Charlemagne's adviser and biographer, praised the emperor's architectural projects in the capital of Aachen. Although other texts refer

8

8. Palatine Chapel, interior. Aachen. Consecrated 805. Inspired by late imperial architecture in Ravenna, Charlemagne's palace chapel gave visual expression to his new status as Holy Roman Emperor.

9

9. Imperial throne. Cathedral, Aachen. Marble. Ca. 800. Charlemagne was crowned Holy Roman Emperor by Pope Leo III on Christmas Day, 800, in St. Peter's, Rome. His simple but imposing throne was designed to reflect his new prestige.

10

10. Carolingian script. Ca. 800. This simple, clear script was introduced by Charlemagne as part of his attempt to standardize the Latin language. Monks were encouraged to copy classical texts, regardless of subject matter, and it is to this tradition that we owe the survival of the literature of antiquity.

to Aachen as the New Rome, it was not classical Rome that Charlemagne sought to recreate. He was the emperor of a Christian Europe, and it was the culture of Early Christian Rome that provided his model. He completed the Frankish abbey church of Saint-Denis in Paris, modeled after the early Christian churches in Rome, as a mausoleum for his father. Charlemagne's palace chapel at Aachen was inspired by the imperial Byzantine church of San Vitale (see chapter 9). The marble columns he brought from Rome and Ravenna to decorate the chapel, which Einhard refers to specifically, were clearly classical in origin. A dedication of the chapel to the Virgin Mary was recorded on Charlemagne's sarcophagus. His imperial throne was placed under the dome, reinforcing the religious foundation of his power.

Culture, Religion, and Figurative Art

Charlemagne encouraged clerical patronage. The gatehouse to the monastery at Lorsch illustrates the revival of classical forms typical of the period, with its Composite capitals and decorative stonework suggesting the influence of Roman masonry. The intellectual and Christian emphasis in Carolingian culture led to the development of manuscript illumination on an unprecedented scale. Charlemagne's role as sovereign of the Holy Roman Empire led him to establish close ties with Rome and Constantinople. Charlemagne, his successors, and clerics all commissioned manuscripts from the monastic schools set up under the guidance of Alcuin, notably in Paris and Rheims. These three influences, Roman, Byzantine, and Northumbrian, were reflected in the stylistic variety of Carolingian manuscripts. With its Roman script and naturalistic treatment of figures in landscape and architectural settings, the *Utrecht Psalter*

11. The Carolingian Empire after its division by the Treaty of Verdun (843):
a) Kingdom of Charles the Bald;
b) Kingdom of Lothair I;
c) Kingdom of Louis the German;
d) Duchy of Spoleto.

11

14

12. Altar. *St. Ambrose, Milan. Ca. 840. Made of gold, silver, and precious stones, this altar was decorated with reliefs depicting the life of Christ and signed by its master craftsman, Vuolvinius.*

13. Utrecht Psalter, Psalm XV. *University Library, Utrecht. Script. Eccl. 484. f. 8r. Parchment. 816–835. The Roman tradition of narrative illustration provided visual images to enhance the literary text of the Bible.*

14. Gatehouse to the Monastery. *Lorsch. Ca. 800. Composite capitals and decorative stonework illustrate Carolingian interest in the architectural language of antiquity.*

12

13

Christianity was the unifying force of Charlemagne's far-flung and culturally diverse empire. Loyalty to the emperor was expressed through adoption of the Christian faith, and the civil service was composed entirely of clerics.

Charlemagne's efforts to standardize religious worship, monastic organization, language, and clerical education are perhaps best understood in a political context. The importance he attached to education and language was reflected

in the growth of monastic schools, whose monks were responsible for copying and decorating religious texts. The variety of techniques and styles reflected the diverse cultural traditions represented in Charlemagne's empire.

Early Carolingian manuscripts were predominantly texts of the Gospels, illuminated with a figure of Christ in Majesty and portraits of the Four Evangelists. Later texts included the Psalms or complete versions of the Old and New Testaments.

Decorative styles varied. The use of tempera paint and gold decoration was an important feature of the scriptoria most closely associated with the imperial court. Elsewhere, narrative pen and ink drawings became the fashion, as used by the illuminator at Reims for the *Utrecht Psalter*. Elaborately decorated manuscripts, especially those produced in the prestigious scriptoria at Reims and Tours, became an essential element of aristocratic patronage in the Carolingian Empire.

This resulted not only in an increasing demand for manuscripts, but also in the development of miniatures to record their patronage and dedication.

THE CAROLINGIAN EMPIRE

15. Diptych. Biblioteca, Vatican. Ivory. Ca. 900. Commissioned by Oldericus, Abbot of the monastery of Rambona. The three patron saints of the abbey were included beneath the image of the Virgin and Child, enthroned on the right. Flat, linear, and stylized, the piece emphasizes decorative effect, not realistic portrayal.

16. San Callisto Bible, Scenes from Genesis. San Paolo fuori le Mura, Rome. Ca. 870. Following the text of Genesis, the images of the San Callisto Bible echoed the words of Pope Gregory I (590–604): "What scripture is to the educated, images are for the illiterate."

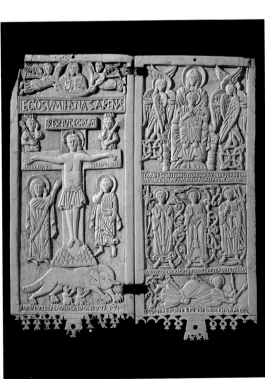

15

16

was clearly derived from the late classical tradition and stands in marked contrast to the more formal style of Northumbrian texts.

After a bitter struggle for succession, Charlemagne's Empire was split between his three grandsons under the Treaty of Verdun (843). Charles the Bald (840–877), who inherited lands corresponding to much of modern France, commissioned a manuscript from Saint-Denis, probably as a present for the pope. The use of manuscripts as important gifts suggests that they were valued no less for their material worth than for their spiritual content. Elaborately decorated, often with carved ivory covers,

they represented the vital and unifying role of Christianity in a politically divided Europe.

Ottonian Art

The Carolingian Empire was short-lived, disintegrating with invasions by Vikings and Magyars in the ninth century. But Charlemagne's concept of a Christian empire survived. Order was restored during the tenth century order by Otto I (912–973). His successors, the Ottonians, recreated much of the cultural splendor of the earlier Carolingian court, most notably in the tradition of richly decorated manuscripts.

Bishop Bernwald of Hildesheim, tutor to Otto III, revived the Roman craft of bronze-casting, commissioning a set of doors for his cathedral and a commemorative column that was decorated with reliefs clearly inspired by ancient Rome. Christianity was now the foundation of European culture, and the reliefs told the story of Christ instead of glorifying the exploits of the emperor. The coronation of Otto I as Holy Roman Emperor in 962 restored the alliance between Church and State established by Charlemagne. It also set the scene for a power struggle between the papacy and the imperial throne for the control of medieval Europe.

17. Scenes from Genesis. *St. Michael's, Hildesheim. Bronze. Completed 1015. Bishop Bernwald's revival of the Roman craft of bronze-casting was almost certainly inspired by classical sculpture he saw while on a trip to Rome.*

18. Adoration of the Magi. *St. Michael's, Hildesheim. Bronze. Completed 1015. The three-dimensional figures of the Virgin and Child with the Three Kings were set against a flat background that combined architectural details with stylized patterns. These reliefs provided pictorial versions of the Biblical stories.*

THE LAWS THAT GOD HANDED TO MOSES on Mount Sinai form the basis not only of the Jewish and Christian faiths, but also of Islam. God's revelations to Muhammad, the Prophet of Islam, expanded these laws into a behavioral code that governs all aspects of Muslim life, from marriage and commerce to war, hygiene, and prayer. These revelations, collected in the Koran, represent the scriptural foundation of Islam. The rigid set of rules was a reaction to social and political changes that wealth had brought to the Arabian Peninsula. The expansion of trade during the sixth

CHAPTER 11

THE RISE OF ISLAM

Art in the Muslim Empire

century had increasingly urbanized the nomadic Arabs, and the old tribal authority had begun to wane. Muhammad's message was aimed at what he saw as the decadence of modern life, preaching repentance before the imminent Day of Judgment, much as Christ had done before him. His monotheism and iconoclastic system of laws were at first greeted with indifference or outright hostility, but Muhammad's success at propagating the new religion proved dramatic. His political and military exploits achieved Muslim dominance of the Arabian Peninsula,

1

secured and expanded after his death (632 C.E.) by his successors, or caliphs. By 750, the Islamic Empire stretched from the Pyrenees Mountains to the Indus River. The newly urbanized Arabs had few artistic traditions of their own and adapted the architectural and decorative styles of the cultures they conquered, such as the temples, churches, and public baths of the Greco-Roman world. The Muslim Empire soon emerged as the preeminent civilization in the Western Hemisphere, united by a strict adherence to the rules laid out in the Koran.

The Dome of the Rock

The vast empire was initially ruled by the Caliphate, established in Damascus by the Umayyad Dynasty in 661. Caliph Abd al-Malik (r. 685–705) built the Dome of the Rock in Jerusalem as a shrine to both Abraham and Muhammad on the former site of Herod's Temple (itself built on the site of Solomon's Temple and destroyed by the Romans in 70 C.E.). Its enduring religious significance to Muslims, Jews, and Christians alike lies in the belief that Abraham led his son Isaac there and offered to sacrifice him to God as a proof of faith. The building's octagonal plan and dome derived from early Christian churches, and its elaborate mosaic decoration was applied by craftsmen trained in Byzantine styles and techniques. Although these and other traditional features illustrate the common religious roots of Islam and Christianity, passages from the Koran were superimposed on the architecture to stress the importance of the new and "correct" path. The shrine, ultimately, was designed as a symbol of Islamic victory over Judaism and Christianity.

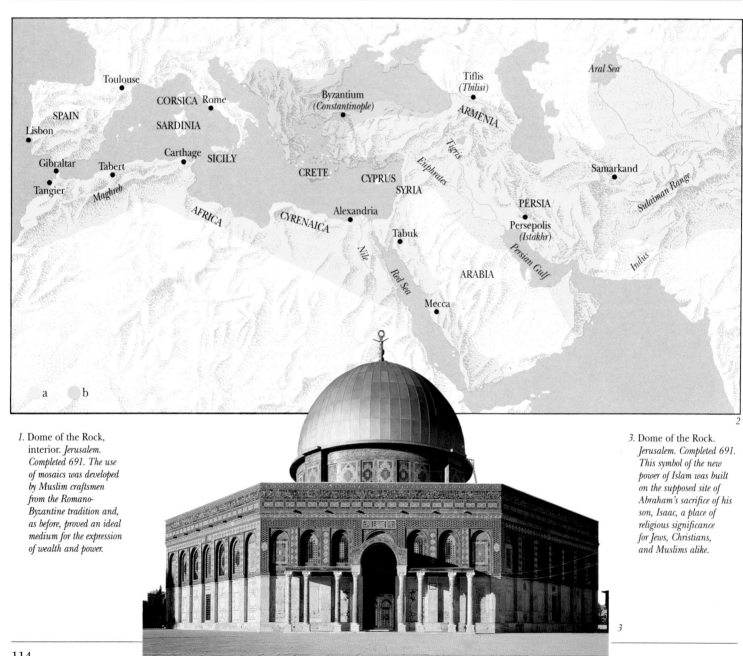

1. Dome of the Rock, interior. *Jerusalem. Completed 691. The use of mosaics was developed by Muslim craftsmen from the Romano-Byzantine tradition and, as before, proved an ideal medium for the expression of wealth and power.*

3. Dome of the Rock. *Jerusalem. Completed 691. This symbol of the new power of Islam was built on the supposed site of Abraham's sacrifice of his son, Isaac, a place of religious significance for Jews, Christians, and Muslims alike.*

Development of the Mosque

New religions invariably need new places of worship, and the mosque had different requirements from those of the pagan temple and Christian church. Islam is a simple religion, a deliberate departure from the hierarchical structure of Christian orthodoxy. Teachers, not priests, play the central clerical role, and there are no liturgical processions or altars before which to pray. Mosque design reflected these differences, being characterized by large open spaces covered for protection from the elements. A niche, or *mihrab*, is placed prominently in the *qibla* wall, which marks the direction of Mecca, toward which Muslims face during prayer. The power of Islam was expressed in the size of the mosques and the splendor of their decoration, which, following Muhammad's condemnation of idolatry, avoided figural representations.

The basic format was established early and changed little, reflecting the inherent conservatism of Islam. Abd al-Malik's successor, al-Walid I (r. 705–715), turned his attention to the capital of the Umayyad Dynasty, Damascus. His Great Mosque, built on the site of a temple of Augustus and a cathedral to Saint John the Baptist, was another example of Islamic triumphalism. It continued many of the traditions of the earlier buildings, most notably in its reuse of classical columns, marble inlay, and acanthus scroll decoration. But the scale of the structure and the richness of the glass mosaics rivaled the churches of the Byzantine Empire and deliberately invoked the new power of the Caliphate.

Luxury and the Umayyad Caliphate

The Umayyad caliphs also adapted classical and Byzantine architecture for secular

2. *Islamic Empire, ca. 750:*
   a) territory occupied
      by Muslims;
   b) the Byzantine Empire.

5. Mosaic floor in bath hall. *Khirbat al-Mafjar. Ca. 730. The contrast between the deer feeding peacefully on the left and the lion attacking on the right was probably intended to symbolize the benefits of Islamic rule.*

5

4. Great Mosque, courtyard. *Damascus. Ca. 715. Built on the site of a pagan temple, subsequently used for a Christian church, this important and early mosque provided another image for the triumph of Islam.*

6. Ceiling fresco. *Qusayr Amra. Ca. 730. These secular frescoes depicting people are some of the relatively rare examples of figurative art in Islamic decoration. Muhammad had condemned idolatry, and figural representation was avoided in Mosque design.*

4

6

As the book of God's revelations to the prophet Muhammad, the Koran is of fundamental importance to Islamic faith and culture. Written in Arabic, its text has been zealously guarded, and translations have been allowed only recently.

The importance of the words of the Prophet was reinforced by the value placed on the script, which embodied religious and ceremonial concepts and soon developed as a means of communication between man and God.

The earliest and most important of these scripts was Kufic, with its characteristic geometric form. Later calligraphic styles developed more rounded forms. Their variety reflected the different cultural traditions at work in the Islamic Empire, and their complexity ensured the high status of scribes.

Muhammad's ban of idolatry prohibited the development of figurative art in a religious context, and the importance of the Koranic text itself was reinforced by its use in decorative schemes for buildings and artifacts. Calligraphers became the artists of the Muslim world.

The idea of ornamenting a building with writing was not new, but the scale and extent to which it was exploited in the Muslim world went far beyond the formal patronal inscriptions of the Romans. Upon closer examination, the ornate mosaic patterns that were used to decorate Islamic mosques were invariably religious texts written in elaborate script.

Using the words of the Prophet as decoration for religious buildings reflected widespread knowledge of the Koranic text in the Islamic world, in contrast to the early Christian West, where direct access to the Bible was restricted to priests.

7. Page from the Book of Antidotes. *Bibliothèque Nationale, Paris. PMS Arabe 2964, f. 22. From Northern Iraq. 1199. While the early Christian Church discouraged scientific research, Islamic faith placed no such restrictions on its adherents, who made important contributions to the development of medicine, astrology, and optics.*

8. Great Mosque. *Samarra. Begun 847. With the rise of the Abbasids, who made Baghdad their capital, the heart of the Islamic world moved east and away from the culture of the Mediterranean. This was reflected in the use of the ancient Mesopotamian ziggurat as a new form for the minaret.*

7

8

buildings. They had acquired enormous wealth through conquest, which encouraged a luxurious and pleasure-loving lifestyle. Although figurative art was avoided in a religious context, secular decoration developed the themes and styles of classical Roman palaces. The caliphal palaces at Qusayr Amra and Khirbat al-Mafjar, both in Jordan, are often associated with the patronage of al-Walid II (r. 743–744). A noted hedonist, he is associated with the introduction of eunuchs and the harem into the Muslim court, and his poetry is noted for its lavish praise of women and wine. These palaces were private residences rather than seats of government, refuges from the formalities of public life and religious buildings. The appointments and decoration have a distinct informality; the leisure activities of a royal prince are depicted in scenes of hunting and music. The most elaborate part of the palace at Khirbat al-Mafjar was the bath. The tradition of baths as a public meeting place had developed in Ancient Rome and was continued in Asia Minor. Al-Walid II's bath at Khirbat al-Mafjar served as an audience chamber and banqueting hall, considerably less formal than the official royal audiences held in city mosques.

Power and the Abbasid Caliphate

The Umayyads were overthrown in 750 by the Abbasids, who claimed the Caliphate through descent from an uncle of Muhammad. The Abbasids ruled through a multiracial salaried bureaucracy, which reflected the increasing power of non-Arabic Muslims in the Islamic world. That power was further reinforced by a shift of the capital from Damascus to Baghdad. Founded by Caliph al-Mansur in 762, Baghdad was built on a circular plan almost 6,562 feet (2000 m) in diameter, with a mosque and royal palace at the center

9. Plate with decorative inscription. *Louvre, Paris. From Samarkand. Abbasid period, tenth century. Inspired by the early Chinese porcelain imported into the Islamic world, Muslim potters began to experiment with ceramic production, developing their own forms of decoration. This plate was ornamented with a pious inscription.*

9

10. Great Mosque. *Qairawan. Begun 836. Pointed arches became common in Islamic architecture during the ninth century.*

11. Mosque of Ibn Tulun. *Cairo. Completed 879. Borrowing the spiral ramp for his minaret from the Great Mosque at Samarra, the governor of Egypt visually reinforced his political links with the Abbasid Caliphate in Baghdad.*

12. Great Mosque (maqsura). *Cordoba. 961–976. Rich, ornate, and explicitly Islamic, the decoration of this royal enclosure reflected the wealth of the Umayyad rulers in Spain.*

10

11

12

and shops and streets at the perimeter to serve them. The plan symbolized the religious and political position of the caliph at the heart of the empire, and its formality underscored the highly structured nature of Islamic society. Baghdad prospered and became an important commercial and administrative center. The Caliphate, however, became increasingly isolated by the proliferation of court officials and moved out of Baghdad to Samarra early in the ninth century. The Great Mosque of the palace at Samarra was the largest ever built, covering nearly ten acres. The spiral ramp of its minaret was derived from the ziggurats of ancient Mesopotamia. This deliberate revival of eastern traditions under the Abbasid Caliphate, which included the popularization of the pointed arch, provided a new image for imperial power that emphasized the growing independence of the Arab world from its Greco-Roman forebears.

Baghdad, meanwhile, had become an important center of Arab learning. Caliph al-Mamun (r. 813–833) built an observatory and a university (House of Wisdom). Works by Aristotle, Plato, Archimedes, Euclid, and other Greek scientists and philosophers were translated into Arabic.

This, in turn, encouraged new research, notably in the fields of optics and medicine. Ptolemy's works on geography, translated in the ninth century, were particularly relevant to Muslims everywhere, as they helped determine the precise direction of Mecca. Paper was introduced from China after 751 and facilitated the dissemination of texts.

The increasing isolation of the caliphs weakened their control of the empire. The extravagant ceremonialism of the court at Samarra was an important influence on later Islamic cultures, but it also illustrated a growing interest in the trappings of imperial power.

14

14. Casket of Abd al-Malik. *Museo de Navarra, Pamplona. Ivory. Ca. 1004. The intricate carving on this casket reflected the high standards of craftsmanship in the Islamic world.*

13. Great Mosque, interior. *Cordoba. 785–987. Using Corinthian and Composite columns from earlier Roman buildings, this mosque was extended three times, finally covering an area of nearly six acres (more than two hectares) and including 581 columns.*

13

Provincial governors became increasingly powerful, and around 900 they began to assert their independence in small states such as Morocco, Tunisia, and Afghanistan. Their links with the Abbasid rulers in Baghdad were reinforced by their choice of architectural and decorative style. The mosque at Qairawan in Tunisia featured extensive use of pointed arches and decorative tiles on the *mihrab* that were imported from Mesopotamia. Ibn Tulun's mosque in Cairo was derived directly from the Great Mosque at Samarra, complete with a spiral ramp on the minaret. The mosque was part of a large complex (most of it since destroyed) that also included a palace, residences, and a hospital.

Muslim Art in Spain

Although part of the Islamic world, Spain was a long way from Baghdad. After the Abbasids had overthrown the Umayyad Dynasty (750), one of the Umayyads, Abd al-Rahman I, established himself as an independent ruler in Spain. His Great Mosque in Cordoba, probably built on the site of an earlier Christian church, was originally an enclosure of approximately 797 square feet (74 square meters). The ornate structure was enlarged by later rulers, with the final additions (987–988) made by al-Mansur, the chief minister to Hisham II. One of the largest mosques in the Muslim world, it was an important statement of power in a country where the dominating power was a minority and conversion to Islam was not compulsory. The unusual two-story elevation was made possible by the use of small columns, readily available in the ruins of Roman buildings. Muslim Spain was an outpost of the Islamic world and needed to give visual emphasis to its power over Christian Europe. The complexity of the interior, with its highly elaborate horseshoe arches, reinforced the superiority of Islamic

15

16

15. Alhambra, courtyard of the lions. *Granada. 1354–1391. Taking its name from the lions around the fountain, the intricate carved details of this arcade illustrate the proliferation of ornament during the last years of Muslim power in Spain.*

16. Alhambra, salon of the Dos Hermanas. *Granada. 1354–1391. The minute attention to detail was overwhelming in its effect and provided a standard that was imitated by later Spanish designers.*

culture both in terms of wealth and technical skill. The same message was conveyed in the decorative arts. The casket carved for the son of al-Mansur, with its royal imagery set against a highly ornate background, reveals a quality of craftsmanship unknown in Europe at the time.

By 1100, however, the situation began to change radically. One of the major priorities of Christian Europe was the reconquest of Spain, and its armies pushed south with that aim. By 1260, the Muslims lost everything but Granada, which Spain recaptured in 1492. As Islamic power waned, its architecture increased in complexity and elaboration.

The Alhambra, built in Granada by the last great Moorish dynasty in Spain, carries a distinct message as well as a timeless extravagance and luxury; its designers used every opportunity to enhance the status of their ruler in a visual attempt to prop up his failing regime.

Fatimid Egypt

The economic power of the Arab world was based on trade in luxury goods. Muhammad, a merchant himself, encouraged trade as an honest means of making money. The rise of the Fatimid Dynasty (915–1171) in Egypt established a rival caliphate to that in Baghdad. The new regime was commemorated in the founding of a new capital, Cairo, whose architecture deliberately competed with the scale and grandeur of that in Baghdad. Cairo soon became a thriving cosmopolitan trading center, shifting the focus of economic power from Mesopotamia back to the Mediterranean. Cairo's location and prominence enabled it to exploit the growing potential for trade with a reviving Christian Europe, attracting Italian merchants eager to supply the new demand for luxury goods with high-quality craftsmanship and costly materials.

18. Griffin. Camposanto, Pisa. Bronze. Tenth century. High-quality bronze casting and intricate chiseling gave visual expression to the wealth of Fatimid Egypt. This splendid object came to Pisa around the middle of the eleventh century.

17

17. Al-Azhar Mosque. Cairo. Founded 969. The establishment of the Shi'ite Fatimids in Egypt in opposition to the Sunni Caliphate in Baghdad reflected the increasing enmity between these two sects, each asserting its own claims to ideological and political descent from Muhammad.

18

CHAPTER 12

AFRICAN ART

Traditions and Old Kingdoms

THE PHYSICAL ENVIRONMENT OF AFRICA is immensely varied. From equatorial rainforests to deserts, from mountains to savannahs and woodlands, the wide range of both climate and terrain has fostered the emergence of many diverse lifestyles and favored the growth of small, isolated communities. Africa's earliest inhabitants were hunters. Both the San of the Kalahari Desert and the Pygmy tribes of Zaire are thought to be their descendants, and their cultures have remained largely unchanged since the Stone Age. Nomadic herdsmen inhabited the Sahara, once lush and fertile, until they were forced to migrate south as it dried up (4000–2000 B.C.E.). Their language, Bantu, forms the basis of most modern African languages. While some peoples continued their pastoral existence, such as the Masai in Kenya and Tanzania, others developed a settled lifestyle as agriculturalists. It was from these communities that the sophisticated urban societies and ancient kingdoms of Africa emerged.

Trade and Conquest

Africa has never been united under a single ruler, but the continent's rich natural

1

resources have formed the basis for the growth of powerful empires and provided a major incentive for foreign domination. One of the earliest empires in Africa, Ancient Egypt (see chapter 3) was conquered by the Romans, whose empire stretched along the North African coast. Egypt's fertile Nile Valley provided the empire with corn, and huge shipments of marble, ivory, and precious metals were exported from the continent to satisfy the Roman appetite for luxury. But the Sahara proved a formidable obstacle to further expansion. Christianity did spread south from Egypt into the neighboring kingdom of Axum (modern Ethiopia), whose rulers, down to the last emperor, Haile Selassie (r. 1930–1974), claimed descent from the union of Solomon and the Queen of Sheba. But with the expansion of the Muslim Empire in the eighth century (see chapter 11), the country was cut off from the mainstream of Christianity and developed its own distinctive traditions.

Arab Merchants and Islam

Attracted by abundant supplies of gold, copper, ivory, frankincense, and other goods, Arab merchants established trade links down the east coast of Africa, stimulating the growth of flourishing cities along the coasts of present-day Kenya and Tanzania. They also brought their religion, Islam, which was adopted by Bantu-speaking Africans. The two cultures merged to create a third, Swahili. Farther north, Arab caravans risked the hazardous desert crossing to reach the cities along the southern border of the Sahara, exchanging luxuries from the Mediterranean for gold, leather, and slaves.

Islam had a major impact in the region, spreading gradually through the Sudan and northern Nigeria, where the rulers of Mali adopted it as the religion of their kingdom

1. Plaque with warrior and attendants. *National Museum, Lagos. Copper. Ca. seventeenth century. The sculptor of this Benin bronze has given visual expression to the relative importance of the figures by varying their physical proportions and the quantity of their ornaments.*

2. Conical tower. *Zimbabwe. The spectacular ruins of this palace-temple complex have been variously identified as King Solomon's Mines and the palace of the Queen of Sheba.*

3. Hunting horn. *Museo Nazionale Luigi Pigorini, Rome. Ivory. Sixteenth century. Carved ivory objects, like this piece made by the Bulom people of Sierra Leone, were popular with Portuguese traders and imported into Europe.*

4. Spoon. *Museo Nazionale Luigi Pigorini, Rome. Ivory. Sixteenth century. Made by the Bini people of Nigeria, this ivory formed part of the Medici collection in Florence.*

2

3

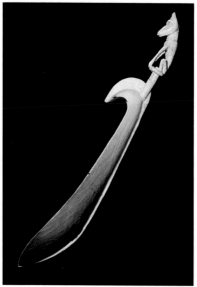

4

in the fourteenth century. Great mosques in the Mali cities of Timbuktu and Jenne gave visual expression to the power and prestige of the country's Islamic rulers. Built of mud and pierced with permanent wooden scaffolding, they had little in common with contemporary Islamic architecture in Cairo or Baghdad (see chapter 32). Nor was the Muslim ban on representational imagery as strictly observed here as elsewhere in the Islamic world. These characteristics reflected the ways in which the new faith was adapted to ensure the continuation of local tribal traditions.

The Arrival of Europeans

In the fifteenth century, Portuguese merchants risked the perils of uncharted ocean to sail around the Atlantic coast of Africa, establishing links with tribes in Guinea and Nigeria. They were soon followed by other Europeans, attracted by the substantial profits to be made in gold, ivory, and slave trade. Vasco da Gama's famous voyage around the Cape of Good Hope (1497–1499) in search of a new route to the markets of the East extended European knowledge of the African continent. But the early

Europeans, like the Arab merchants, largely confined themselves to markets on the coast or just south of the Sahara. It was only in the nineteenth century, when the Industrial Revolution dramatically increased Europe's need for raw materials, that intrepid explorers ventured into Africa's inhospitable interior. By then, the highly profitable slave trade had had a catastrophic effect on West African societies, and political domination proved comparatively easy. By 1914, the entire continent, with the exception of Liberia and Ethiopia, was under the control of European powers.

AFRICAN ART

5. Reliquary figure (mbulungulu). *Wood covered with bronze and copper. These wooden carvings, covered with sheets of precious metals, were placed by the Kota people over the relics of their important ancestors.*

6. Reliquary figure (mbulungulu). *Wood covered with bronze and copper.*

7. Mask. *Wood. White-faced masks, like this example from Gabon, were used by several neighboring peoples in the rainforests of Gabon and Zaire, including the Kota, Lumbo, Punu, and Mpongwe.*

5

6

7

AFRICAN MASKS

African masks were not designed simply as works of art. A central feature of African tribal culture, they were imbued with mystical powers and invariably played a part in distinctive ceremonies and tribal rites, many of which involved elaborate and colorful costumes. Masks have served many functions in African societies, but in all cases they have provided a link between the real and invisible worlds, reinforcing the social structure of the community. Although stylistic and functional connections have been traced between the masks of neighboring peoples, each community developed distinctive artistic traditions. Ranging from the realistic to the abstract, the masks typically represent the facial features of humans and animals. They were designed specifically for use in initiation ceremonies, funerals, and the rites of secret societies. Some were used for didactic purposes, others for entertainment.

By no means were all of them intended to be beautiful; many were designed specifically to invoke awe or terror. Some masks were designed to represent ancestral spirits, who could be invoked against fire, disease, or natural disasters. Others served as peace offerings. Many were conspicuously displayed in dances, but others were deliberately hidden to enhance their mystical qualities.

Masks generally could be worn in three different ways: face masks, vertically covering the face; helmets, encasing the entire head; and crest, resting upon the head, usually covered by material as part of the disguise. Both visually and historically independent from the aesthetic canons of Western art, African masks were both appealing and inspiration to the nineteenth-century avant-garde, and they were a formative influence on the development of Cubism and the other modern art movements (see chapter 50).

9. *Pablo Picasso,* Head with scarifications. *Oil and sand on panel. 1907. Picasso was one of many Western artists who were influenced by African sculpture.*

10. *Max Ernst,* Head of a bird. *Bronze. 1934–1935. Ernst's sculpture was directly influenced by his experience of African art.*

8. Mask. *Musée Barbier-Müller, Geneva. Wood and vegetable fibers. This Tusyan tribal mask from Upper Volta is characterized by the highly abstract and geometric representation of the face.*

8

9

10

124

Geographical and Cultural Diversity

Exploration of the African interior brought Europe into contact with an enormous landmass and peoples whose religious, social, and cultural traditions had developed largely independently of the outside world. Africa's natural environment had not only proved an effective barrier to outsiders but had also encouraged the development of a multitude of cultures. The dramatic decline in elevation from the inland plateaus of East Africa to its narrow coastal plains had protected the rich mineral resources of Zimbabwe from Arab and European traders. Tropical rainforests along the southern coast of West Africa and in the Congo basin protected area tribes from the powerful Islamic states farther north and fostered the growth of isolated communities, such as the Kota in Gabon and the Kwele in Zaire, as well as the powerful kingdom of Benin near the Nigerian coast.

The European invaders of the nineteenth century may have seen Africa as the "Dark Continent," peopled by tribes of uncivilized savages, and assumed that outsiders were responsible for anything they perceived as "civilized," but this view has obscured the facts. Anthropological research has provided evidence of both primitive and sophisticated communities. It has also given evidence of highly developed and well-established artistic traditions. Evolving in response to the needs of highly diverse lifestyles, social structures, and religious beliefs, the range of African art is considerable. Generalizations are inevitably misleading, but one important characteristic is a strong reliance on tradition. Nevertheless, our understanding of African art is hampered not only by the lack of written records but also by the relatively small amount of research so far carried out.

AFRICAN ART

11. Zoomorphic mask. *Metropolitan Museum of Modern Art, New York. Wood. Animal masks, like this example from the Mambila people of Cameroon, were used in African ceremonies to frighten or amuse.*

12. Mask. *Metropolitan Museum of Modern Art, New York. Wood. It was the almost abstract qualities of African masks, like this one from the Grebo people of the Ivory Coast, that had a direct appeal to the artists of the modern art movements of the twentieth century.*

13. Mask. *Metropolitan Museum of Modern Art, New York. Wood. The white coloring on this mask, made by the Kwele people of Zaire, was derived from kaolin.*

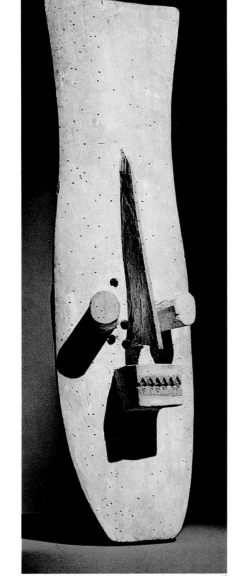

11   12   13

Hunters and Herdsmen

The Rift Valley in East Africa has provided fossil evidence of the earliest human ancestors, but the continent has also revealed some of the oldest examples of artistic creation. Prehistoric hunters in southern Africa painted images of zebras and rhinoceroses on cave walls, and the herdsmen of the once-fertile Sahara decorated rocks with pictures and engravings of elephants, horses, gazelles, and camels. But the nomadic lifestyle of hunters and herdsmen, who have long populated large tracts of Africa, is not ideally suited to the development of large-scale art. The San of the Kalahari continue to paint and engrave rock, but nomadic communities generally have concentrated on more portable forms of artistic expression. Notable among these are the elaborate personal adornments—hairstyles, jewelry, and shields—of the Masai in Kenya and Tanzania. The major developments in African art have taken place in the more settled agricultural and mercantile communities.

Zimbabwe

The lack of suitable and readily available building stone in Africa encouraged the use of wood, mud, and other less permanent materials for use in construction. Thus, few examples of ancient African architecture survive today. A notable exception is the stone-built Zimbabwe Ruins complex in the present-day nation of Zimbabwe. As capital of the prosperous Monomatapa Empire, the settlement amassed great wealth from the area's mineral resources, especially gold and copper, which it bartered with east African traders. Archaeological research

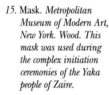

14. Mask. *Metropolitan Museum of Modern Art, New York. Wood. Made for members of the Lo society of the Senufo people in the Ivory Coast, this complex mask was decorated with vegetable fibers and was probably intended to be worn with a distinctive costume.*

16. Human Head. *National Museum, Lagos. Terracotta. Ca. 500–200 B.C.E. Found in Rufin Kura (Nok, Nigeria), this head is approximately 14 inches (36 cm) high. It is an example of the earliest known terracotta sculptures in Africa.*

15. Mask. *Metropolitan Museum of Modern Art, New York. Wood. This mask was used during the complex initiation ceremonies of the Yaka people of Zaire.*

14

15

16

has revealed that the site was occupied as early as the second century C.E., but the existing structures date to the fifteenth century. Like their counterparts in Mesoamerica (see chapter 35), the builders at Zimbabwe exploited the potential of mortarless block walls to create an enclosed complex that contained a royal palace and temple. Fine metal ornaments are among the local manufactures discovered at the site.

Sculpture

African artists and their patrons have concentrated on sculpture, and it is in this area that the artists have made the greatest contribution to the history of art. Free-standing statuettes, decorative weights for measuring gold, ceremonial cups, royal thrones, decorative panels for doors, carved lintels, portrait heads, and, above all, masks have given African craftsmen the opportunity to exploit the potential of a wide variety of media and develop a corresponding diversity of styles. Although subject to local availability, materials commonly used in African sculpture have included wood, ivory, clay, vegetable fibers, bronze, copper, and gold. The diversity of media required the development of specialized skills in both carving and modeling, as well as a variety of embellishment techniques.

Nok

The oldest known African sculptures outside Egypt were found at Nok in Nigeria during the 1940s. These terracotta figures of humans and animals have been dated to as early as 500 B.C.E. Their strongly incised features suggest that the style derived from an older wood-carving tradition, but much research is still needed to confirm their place in the development of African art.

17. Vase. *National Museum, Lagos. Bronze. Ninth–tenth century C.E. African bronze workers displayed a high degree of skill in their work. This vase in the form of a shell surmounted by a leopard was excavated at Igbo-Isaiah (Igbo-Ukwo) in Nigeria.*

18. Vessel. *National Museum, Lagos. Bronze. Ninth–tenth century C.E. Elaborately decorated, this vase was also excavated at Igbo-Isaiah.*

17

18

Little else is known about the culture in which these sculptures were produced, but the tin mine in which they were discovered has revealed evidence of an ironworks industry.

Use of Metals

Throughout Africa, Bantu-speaking tribes were beginning to work the continent's rich metal resources by 500 B.C.E. These provided not only an important source of wealth but also a new material for sculpture. The terracotta sculpture in Ife, capital of the Yoruba people of southern Nigeria, shows a strong resemblance to the Nok tradition, which continued when the Ife adopted bronze as a sculpting medium. The earliest bronze sculptures found in Ife have been dated to the sixth century C.E. Ife bronzes were cast by the "lost-wax" process: a wax model was covered with clay to reproduce the image, which was heated to remove the wax and then refilled with molten metal. Ife culture flourished from the twelfth to the sixteenth centuries. Later Ife bronzes show a distinct trend toward naturalism, culminating in a series of masks, statuettes, and portrait heads associated with the royal court.

Benin

Arguably the greatest African bronze sculptures were crafted in the old city of Benin, in southern Nigeria. Powerful and rich, Benin prospered (ca. 1400–1700) from trade with neighboring tribes and European merchants on the coast. By 1600, Benin was a vast walled city with an imposing royal palace. European visitors were full of praise for the city, its architecture, and the high quality

19. Figure of an Oni of Ife. *Museum of Ife Antiquities, Ife. Copper alloy. Fourteenth–fifteenth century. This famous statuette of a ruler of Ife reflects the growing trend toward naturalism in Ife sculpture.*

19

20. Head of an Oni. *National Museum, Lagos. Copper alloy. Twelfth–fifteenth century. Belonging to the early period of Benin culture, this portrait head illustrates the influence of the naturalistic tradition of Ife sculpture.*

20

21. Head of an Oni. *Museum of Ife Antiquities, Ife. Copper alloy. Twelfth–fifteenth century. Often praised as the peak of African sculpture, Ife portrait heads display a high degree of naturalism that has long appealed to Western European aesthetic taste.*

21

of craftsmanship in its sculptural decoration (even if they were shocked at the pagan practices of its inhabitants). The Benin tradition of bronze sculpture owed much to that of Ife. Royal patronage of court craftsmen encouraged the development of naturalistic portrait heads as well as a tradition of high-quality relief sculpture, both in wood and metal, to decorate the doors, lintels, and other appointments of royal palaces. Bronze required not only material wealth but technical skill, making it an ideal material to promote an image of power and authority.

Style and Function

The lack of naturalistic proportion in much African art was seen by nineteenth-century Europeans as evidence of a lack of skill, and they derided it as primitive and uncivilized. It should have come as no surprise, however, that African art did not conform to the aesthetic canons of the West. After all, it had developed its own traditions largely independent of external influences. Moreover, even in the history of Western art, there have been long periods when naturalism was not an artistic goal. Indeed, a lack of interest in naturalism has often been associated with a desire to express the spiritual and supernatural aspects of religious belief; this was certainly the case in the development of early Christian and Byzantine art (see chapter 9). In this context, it is significant that the African tradition of naturalistic sculpture developed mainly in the royal courts of Ife and Benin.

Very different traditions emerged in the smaller tribal communities that populated the rest of the continent. The reliquary figures of the Kota people in Gabon, with their simplified and stylized faces resting on "legs" and the almost abstract masks

---

AFRICAN ART

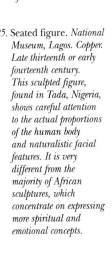

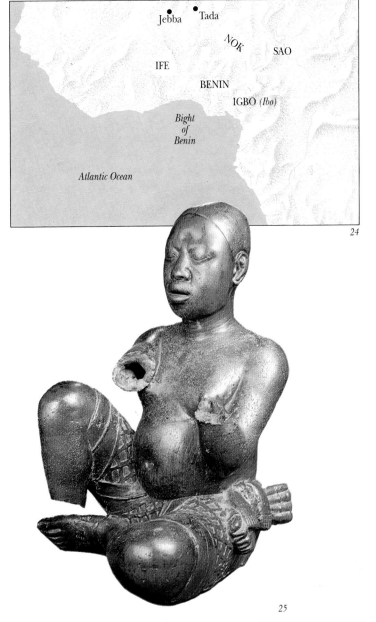

22. Head of a Queen Mother. *National Museum, Lagos. Copper alloy. Early sixteenth century. Detailed and naturalistic, this portrait head was typical of early Benin bronzes.*

23. Mask. *Metropolitan Museum of Art, New York. Ivory. Ca. sixteenth century. The kings of Benin carried small masks such as this on their belts as symbols of royal power.*

24. *Map of the principal centers of western African culture.*

25. Seated figure. *National Museum, Lagos. Copper. Late thirteenth or early fourteenth century. This sculpted figure, found in Tada, Nigeria, shows careful attention to the actual proportions of the human body and naturalistic facial features. It is very different from the majority of African sculptures, which concentrate on expressing more spiritual and emotional concepts.*

of the Grebo people in the Ivory Coast both display a profoundly different approach to the portrayal of facial features.

Far from attempting to represent actual personalities, the sculptors of these small, independent communities sought to give visual expression to more spiritual and intangible concepts, ranging from fear, respect, and revenge to peacefulness and amusement. Masks, while an integral part of the ceremonies and rituals that unified particular societies, were only one element of the wide range of works produced by African sculptors. The many others included wooden figures to contain magical substances believed to ward off disease and natural disaster, memorial screens for important ancestors, and ceremonial cups and plates for tribal chiefs.

The most important contribution of African sculpture to the history of art lies precisely in its variety of materials, functions, and styles that conform to no single set of representational rules.

26

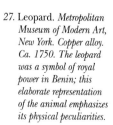

26. Olowe of Ise, Bowl. *Private Collection. Wood. Ca. 1925. One of the greatest of the Yoruba sculptors, Olowe of Ise (died 1938) carved many decorative doors for Yoruba royal palaces, often incorporating figures that represented British colonial administrators.*

27. Leopard. *Metropolitan Museum of Modern Art, New York. Copper alloy. Ca. 1750. The leopard was a symbol of royal power in Benin; this elaborate representation of the animal emphasizes its physical peculiarities.*

27

INDIA CAN CLAIM ONE OF THE OLDEST civilizations in the world. By 4000 B.C.E., farmers were cultivating the fertile soils of the upper Indus Valley, their surplus wealth stimulating the development of a sophisticated urban culture (ca. 2500 B.C.E.). Archaeologists have discovered a number of early Indus sites, including the twin capitals of Mohenjo-daro and Harappa, and a large quantity of pottery, small-scale sculptures, and jewelry that provide evidence of a wealthy elite. The drainage systems at Mohenjo-daro and Harappa were unparalleled in contemporary Sumerian and Egyptian cultures, with

CHAPTER 13

BUDDHISM, JAINISM, AND HINDUISM

The Development of Indian Art

which they had established trading links. A huge stone bath on top of the citadel at Mohenjo-daro suggests that cleanliness also played an important role in religion. Laid out in a grid plan with well-defined areas for rich and poor, these cities suggest a highly structured society but have so far provided scant evidence of temples, palaces, royal tombs, or other evidence of societies' political or religious organization. The language appears on seal inscriptions but it is still not deciphered, severely restricting our knowledge of the culture and the reasons for its economic decline after ten centuries of relative stability.

The Indus civilization was finally overwhelmed by invading Aryan tribes from Central Asia (ca. 1500 B.C.E.).

Early Indian Culture

The Aryans imposed a new culture on India. The word "India" is derived from the Sanskrit *Sindhu*, the Aryan name for the Indus. From their religious texts, the Vedas, it is clear that the fair-skinned Aryans considered themselves superior to the darker indigenous populations. Racial distinctions eventually became blurred, but color remained the basis of a complex four-tiered class system that developed in response to the growth of towns in the Ganges Plain. Priests (*brahmans*) represented the highest class, followed by warriors and secular rulers (*kshatriyas*), farmers and merchants (*vaishayas*), and serfs (*shudras*). Status was determined by birth and based on race. It could only change with reincarnation, a fundamental Vedic belief that gave religious justification to the structure of society. In the sixth century B.C.E., growing dissatisfaction with the rigidity of the caste system found an outlet in two fledgling movements: Jainism and Buddhism. Both rejected the need for priests or specific deities, promoting a moral lifestyle that aimed at providing release from the endless cycle of rebirth through spiritual purification. Jainism, founded by Mahavira (ca. 599–527 B.C.E.), reacted against violence to animals as well as to people and insisted on strict vegetarianism. Buddha, "The Enlightened One," was born Siddhartha Gautama (ca. 556 B.C.E.), a warrior-caste prince who rejected his wealthy background and sought salvation through self-denial and meditation. After his achievement of *nirvana*, or release from earthly desires, he wandered and preached in northern India. His message attracted converts and donations from all

1. Buddha. *Museum, Mathura. Sandstone. Gupta, fifth century. The image of the Buddha became increasingly removed from his human form, as reflected in the increasing stylization of his facial features as well as his clothes, hair, and halo.*

2. Dancer. *National Museum, New Delhi. Bronze. Ca. 2000 B.C.E. Archaeological research has provided evidence of a highly structured society in the Indus Valley at this time, but our inability to decipher its texts has made identification of this dancer from Mohenjo-daro impossible.*

3. Neminatha. *Museo Nazionale d'Arte Orientale, Rome. Bronze. Ca. 1450. One of the twenty-four saints, or Tirthantharas, of the Jain religion. The characteristically rigid poses of these figures reflect the austerity and severity of the Jainist faith.*

4. and 5. Seal impressions with sacred bulls. *National Museum, New Delhi. Ca. 3000 B.C.E. The appearance of the distinctive humped cattle of India on these seals from Mohenjo-daro suggests that these animals acquired their religious significance at a very early stage in the development of Indian civilization.*

3

2

4

5

levels of society, and by his death (ca. 486 B.C.E.), he had organized a monastic order.

Asoka and the Mauryan Empire

The power of Buddhism was considerably enhanced by the conversion of Asoka (r. 273–232 B.C.E.), the third and greatest ruler of the Mauryan Empire. The Mauryan Empire had been founded by Chandragupta Maurya (r. 322–298 B.C.E.), who had expanded his lands in northeast India to the fringes of the Greek Seleucid Empire. Greek writers compared the extravagance of his capital, Pataliputra, with the cities of Persia, but little remains of its wooden structures. Asoka explained his conversion to Buddhism as an expression of remorse after a particularly bloody victory, but it had political advantages as well, lessening both the power of the priests and the rigidity of the caste system. Inscriptions on his edict pillars announced the new laws and moral precepts of his reign. Their capitals show distinctive Persian and even Greek details, testifying to cultural and economic links with the Hellenistic Empires. Asoka reinforced his new faith by locating these pillars on sites marking the key events in the Buddha's life and by building a network of stupas (shrines) —84,000 in all, according to legend— over relics of the Buddha. Under Asoka's patronage, Buddhism began to change from a way of life to a ritualistic religion.

The Spread of Buddhism

Buddhism survived the collapse of the Mauryan Empire. The political vacuum was filled by the Andhrans in central India and by the Kushans in the north. Although power was fragmented, India's supply of spices, pearls, and ivory ensured flourishing trade with the Roman Empire

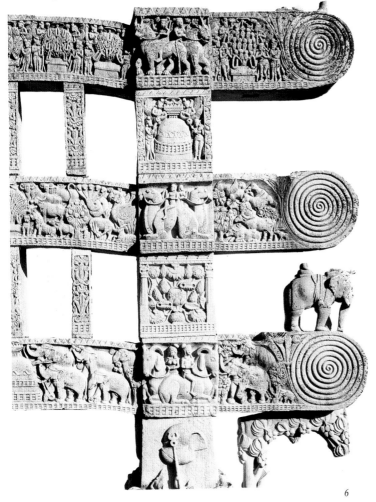

6. Stupa I, eastern torana. *Sanchi. First century C.E. These stone gateways were carved with scenes from the life of the Buddha. He is represented by symbols only, however, such as a footprint or an empty throne.*

7. Stupa I. *Sanchi. Begun second century B.C.E. Founded by the Emperor Asoka, the structure today represents a considerable enlargement of his original project. The three-tiered umbrella crowning the building symbolizes the three jewels of Buddhism: Buddha himself, the Law, and monastic communities.*

8. Lion capital. *Archaeological Museum, Sarnath. Sandstone. Third century B.C.E. From Asoka's column at Sarnath, this capital testifies to the economic links between Asoka's empire and the Hellenistic world.*

and elsewhere. The Andhrans controlled the sea routes to the West, and the Kushans exploited their position between China and the Mediterranean. The wealth of the Andhra rulers was reflected in their embellishment of Asoka's stupa at Sanchi, adding stone *toranas* (gateways) decorated with scenes from the life of Buddha. The Buddha himself was represented by symbols, such as footprints and an empty throne. The railing around the stupa enclosed the sacred precinct, providing an area for clockwise circumambulation of the shrine. This was an essential element in the new Buddhist ritual.

Through his imitation of the movement of the sun, the worshiper was put in harmony with the cosmos, symbolized by the mound of the stupa.

The Buddhist Empire established by the Kushans in northern India and Afghanistan during the first century C.E. coincided with a fundamental change in the nature of Buddhism. The Buddha was no longer revered as a merely exemplary human being but worshiped as a god in his own right. Symbolic images were inadequate for this new approach, and the Buddha was given human form. Early statues emphasized his physical reality with heavy drapery, closely modeled

on Greek or Roman prototypes. But this image underwent an evolution. The simple solar disc was soon elaborately carved, and the drapery became increasingly stylized and transparent. The ageless spirituality of the new image reinforced the Buddha's attainment of *nirvana*. Colossal statues provided easily recognizable images of his power and enlightenment. The increasing wealth and power of Buddhism were also expressed in the development of Buddhist architecture. The tradition of rock-cut *chaityas*, or worship halls, and *viharas*, or monasteries, dates to the early Buddhist custom of seeking refuge in caves during the monsoon. But the growing

9. Yakshi. *Indian Museum, Calcutta. Pink sandstone. Third century C.E. Female earth spirits were common in Buddhist temples, and this example from Mathura was typical in its celebration of the female form.*

10. The caves at Ajanta. *Second century B.C.E. to seventh century C.E. This remarkable complex of rock-cut cave temples was rediscovered by soldiers hunting tigers in 1817.*

10

11. Cave 26, Ajanta. *Early sixth century. Originally derived from Western architectural traditions, the columns and capitals of Indian temples soon developed their own distinctive forms.*

9

11

emphasis on ritual encouraged more elaborate, custom-built structures. The earliest attempts at cutting large chambers out of living rock date to the second century B.C.E. One of the largest complexes of this type are the caves at Ajanta, with twenty-nine *chaityas* and *viharas*, built between the second century B.C.E. and the seventh century C.E. The façades and interior rectangular halls of the *chaityas* were elaborately decorated with sculpture and wall paintings, whose contemporary settings reflected the wealthy lifestyle of their patrons.

The Rise of Hindu Art

The idealized image of Buddha and the courtly decoration of the caves at Ajanta are associated with India's Gupta Dynasty (ca. 320–540 C.E.). Little remains of the art of this period, but its importance as an expression of Gupta power survives in the *Vishnudharmottaram*, a treatise on art that outlines appropriate decoration for palaces, private houses, and temples. Consciously reviving ancient Mauryan culture, the Gupta rulers adopted pre-Buddhist Vedic traditions, which by now had been formalized into Hinduism. Although tolerant of Buddhism,

the Guptas supported the new Hindu religion and thereby ensured its predominance. Buddhism began to decline in India, despite its continuing popularity in Southeast Asia.

Hinduism can be seen as a reaction to the monotheistic worship of Buddha, with worshipers choosing their personal deity from the enormously complex Hindu pantheon. Headed by the trinity of Brahma, Vishnu, and Shiva, it incorporates figures from the Vedic past as well as legendary Indian heroes and local spirits. Many of the deities have more than one incarnation. The Buddha was included as the ninth incarnation of Vishnu, who is also embodied in Rama and Krishna.

BUDDHISM, JAINISM, AND HINDUISM

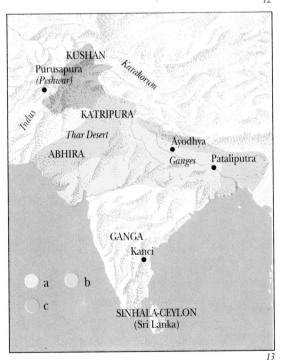

12

12. Harem scene. *Cave 17, Ajanta. Wall painting. Fifth century. The celebration of physical love was a common theme in Indian culture, according to which the pleasures of the flesh are not sinful.*

14. Buddha. *National Museum, New Delhi. Black marble. Second century C.E. (?). Like the Christian halo, the circular form representing the sanctity of Buddha —as in this statue from Gandhara—derived from the Persian symbol of divinity, the solar disc.*

13. *Map of India:*
a) Gupta Empire;
b) states owing allegiance to the Gupta emperors;
c) Kushan Empire.

13

14

Indian art was created above all in a religious context. Shiva, one of the three supreme deities (with Brahma and Vishnu) in the extensive Hindu pantheon, was a particularly popular subject among adherents. Hindu religion emphasizes the transcendental and cyclical forces of life.

Unlike Western religious traditions, which make a clear distinction between good and evil, Hinduism invests many of its deities with opposing forces. Thus, Shiva is not only seen as the creator and maintainer of the cosmos but also as its destroyer, for he represents the renewel of Nature. Even for this reason Shiva was at times considered the god Kala, who symbolized Time.

Statues of Shiva in these three aspects depict his contrasting roles in visual terms: as the creator, Vamadeva, he is depicted as feminine and gentle; as the maintainer, Mahadeva, he seems benign and tranquil; as the destroyer, Bhairava, he is inevitably ugly. Also the god of fertility and regeneration, he is often represented by a phallus, or lingam.

The common image of Shiva dancing is a direct expression of the cosmic forces of creation and destruction. Extra pairs of arms reinforce his supernatural power. The act of creation within the circle of the cosmos is contrasted by its simultaneous destruction, symbolized by the flames surrounding it. Shiva's complicated pose, with one foot resting on the demon Ignorance, includes gestures of benediction that were a standard element in Hindu dance ritual.

The triad of deities represented (Shiva, Brahma, and Vishnu) is common in Indian epic and was often depicted in a single image: one body with three heads.

15. Dancing Shiva.
Rijksmuseum, Amsterdam.
Bronze. Chola,
twelfth century.

15

The various incarnations often incorporate opposing forces in the universe, such as good and evil. Thus, Shiva is both the creator and destroyer; his wife appears as the gentle Parvati but also as the violent, bloodthirsty Kali. Hinduism survived the collapse of the Gupta Empire in the sixth century to become the major religion in India, which it remains today.

Style and Conformity

Indian art came to be criticized for a lack of originality or dynamic change. The criticism is both misleading and misguided. There was a close relationship between sculptors and the Hindu priests, who established the formal guidelines for temple decoration from their religious texts. Hindu sculptors not only received training in technique but also studied the sacred texts and their interpretation. The basic images and stylistic models were fixed by tradition, and the concept of originality as understood in the West had little meaning for them. A work achieved excellence if the sculpture succeeded in penetrating the spiritual significance of the image. This was expressed through subtle distinctions of gesture, proportion, and pose, reflecting the importance of dancing as part of the Hindu ritual.

Hindu Temples

Hindu art and architecture developed slowly. Influenced by Buddhist tradition, the Hindus continued the construction of rock-cut temples for some time. The thirty-five "caves" at Ellora (in present-day Maharashtra state)—one of the architectural wonders of India—include Hindu as well as Buddhist and Jain temples. But the new religion soon developed its own forms of artistic and architectural expression. The earliest surviving freestanding Hindu temples date from the fifth century. With their square cells,

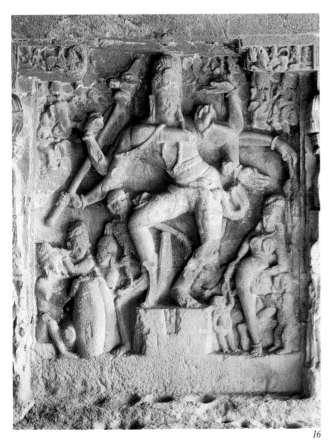

16. Shiva dancing for Parvati. *Kailasanatha Temple, Ellora. Stone. Ca. 757–790.*

17. Vishnu with crown and royal jewels. *National Museum, New Delhi. Stone. Gupta, fifth century. A jeweled crown, armlets, and necklaces were used to reinforce the power of Vishnu.*

17

18. Couple. *Kailasanatha Temple, Ellora. Stone. Ca. 757–783. The solid broad chest and shoulders of the man are a marked contrast to the rounded form of the female he embraces.*

18

137

fronted by a porch, they owed much to Hellenistic and Roman prototypes. But the formal outline was soon disguised by elaborate sculpted decoration dominated by an ornate *shikhara*, or tower over the sacred cell. The emergence of gently curving *shikharas* in northern areas of country contrasted sharply with the angular slab tiers typically seen in the south, reflecting divergent political developments in the two parts of the Indian subcontinent. Political power in the north was claimed by Muslim invaders, who achieved dominance by the thirteenth century and imposed a new and very different culture (see chapter 32).

But Hindu traditions continued in the south under the Chola and Pallava dynasties, and Hindu artists continued to develop a characteristic style.

19. Durga Temple. *Aihole. Ca. 550. Indian craftsmen used architecture as a vehicle for sculptural decoration.*

20. Kandariya Mahadeo Temple. *Khajuraho. Ca. 1025–1050. Later Hindu temples became increasingly elaborate in both form and decoration.*

21. Shore Temple. *Mamallapuram. Early eighth century. Much of the original sculptural decoration has been eroded, but the bulls and the angular slabs of the tower are still clearly identifiable.*

19

20

21

CHAPTER 14

BUDDHISM, TAOISM, AND CONFUCIANISM

Art in China, 600–1368

CHINA REMAINED POLITICALLY DIVIDED for nearly four hundred years following the collapse of the Han Empire in 220 C.E. In the north, invading barbarians established their own kingdoms, adopting Chinese culture as an expression of their supremacy. But the barbarian conquests had led to mass migration to the south, which now took over as the center of Chinese intellectual and cultural life. The instability and unrest undermined Confucian belief that an ordered bureaucratic society, based on loyalty and respect, would vouchsafe peace and stability. It also fostered the growth of religious systems based on spirituality rather than ethical precepts, notably Buddhism, which had been introduced into China from India during the Han Dynasty. The substantial funds lavished on Buddhist monasteries, temples, and colossal statues reflected the increasing popularity of the new religion. Its defining images, which relied strongly on Indian prototypes, introduced a distinctly foreign element into Chinese culture.

The conceptual framework of Buddhism had a profound influence on the development of Taoism, which evolved from a school of philosophy based on the worship

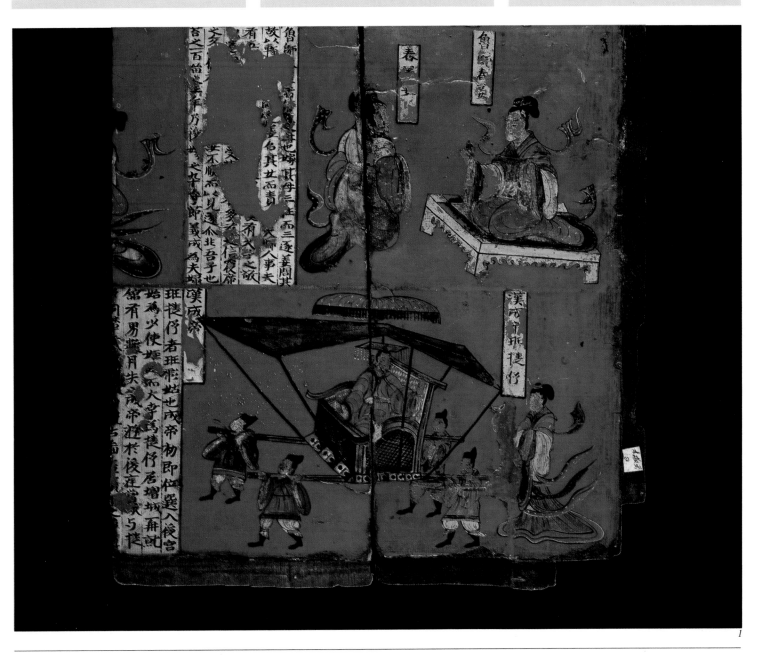

1

of nature into an organized religion with its own temples and sacred texts. Buddhism and Taoism did not replace Confucian tradition but enriched Chinese religious life, allowing individuals to adopt elements from each to suit their own beliefs. Taoist ideas, which emphasized self-expression, became the dominant intellectual force in China during this period and had a major impact on attitudes toward art. Strict adherence to Confucian rules and traditions was replaced by a more imaginative approach that judged art according to aesthetic criteria. Calligraphy, poetry, and especially landscape painting developed as intellectual responses to the Taoist desire to express the concept of *ch'i*, the cosmic spirit that gives life to living things. The landscapes are now lost, but the ideas formulated at this time were crucial to the later development of Chinese art.

The T'ang Dynasty

China was reunited under the short-lived Sui Dynasty (581–618), but it was only with the T'ang Dynasty (618–906) that stability and prosperity returned. The T'ang emperors restored China to centralized rule, which they emphasized by enlarging and embellishing the Sui capital in the north at Ch'ang-an with government buildings And royal palaces (now destroyed). They reorganized the administration according to traditional Confucian principles, selecting the civil service cadres on the basis of examination and merit. Confident and secure, the T'ang Empire flourished on trade and was notable for its tolerance of foreigners and their religions. The Muslims in Ch'ang-an had their own mosque, and Buddhist monasteries continued to attract donations, which paid for monastic buildings, statues, and wall paintings. The Buddhist desire to create

2

4

3

5

1. Scenes of exemplary lives. *Wood and lacquer. Northern Wei Dynasty, 484. Words and images reinforced Confucian doctrine, which stressed the importance of filial piety and a moral life.*

2. Buddha. *Yün-Kang, Shansi province. Northern Wei Dynasty, ca. 470–480. Nearly 46 feet (14 m) high, this colossal statue of the Buddha emphasizes his superhuman status.*

3. Buddhist stele. *British Museum, London. Limestone. 544. The spread of Buddhism in China after the fall of the Han Empire was aided by a breakdown of the established order.*

4. Admonitions of the Instructress to the Court Ladies. *British Museum, London. Ink on silk. Ninth- or tenth-century copy of fourth-century work by Ku K'ai-chih (ca. 344–406). The text encouraged ladies of the court to behave in a way that would be attractive to men.*

5. Horse and Rider. *Giuganno Collection, Rome. Terracotta. T'ang Dynasty, ninth century (?). Terracotta figurines were common in T'ang tombs.*

precise duplications of their sacred images led to the development of printing, soon adopted by the government for its own purposes. Imported goods, especially from the Near East and Persia, stimulated the development of new styles and motifs in the decorative arts. Pottery figurines from T'ang graves show a wide variety of racial types. The earliest examples of Chinese porcelain also date from this period.

The T'ang Dynasty reached its cultural peak under the Emperor Ming Huang (r. 713–756). Himself a renowned calligrapher, Ming founded the Imperial Academy of Letters (Han-lin Academy) and heavily patronized the work of scholars, poets, and artists. His court painters concentrated on depicting court life, even creating portraits of the emperor's horses. Professional artists at court took up the scholarly tradition of landscape painting, while intellectuals such as Wang Wei (699–759) continued to develop their ideas in both painting and poetry. The two trends later became formalized in the establishment of northern (professional) and southern (scholarly) schools. Although the divergence was not entirely clear at this stage, it marked an important development in the history of Chinese art.

Ming Huang's reign ended after a Chinese defeat at the hands of Muslim armies in Central Asia (751) and the rebellion of one of his generals (755). The instability that followed adversely affected trade and prosperity. It also increased religious intolerance and, in 845, all foreign religions were banned. Buddhist monasteries were confiscated and their bronzes melted down. Buddhism survived in China, but it never regained its former prestige. The T'ang Dynasty remained in decline, and by early the next century (907) the empire once again dissolved.

BUDDHISM, TAOISM, AND CONFUCIANISM

6

7

6. *Kuo Hsi*, Clear Autumn Skies Over Mountains and Valleys. *Smithsonian Institution, Freer Gallery of Art, Washington, D.C. Ink on silk. Sung Dynasty. One of the leading artists at the Sung court, Kuo Hsi (ca. 1020–1090) made important contributions to the development of landscape painting.*

7. *Li Ch'eng*, Buddhist Temple in the Hills after Rain. *Atkins Museum, Nelson Art Gallery, Kansas City. Ink and color on silk. Sung Dynasty, ca. 960. An imaginary scene, this spiritual landscape is almost certainly the work of Li Che'ng (940–967), a leading scholar-painter of the period.*

8. Ladies Ironing Silk. *Museum of Fine Arts, Boston. Sung Dynasty, ca. 1120. From an original by the T'ang painter Chang Hsüan, this copy was reputedly made by the Sung Emperor Hui-tsung himself.*

8

The Sung Dynasty

Order was restored by the Sung Dynasty (960–1279). Under the Sung emperors, the Confucian ideal of a meritocratic ruling class became a reality at the expense of the hereditary aristocracies, who had managed to maintain their influence under earlier dynasties. The importance of the exam —the passing of which conferred status as well as a means of livelihood for many— gave rise to elaborate precautions against cheating. Although many scholars opted not to accept civil service positions and retired to cultural pursuits on their country estates, Sung culture was dominated by the intellectual elite. The important state officials were also the leading poets, writers, painters, and calligraphers. Emphasis on intellectual achievement stimulated the writing of treatises on a wide variety of subjects, from war to medicine and architecture. Confucian reverence for the past encouraged the collection, imitation, and even forging of ancient ritual bronzes and jade objects. Painters were encouraged to study and copy earlier masters. The fact that Emperor Hui-tsung (r. 1101–1125) could put his own name to a copy of a T'ang masterpiece indicates the high status accorded to the art of that period.

Imperial Patron and Collector

The Emperor Hui-tsung was a great patron and connoisseur of the arts. He collected more than 6,000 paintings from the Han Dynasty onward. His inventory listed the possessions under ten subject headings, such as Taoist and Buddhist themes, landscapes, foreign tribes, animals or birds, and flowers. His court painters were given official status and admitted to the Han-lin Academy. Their production was closely supervised by the

9. Liang K'ai, Portrait of the Poet Li Po. *National Museum, Tokyo. Ink on paper. Sung Dynasty, thirteenth century. Executed in simple brushstrokes, this portrait of the eighth-century poet by Liang K'ai (ca. 1260–1310) was closely related to the scholarly art of calligraphy.*

10. Mu-ch'i, Six Persimmons. *Daitokuji, Kyoto. Ink on paper. Sung Dynasty, mid-thirteenth century. Under the influence of Ch'an (Zen) Buddhism, artists like Mu-ch'i (active mid-thirteenth century) attempted to convey the intensity of a rare moment of enlightenment.*

11. Mongol Groom Leading Chinese Horse. *Smithsonian Institution, Freer Gallery of Art, Washington, D.C. Ink on paper. Yan Dynasty. The Mongol Yan dynasty was noticeably less interested in the intellectual content of Chinese culture.*

10

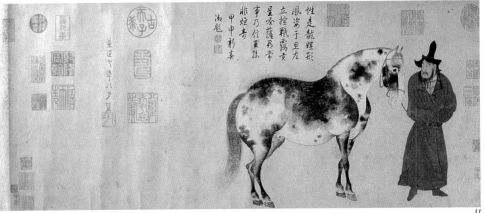

9

11

emperor himself, who set standards of style and subject matter. The court artists were not just craftsmen. Their approach was intellectual: paintings were not intended so much to represent the scene or object itself but to express a deeper spiritual reality. The public response was intellectually inclined, and the artists themselves discussed the aesthetic merits of individual works, as well as varieties of style and modes of expression.

Development of Landscape Painting

Landscape painting became the means by which the artist could fulfill his Confucian obligations as an urban official and still experience his Taoist yearning for rural retreat. The influential landscape painter and art theorist Kuo Hsi encouraged the study of changes in the same scene through its daily and seasonal variations. Outside the court circle, painters were free to experiment. The scholar-painters consciously pursued different aims from those of the professional artists at court. Preferring ink on paper to the luxury of color on silk, they reinforced the link between painting and the other scholarly arts of poetry and calligraphy. To the scholar-artist, painting was more a form of self-expression. This was also true of the painters who belonged to the Ch'an (Zen) sect of Buddhism, such as Liang K'ai and Mu-ch'i, who sought to convey the momentary experience of simple truth as achieved through meditation. Concentration on intellectual pursuits at the expense of defense proved disastrous for the Sung Dynasty. Barbarian invaders captured Emperor Hui-tsung's court in 1125, forcing the Sung to retreat south to a new capital at Hangchow. The final blow came with the Mongol invasion of 1210–1279.

BUDDHISM, TAOISM, AND CONFUCIANISM

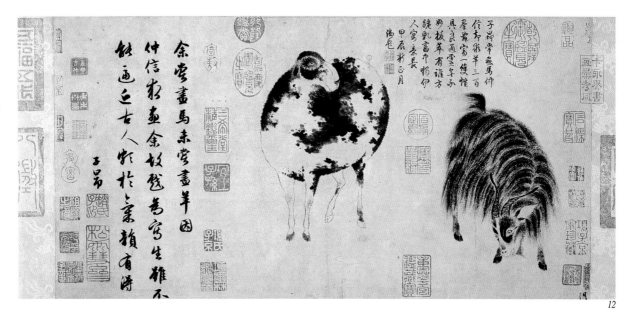

12. Chao Meng-fu, Sheep and Goat. *Smithsonian Institution, Freer Gallery of Art, Washington, D.C. Ink on paper. Yan Dynasty. Chao Meng-fu (1254–1322) was one of the few official artists who remained at court after the arrival of the Mongols.*

12

13. Ch'ien Hsüan, Flowers. *Smithsonian Institution, Freer Gallery of Art, Washington, D.C. Color on paper. Yan Dynasty. After the Mongol conquest, many scholar-painters retreated south to pursue their individual paths. Ch'ien Hsüan (ca. 1235–1301) concentrated on reviving the styles of the past.*

13

The existence of an intellectual elite in China was a powerful influence on the development of calligraphy. Under the influence of Confucianism, the Han emperors had established a civil service bureaucracy whose members were determined by examination; scholarship had become an integral element of Chinese culture. The growing popularity of Taoism after the fall of the Han dynasty enriched the stricter moral codes of Confucian-

CALLIGRAPHY AND THE SCHOLAR-PAINTER

ism with concepts of self-expression and aesthetic merit. The development of landscape painting, poetry, and calligraphy as upper-class intellectual pursuits reflected the new Taoist ideals.

Calligraphy had been developed by clerks in the imperial administration, but in the hands of these scholars it evolved into an art form

capable of expressing far more than words. Produced alone or in combination with painting and poetry, calligraphy conveyed not only the personality of its creator but also his search for universal truth. The scholar-painter exploited all three art forms, blurring the lines of distinction. A painting was frequently enriched not only by an accompanying poem but also by the style of the calligraphy in which the poem was written.

The Mongol Yan Dynasty

Under their supreme leader, Genghis Khan (1167–1227), the Mongols captured Peking in 1215 and soon conquered the rest of China. Under their first ruler, Kublai Khan (r. 1260–1294), the Mongols established the Yan Dynasty (1260–1368). Mongol control of Central Asia led to the reopening of the Silk Road and the reestablishment of trade with the West. Kublai Khan adapted the Chinese administrative system to suit his own purposes, employing only a few Chinese officials and encouraging foreigners to take

14

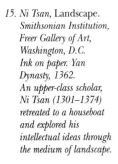

14. *Li K'an*, Bamboo.
*Atkins Museum,
Nelson Art Gallery,
Kansas City. Ink
on paper. Yan Dynasty.
Li K'an (1260–1310)
specialized in paintings
of bamboo, which bent*

*under the force of the
wind but did not break.
The image had a special
significance for
the survival of Chinese
culture under the
domination of the foreign
Yan Dynasty.*

16. *Map of China:*
  *a) maximum extent
     of Mongol Empire;*
  b) Sung Empire.

15. *Ni Tsan*, Landscape.
*Smithsonian Institution,
Freer Gallery of Art,
Washington, D.C.
Ink on paper. Yan
Dynasty, 1362.
An upper-class scholar,
Ni Tsan (1301–1374)
retreated to a houseboat
and explored his
intellectual ideas through
the medium of landscape.*

15

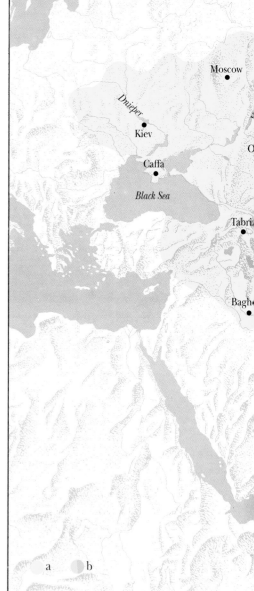

posts in the civil service. One of these was Marco Polo, a Venetian merchant and adventurer who arrived in China in 1275. Polo's description of Kublai Khan's capital at Peking testified to its grandeur and splendor. The buildings of the walled palace city were recognizably Chinese in style but noticeably grander than Sung architecture, a direct reflection of Mongol domination. The Yan emperors were little interested in the intellectual culture of the Sung, and they employed artists to paint scenes of contemporary court life. The scholarly painter Chao Meng-fu had been employed by the Sung emperors and was one of the few to continue working for the new rulers, becoming a confidential advisor to the emperor and head of the Han-lin Academy.

Foreign domination was anathema to the Chinese. Most scholars avoided association with the Mongol court and retreated into private life. Scholar-painters, who had already separated themselves from the traditions of professional artists under the Sung Dynasty, were now convinced of their elite status. Many of them sought inspiration and solace in earlier styles; Ch'ien Hsüan worked in the T'ang tradition as a deliberate reminder of China's past glory.

They developed the scholarly traditions of calligraphy and poetry, invariably adding a poem or inscription to their paintings. Careful observation of nature was an essential element in their art. Li K'an dedicated his life to the study of bamboo. Others, like Ni Tsan, concentrated on expressing the essence of nature through landscape. Paintings of bamboo that bent but did not break or of plum blossoms that flowered in winter took on a special significance in a culture that struggled to survive.

BUDDHISM, TAOISM, AND CONFUCIANISM

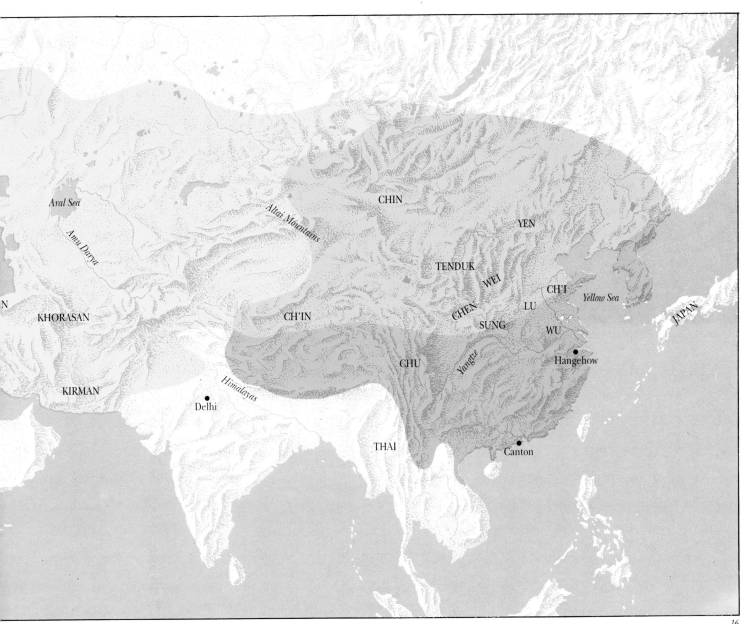

THE MIDDLE AGES: TIME OF FAITH

According to the description by the learned chronicler Rudolph the Bald, around the year 1000 a white mantle of churches had clothed all of Europe. In fact, after the Barbarian invasions, the Christian West entered a new and constructive phase. After five critical centuries that followed the fall of the Roman Empire, Europe finally acquired a physiognomy of its own. Compared with the enormous area dominated by Islam, the Christian West was relatively small, extending from the Pyrenees to the Island of Elba.

At the beginning of this new era, Europe was also behind in farming techniques, economics and culture. However, first the spread of monasticism and then the development of the city-states led to the birth of a new architectural and artistic civilization. Large abbeys organized into autonomous strongholds were the reference points for the lives of thousands. Then, the building of the great cathedrals became just as important. They began to rise up almost everywhere, from Spain to France, Italy to Germany to England.

Notwithstanding enormous difficulties of every type, the travels of monks, pilgrims, crusaders, artisans and architects contributed to the spread of techniques, styles, and symbols that shared a common denominator: the Christian faith.

	1040	1055	1070	1085	1100	1115	1130	1145	1160	1180	1200	1220	1240	1260	1280

FRANCE

910 | Founding of the Abbey of Cluny
1050 | Saintè-Foi, Conques
1080 | Saint-Sernin, Toulouse
1088 | Cluny III
1104 | Sainte-Madeleine, Vézelay
1120 | Saint-Front, Périgueux, Saint-Lazare, Autun
1122 | *Suger, Abbot of Saint-Denis*
1137–1180 | Reconstruction of the abbey of Saint-Denis
1145–1170 | Chartres Cathedral
1163 | Notre Dame, Paris
1165 | Laon Cathedral
1170–1180 | Saint-Trophîme, Arles
1200 | Rheims Cathedral

ITALY

1046–1115 | *Matilde of Canossa*
San Miniato, Florence
1059 | The Baptistry, Florence
1071 | Montecassino consecrated
1075 | Sant'Angelo in Formis, Santa Maria Capua Vetere
1093 | St. Mark's, Venice
1095 | *Start of the First Crusade*
1099–1110 | Cathedral of Modena
1100 | Basilica of San Piero, Grado, frescoes
1131–1200 | Cefalù Cathedral
1132–1189 | Palatine Chapel, Palermo
1138 | San Zeno, Verona
1153 | Santo Sepolcro, Pisa

Arnolfo di Cambio: Florence, | 1245–1302
Siena, Perugia, Rome
Giovanni Pisano: Pisa, | 1248–1314
Siena, Perugia
Giotto: Padua, Florence, | 1267–1337
Assisi, Rome, Naples
Pietro Cavallini: Rome, Naples | 1273–1321

1200 | *Jacopo Torriti: Assisi, Rome*

SPAIN

1075 | Santiago de Compostela

1085 | *Toledo liberated from the Moors*
San Domingo de Silos

BRITAIN

1066 | *William of Orange, King of the Normans, invades England, Battle of Hastings*
1078 | The Tower of London
1086 | *The Domesday Book*
1090 | Norwich Cathedral
1093 | Durham Cathedral
1120 | Wells Cathedral

1170 | *Thomas Becket assassinated*
1175–1178 | Canterbury Cathedral

Lincoln Cathedral | 1240–1250

THE YEAR 1000 MARKED A RETURN to stability in Europe. The first millennium, predicted as the Day of Judgment, had safely passed. The invasions of the ninth and tenth centuries were over. The climate improved, and higher crop yields led to greater prosperity. Christian Europe entered a new phase in its development. In theory, at least, the pope was Europe's spiritual leader, and political power was divided among secular rulers. The distinction was ambiguous, however, as bishops and abbots often played both spiritual and political roles. Since Charlemagne, feudal nobles had been

CHAPTER 15

MONASTERIES AND PILGRIMS

Romanesque Art in France and Spain

appointed as bishops and abbots by their kings, to whom they owed temporal allegiance. This posed a threat to Rome, which had ambitions in the political arena. During the eleventh century, the papacy reasserted its power through a series of reforms aimed at freeing the Church from secular control. Clerical marriage was abolished, freeing priests from dynastic ambitions, and the appointment of bishops and other important Church positions increasingly became a papal prerogative. The founding of the Benedictine Abbey of Cluny in France (910) was another important step in this direction.

1

Earlier Benedictine monasteries had been controlled by secular rulers, but Cluny owed its allegiance directly to Rome. The success of Cluny was immediate. Cluniac abbots advised other monasteries on reform and founded a series of monasteries and priories owing allegiance directly to Cluny, thereby putting them under papal control.

The Importance of Relics

Monastic wealth depended mainly on donations. King Alfonso of Spain contributed to the rebuilding of the abbey of Cluny with a large donation in gratitude for his liberation of Toledo from the Moors (1085) and with an annuity to be paid by his heirs. Pilgrims traveled widely to visit holy shrines and to see the relics preserved inside them; belief in the miraculous properties of these objects was encouraged by the Church. Important relics inevitably attracted both pilgrims and income. Richer monasteries could afford to acquire more valuable relics and thereby increase their wealth. The desire to possess "important" relics was evidenced by the frequent incidence of theft.

The Benedictine abbot of Conques, for example, stole the relics of Sainte-Foi and enshrined them in a magnificent gold statue to convey their importance. Santiago de Compostela, in northern Spain, became a major pilgrimage center after the miraculous discovery there of the body of Saint James, who died in Jerusalem. Pilgrims flowed into Compostela through France, following routes that enabled them to see other important relics, such as the body of Saint Martin at Tours and of Saint-Rémi at Reims. Roads, bridges, and hospices were built or repaired, and new monasteries sprouted up along the way.

1. Capital with monks constructing a building. *Sainte-Foi, Conques. Ca. 1100. The importance of architecture as the visual expression of the power of the Church was reinforced by this nonbiblical image.*

2. Crucifixion. *Museo Arqueológico, Madrid. Ivory. Ca. 1063. Precious materials and skilled craftsmanship gave visual expression to the wealth and authority of the Church.*

3

2

4

3. Reliquary. *Germanisches Nationalmuseum, Nüremberg. Brass. Ca. 1100. Relics were the major tourist attraction in the Middle Ages; the most important ones attracted flocks of pilgrims and abundant offerings.*

4. San Domingo, cloisters. *Silos. Begun ca. 1085. Places of prayer and meditation, cloisters were ornamented with elaborately decorated capitals, often following a precise Christian iconographic program.*

5. Sainte-Foi. *Conques. Begun ca. 1050. Small round-headed windows and blind arcading against the walls were typical of Romanesque architecture.*

6. Santiago de Compostela, Cathedral, nave. *Begun ca. 1075. After Jerusalem and Rome, Santiago de Compostela in Spain was the third most important center of Christian pilgrimage following the miraculous discovery there of the body of Saint James (ca. 810).*

7. Saint-Front. *Périgueux. Begun after 1120. In contrast to the new Romanesque style developing in France, some abbots preferred older Christian prototypes. Saint-Front owes its design to the influence of Christian Byzantium.*

Pilgrimage Churches

By 1100, most of the great monasteries in Europe had become centers of pilgrimage. The desire to assert the growing wealth and power of the Church led to a boom in construction. Monasteries were self-supporting communities that required residential and administrative buildings, notably a chapter house, refectory, dormitories, and cloisters. By far the most important building in any monastic complex was the church, and it was here that the building funds were concentrated. The simple, semicircular apse of the early Christian basilica was proving inadequate to the special requirements of monastic life and pilgrimage. Abbots therefore commissioned craftsmen to build new east ends for their churches, incorporating an enlarged choir and an ambulatory in the rear to provide easier access to the relics; a series of subsidiary chapels was built around the outside. In the most visited pilgrimage churches, transepts were lengthened to allow for extra altars and additional space for pilgrims attending services. Other abbots looked to alternate prototypes. Equally Christian in inspiration, the multidomed Greek Cross plan of Saint-Front in Périgueux was influenced by the churches of the Byzantine Empire and Constantinople.

In an age when most buildings were small and built of wood, the scale of church architecture and the use of stone for construction gave visual expression to the power of Christianity. The development of stone vaults was important for a number of reasons. At a practical level, they greatly reduced the risk of fire. At the aesthetic level, they responded to the challenge of ancient Roman architecture, examples of which

7

8. *Map of principal pilgrimage routes to Santiago de Compostela.*

6

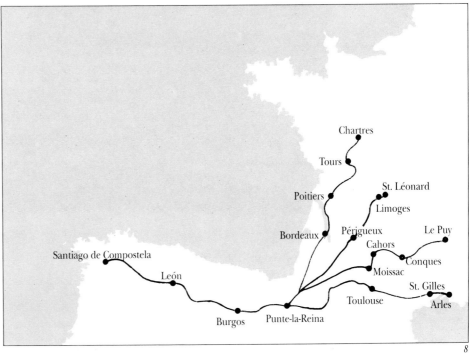

8

were still to be seen in major French cities. Moreover, they were consciously grander than the wooden roofs of early Christian churches in Rome. Stone vaults were heavy and required the solid support of the arched walls of the nave and gallery. At Santiago de Compostela and Saint-Sernin in Toulouse, the barrel vaults were further reinforced by transverse ribs supported by half-columns attached to the nave piers, and the nave itself was buttressed by the side aisle walls. The builders of Sainte-Madeleine in Vézelay improved on vaulting technique with the introduction of groin vaults to replace the more common barrel vaults. Both systems derived from Roman architecture, but so much expertise had been lost that the first attempts at rivaling the ancient structures were inevitably tentative. Groin vaults distributed the weight more directly into the corners, supported by the nave piers. This allowed windows to be pierced in the wall without endangering the stability of the structure; the creation of a clerestory made the interiors much brighter.

The Abbey of Cluny

The most powerful monastery at this time was Cluny. Its enormous wealth and prestige, due in part to papal support, was emphasized in an elaboration of the liturgy and the development of Cluniac chant. It was given visual expression in the increasing grandeur of the abbey church, rebuilt twice since its founding in 910. Cluny III, dedicated to Saint Peter, was enormous. Its double-aisled plan recalled Saint Peter's in Rome, but it was conspicuously larger. It was commissioned (ca. 1088) by Abbot Hugh (1049–1109), whose massive reorganization of the order was reflected in his architectural ambitions for the abbey, which grew from 70 monks in 1042 to 300 at his death.

9

10

9. Reconstruction of Cluny III and monastic buildings: the large church on the right was the third built at the influential abbey of Cluny (1088–1130).

10. Plan of Cluny III and monastic buildings in the mid-twelfth century.

11. Saint-Lazare, nave. Autun. Begun 1120. Pointed arches, introduced in France by the abbot of Cluny, became a popular feature of Burgundian Romanesque architecture.

12. Saint-Sernin, nave. Toulouse. Begun ca. 1080. The use of arches, piers, and half-columns was derived from Roman architecture.

13. Sainte-Madeleine, nave. Vézelay. Begun ca. 1104. The polychrome transverse arches suggest Arabic influence from Spain; they were used here to support groin vaults.

Cluny III (destroyed during the French Revolution) included a number of stylistic features that were to become highly influential. Pointed arches not only increased the height of the nave, but their use in the side aisle vaults was an important structural improvement. Pointed arches had already been incorporated in a new church at Montecassino in Italy (consecrated 1071; see chapter 18), originally founded by Saint Benedict in the sixth century and the most important Benedictine monastery in Europe. It was no coincidence that Abbot Hugh had visited Montecassino in 1083, and he adopted other of its features for Cluny III. Notable among these was an apse fresco of *Christ in Glory*, since destroyed but known to us from a smaller version in the Cluniac chapel at Berzé-la-Ville. Cluny III was completed by Abbot Hugh's successors, who added one of the first grand allegorical portals —a prominent feature of Romanesque architecture.

Depictions of Wealth and Power

If the scale of Romanesque architecture emphasized the power and wealth of the Church, its exterior decoration conveyed distinct Christian themes. Highly elaborate entrance portals derived from the Roman tradition of carved triumphal arches. These expensive sculptural portals were typically painted, at once demonstrating the wealth of the Church and communicating a strong Christian message. Architecture and sculpture were integrally connected, and the decoration of the portals was a vital element of building design, reinforcing the power of Christianity with easily understood visual images. Directly above the entrance to Sainte-Foi

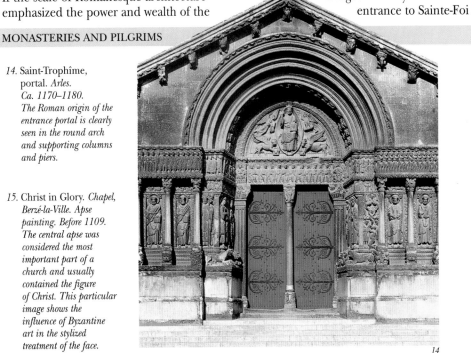

14. Saint-Trophîme, portal. *Arles. Ca. 1170–1180. The Roman origin of the entrance portal is clearly seen in the round arch and supporting columns and piers.*

15. Christ in Glory. *Chapel, Berzé-la-Ville. Apse painting. Before 1109. The central apse was considered the most important part of a church and usually contained the figure of Christ. This particular image shows the influence of Byzantine art in the stylized treatment of the face.*

11

12

13

14

15

The church portal was an important vehicle for conveying the image and religious orthodoxy of the Church. Not only did it reinforce the power of Christianity through its visual imagery, but it also expressed the wealth of the Church through the proliferation of sculptural detail. Expensive to produce and didactic in purpose, the decorative elements of these portals were not left to the imagination of the artist; they were designed by monastic authorities before being carved and painted by skilled craftsmen.

THE PORTAL OF SAINTE-MADELEINE, VÉZELAY

The upper part of the arched opening was filled in to provide a semicircular arena, or *tympanum*, for sculptural decoration. As churches became grander, these openings became correspondingly larger, and the increasing weight of the tympanum required extra support. The central pier, or *trumeau*, introduced in about 1130, offered new surfaces for sculpture, which already covered the lintels, the archivolts (arched moldings around the tympanum), and their supporting columns on either side. At Vézelay, the architectural language of ancient Rome was still visible in the fluted columns and quasi-Corinthian capitals. But architectural features were no longer the primary means of articulation. The sculpted image of Saint John the Baptist on the *trumeau* reveals the Romanesque preference for figurative decoration. The tympanum at Vézelay depicts *Christ's Mission to the Apostles*, instructing them to convert the heathens, heal the sick, and exorcize the demons. The objects of their tasks are depicted in the lintel and inner archivolt. On the outer archivolt are scenes of the *Labors of the Months* and astronomical signs, reinforcing Christ's power over the human world. The proliferation of figurative ornamentation at Vézelay has earned it an important place in the history of sculpture.

17. Last Judgment.
Sainte-Foi, tympanum of portal, Conques. Stone. Ca. 1120. The first known sculptural version of the Last Judgment, this image appeared in the tympanum above the main entrance portal and held a clear message for those entering the church.

16. Sainte-Madeleine, interior portal. *Vézelay. Ca. 1120.*

18. Christ in Glory. *Saint-Pierre, tympanum of south portal, Moissac. Stone. Ca. 1120. According to official Church doctrine, "the composition is not the invention of the artist but the result of Church legislation and custom. The skill alone belongs to the artist; the choice and arrangement are due to the patrons who build the churches."*

16

17

18

in Conques was a depiction of the *Last Judgment,* the earliest known sculptural representation of that theme. In the scene, Christ raises his right hand to the saved and casts the damned to hell with his left; below the two gable lintels are depictions of heaven, presided over by Abraham, and hell, with Satan in charge. A painted version was included in the decoration of the refectory at Cluny.

More common was the image of Christ in glory with the Four Evangelists. The association of the Four Beasts of the Apocalypse (man, lion, ox, and eagle) with the Four Evangelists (Matthew, Mark, Luke, and John) had been established in the second century and was now standard Christian iconography. The many large illustrations typically found in eleventh-century copies of Beatus's *Commentary on the Apocalypse,* written in the eighth century, underlines the importance of Apocalyptic imagery at the time. The *Commentary* was a major source of such imagery, and new manuscripts were produced in abundance. Fear of the end of the world helped reinforce the power of the Church.

Interior Imagery

Romanesque church interiors continued the Christian theme. Little remains of painted decoration inside monastic churches, but the images typically reinforced two messages: salvation through belief and the necessity of obedience to the Church and its teachings. The image of Christ in glory, popularized by its use at Cluny, often appeared in a prominent position. Scenes from the Hebrew Bible and New Testament decorated the nave aisles and had a didactic purpose, aimed specifically at the illiterate.

19. The Lamb, the Four Beasts, and the Elders. *British Museum, London. Add MS 11695, f. 86b. Completed 1109. This manuscript from San Domingo de Silos was one of many versions of Beatus's* Commentary on the Apocalypse *(ca. 780), an important source of the Apocalyptic imagery that became popular in Romanesque France.*

20. Visions of the Apocalypse. *Saint-Savin-sur-Gartempe, porch. Fresco. Ca. 1100. Scenes from the Book of Revelation —the Four Horsemen of the Apocalypse (Conquest, War, Famine, and Death) and the seven-headed dragon— were frequently depicted in Romanesque church decoration.*

The introduction of pointed arches was a decisive break with classical tradition, which survived only in occasional details, such as the use of more elaborate capitals above the simpler ones at ground level.

Whereas Carolingian patrons had deliberately chosen Roman capital types, Romanesque patrons developed their own themes. Using biblical imagery, these elaborately sculpted capitals were designed by abbots and carved by craftsmen, many of whom were monks. Some capitals show a distinct Byzantine influence, but most convey a clear Christian message. The combination of Moses descending from Mount Sinai and the Adoration of the Golden Calf stressed the importance of obedience to the Ten Commandments. The Angel appearing to the Three Kings represented the coming of Christ. More modern images also appeared. The depiction of monks at work and their use of stone for building emphasized the skill and wealth at the disposal of the Church. Generally, however, the sculptures did not aim at realism. In the old Celtic tradition, the images were designed and carved to represent events in a highly decorative style.

The development of a Christian aesthetic independent of the pagan past took its first tentative steps during the eleventh century. The Church used art and architecture to reinforce both its religious authority and its material wealth—a combination of secular and spiritual power that was to have important implications in later times.

21. Capital with Moses and the Golden Calf. *Sainte-Madeleine, Vézelay. Ca. 1100. This capital specifically recalled God's ban on the worship of images. The Christian Church circumvented this prohibition by insisting on their educational value to the illiterate.*

22. Capital. *Saint-Sernin, Toulouse. Ca. 1080. Despite the addition of figural decoration, the small volutes above illustrate the Corinthian origins of this capital.*

23. Capital with the Angel appearing to the Three Kings. *Saint-Lazare, Autun. Ca. 1100. Stylized and unrealistic, this image nevertheless conveys the key elements of the scene, notably the star in the East and the angel waking the sleeping Kings, all wearing crowns.*

21

22

23

VIKING RAIDS IN NORTHERN EUROPE began with the destruction of the monastery at Lindisfarne in 793 and continued throughout the ninth century. The Vikings grew rich on the spoils of the monasteries they sacked, and their search for new land took them as far as Greenland and Canada. On the European mainland, they were temporarily pacified by a grant of land (911) that became known as Normandy ("land of the North men"). Removed from their Scandinavian homeland, the Normans converted to Christianity and turned their military skills and determination to the cause

CHAPTER 16

CONQUERORS AND CRUSADERS

The Influence of the Normans

of the Church. Like their ancestors, they never established a unified empire. During the course of the twelfth century, however, Norman rulers gained control of England, most of France, southern Italy, and Sicily. They also played a major role in the Crusades and the colonization of the Holy Land.

Normandy

The Norman dukes soon became a powerful political force, integrating with other European rulers through the common custom of strategic marriage. Duke William

1

(r. 1035–1087) was related to the English king Edward the Confessor and had been named as his heir. William's wife, Mathilda, was the daughter of the Count of Flanders and traced her descent back to Charlemagne. But William and Mathilda were cousins, and their marriage was outside the bounds of consanguinity prescribed by the Church. Papal dispensation was granted after the couple commissioned two abbeys in Caen: William's Abbaye-aux-Hommes (Saint-Etienne) and Mathilda's Abbaye-aux-Dames (Sainte-Trinité). The Church played an important role in the efficiently organized ducal administration. Cluniac reforms had been introduced by William's father, and the plan of Sainte-Trinité derived from Cluny II. William's closest advisor was Lanfranc, a monk from Pavia whom he had appointed abbot of Saint-Etienne. Its west towers and relative lack of ornamentation suggest Ottonian and Lombard influence. Deliberately plain, both monasteries avoided the elaborate sculptured portals and capitals of the pilgrimage churches of Burgundy. Physical power and strength rather than an explicitly Christian message provided an image for the Norman Church, a tool of state machinery.

Norman Conquest of England

William's conquest of England in 1066 was precipitated by the seizure of the English crown by Harold Godwineson, brother of the wife of the dead king Edward the Confessor and head of the most powerful Anglo-Saxon family at the English court. Lanfranc justified the invasion on both temporal and spiritual grounds: not only was William the rightful heir, but his accession would lead to the establishment of the pro-papal Norman Church in England and the dismissal of the schismatic Anglo-Saxon archbishop of Canterbury.

1. Bayeux Tapestry, detail. *Bibliothèque Municipale, Bayeux. Wool embroidery on linen. Ca. 1073–1083. This record of the events leading up to the Norman Conquest of England is remarkable for its detailed narrative scenes and inexpensive materials.*

2. Abbaye-aux-Hommes (Saint-Etienne), nave. *Caen. Begun ca. 1068. Imposing but plainly decorated, Norman Romanesque architecture in France was less ornamented than the monasteries farther south.*

3. Abbaye-aux-Hommes (Saint-Etienne). *Caen. Begun ca. 1068. Although much altered, Romanesque detail can still be seen in the round arches that decorate the great square towers of the west façade.*

2

3

Harold was defeated at the Battle of Hastings on October 14, 1066. The importance of the conquest was illustrated in an approximately 230-foot (70-m) commemorative tapestry. This remarkable piece of political propaganda was not a glorification of William but recounted the events leading up to the conquest, stressing the practical aspects of the Norman achievement. The Anglo-Saxon nobles were firmly opposed to Norman rule, and William ruthlessly imposed his own culture. Norman French replaced Old English as the language of the court. One of William's first projects was the *Domesday Book* (1086), a systematic account of landholdings and other assets throughout the kingdom. Normans replaced Anglo-Saxons in positions of power. Lanfranc was appointed archbishop of Canterbury, and other key posts were filled by William's friends and relations. For the first time in its history, England was organized under a highly centralized monarchy.

Inevitably, architecture also became a medium of expression for the new regime. Huge stone fortresses were built in towns throughout the kingdom as symbols of Norman strength. Anglo-Saxon cathedrals and churches were destroyed and replaced by Norman buildings. Changes in scale, location, style, and material reinforced Norman domination. The old cathedral of East Anglia had been located at North Elmham, but the Normans built a new and considerably larger one in Norwich. Norman style replaced Anglo-Saxon traditions. Lanfranc's new cathedral at Canterbury was based on the design of Saint-Etienne in Caen. Many of the new cathedrals were built with Caen stone imported from Normandy. The cost of transporting it was considerable, and its very use was a conspicuous statement

4

6

7

4. Tower of London, the White Tower. *Begun 1078. Stone fortresses on this scale were unknown in England before the arrival of the Normans. The castles they erected throughout the kingdom provided potent images of power.*

5. Cathedral, nave. *Norwich. Begun 1090. Importing stone from Caen in Normandy, the Normans imposed their own architectural style in England to reinforce their authority.*

6. Cathedral. *Durham. Begun 1093. Vast and imposing, this building proclaimed the political role of the Church during the Norman domination of England.*

7. Cathedral, nave. *Durham. Begun 1093. Compound piers alternating with decorated columns reflect the position of the transverse arches supporting the vaults.*

of Norman wealth and power. William established a major ecclesiastical and military center at Durham to defend his kingdom from northern attack. The formidable cathedral was considerably larger than the adjoining castle and provided an ideal image for the Norman Church as an arm of temporal power. The lack of figural sculpture and preference for architectural decoration, including blind arcading and cushion capitals, was typically Norman. Interest in structure rather than decoration encouraged the development of rib vaults, which appeared first at Durham (ca. 1093) and later at Saint-Etienne (ca. 1120). An improvement on the structural innovations of Cluny III, the rib vault had important implications for the development of Gothic architecture (see chapter 17).

Normans in Southern Italy

The Normans were highly skilled fighters and much in demand as mercenaries. It was in this capacity that they were first recorded in southern Italy during the early eleventh century. Taking shrewd advantage of disputes between the Holy Roman Empire and the papacy, they soon claimed territorial rights and were confirmed as rulers of Apulia, Calabria, and Sicily (1059). The Normans conquered land nominally controlled by the Lombard rulers of the Holy Roman Empire, as well as Byzantine territory in southern Italy and the Muslim island of Sicily (completed 1091). To affirm their allegiance to the papacy, they imposed the Latin Church throughout their domain. Like their counterparts in England, the Normans in southern Italy were a ruling elite. Their kingdom was composed of distinct Lombard, Byzantine, and Arabic elements but, unlike the Anglo-Normans, they were confident enough to assimilate

8. Palatine chapel, interior. *Palermo. 1132–1189. The Norman conquest of Sicily produced a variety of images. Influenced by the splendor of Islamic and Byzantine cultures, the new rulers adopted local traditions of extravagant mosaic decoration.*

8

In the year 1000, one of the most advanced civilizations in the world was the Middle East. The Christian Byzantine Empire, with its capital at Constantinople, and the extravagant courts of the Islamic world both achieved standards of wealth and luxury unknown in Europe. By the end of the eleventh century, the situation began to change. An increasingly prosperous and powerful Europe began to assert itself, its newfound confidence epitomized by the First Crusade in 1095. The split between the Eastern and Western

Churches was formalized in 1054, but the common heritage of the two Christian cultures was reflected in the adoption of Byzantine art as a visual expression of Europe's new power and prestige.

In works of mosaic, Byzantine patrons had exploited the use of gold and colored glass to produce images that evidenced their enormous wealth and conveyed the mystical and spiritual dimensions of

Christianity. The mosaic tradition in Europe was revived at Montecassino by Abbot Desiderius, who imported Byzantine craftsmen to decorate his church. Nothing remains of these mosaics, but they were an important influence on Abbot Hugh, who adapted their style for frescoes in his churches at Cluny and Berzé-la-Ville. The papacy developed mosaic art to communicate doctrine and

to project its own authority. The Normans in Sicily, who sought to rival the prestige of Constantinople, adapted both the style and the medium of Byzantine art for the elaborate decoration of church interiors. In Venice, the extensive mosaic decoration inside Saint Mark's and other churches reflected the city's economic and cultural links with the empires of the East, which were crucial to its continuing independence. Some Venetian patrons even adopted the distinctive iconography of the Eastern Church.

CONQUERORS AND CRUSADERS

9

11

11. Cathedral. *Cefalù. 1131–1200. The combination of round and pointed arches on the façade was typical of southern Italian Romanesque portals.*

9. Hunting scenes. *Palazzo dei Normanni, Palermo. Mosaic. Twelfth century. Peacocks, leopards, and centaurs provided exotic images for the secular decoration of the royal palace.*

10

10. Cathedral, interior. *Cefalù. 1131–1200. Pointed arches derived from Islamic architecture, but they had already been used in the Benedictine abbey of Montecassino and were soon to become an important feature of the specifically Christian Gothic style in northern Europe.*

local traditions. Under their rule, southern Italy became a vital center for the dissemination of Greek and Arabic learning. Greek philosophy was translated into Latin, and Salerno developed a leading medical school under the influence of the Arabs.

Southern Italy and Sicily prospered from trade with North Africa and the East. Direct contact with Byzantine and Arabic cultures stimulated a taste for luxury. The court of Roger II (r. 1113–1154) was tolerant by Western standards, encouraging Islamic and Byzantine as well as Latin scholars. Roger's patronage of the arts reflected this eclectic culture. Both the chapel

in his palace at Palermo and the cathedral at Cefalù were built on Roman basilical plans. The proportions of the nave arcade in the chapel had a distinct Arabic influence, but the more public cathedral conformed with Christian tradition. The combination of pointed arches and classical columns and capitals had been established in church architecture by its use in the Benedictine abbey of Montecassino, built during the early years of Norman rule in southern Italy (ca. 1070). As at Montecassino, the apse mosaic of *Christ Pantocrator* was directly inspired by Byzantine prototypes and made by Byzantine craftsmen. The text in Christ's hand was

written in Latin as well as Greek (the language of the Byzantine Church), emphasizing the adoption of this image into the Western Church. A more direct example of Byzantine influence was the mosaic of *Christ Crowning Roger II King of Sicily*, commissioned by Roger's admiral, George of Antioch. This sacral image of imperial power was not common in northern Europe and made an interesting comment on Roger's aspirations. The secular images of imperial Constantinople, derived from Ancient Rome, also influenced the decoration of Roger's palace with its hunting scenes and exotic wild animals.

12

14

12. Christ Crowning King Roger II of Sicily. *Santa Maria dell'Ammiraglio (La Martorana), Palermo. Mosaic. Ca. 1148. The concept of kingship as a divine right provided an important justification for royal power. King Roger's small size and gestures reinforce his submission to Christ.*

13. Christ Pantocrator. *Abbey Church, Monreale. Apse mosaic. Before 1183. The words "I am the light of the world..." are given in both Latin and Greek, reflecting fusion of the two traditions in Norman-Sicilian culture.*

14. Capital with soldiers. *Sainte-Foi, Conques. Ca. 1100. The Church divided its flock into those who worked, those who prayed, and those who fought.*

15. Santo Sepolcro, interior. *Pisa. Begun 1153. Churches dedicated to the Holy Sepulchre invariably had a central plan, usually octagonal or circular. Built by quasi-monastic orders of knights, they symbolized the importance of the Christian reconquest of the Holy Land.*

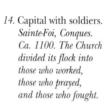

13

15

The Crusades

The Normans had established their empires with the support of the papacy, which justified war for religious causes—whether against dissent and heresy within the Church, or against non-Christians. Its goals were temporal as well as spiritual. When Pope Urban II declared the First Crusade (1095), he was responding to a request from the Byzantine Emperor for help against the Turks; he neatly translated the emperor's request into the mission of liberating Jerusalem from the Muslims. His intention was the expansion of a confident Christian Europe, and it was strongly supported by the monastic reformer Saint Bernard. Armies were raised by independent rulers, including Robert, the son of William the Conqueror, and Bohemond, an Italo-Norman prince. Contemporary chronicles are unreliable, but modern historians have estimated that about 50,000 people set forth on the First Crusade. Highly disorganized, they nevertheless managed to capture Jerusalem (1099) and much of Palestine. Most of the Crusaders had commitments at home and soon left, but some stayed behind to establish a Latin kingdom, imposing the Western Church and European-style administration. Mosques were converted into churches, and new ones—such as the Church of the Holy Sepulchre in Jerusalem—were built as symbols of Christian reconquest. Castles were constructed throughout the Holy Land to reinforce the power of the new regime and to safeguard valuable trade routes with Arabia and the East. One immediate result of the Crusades was the founding of a number of military orders, such as the Knights Templar and the Knights of Saint John. Members were bound by monastic vows of poverty, chastity, and obedience

16. Bayeux Tapestry, detail. *Bibliothèque Municipale, Bayeux. Wool embroidery on linen. Ca. 1073–1083. The appearance of a comet has long been seen as the portent of an important event, and the arrival of Halley's Comet in 1065 was no exception.*

17. Montreal. *Shobak. Twelfth century. Crusader castles were erected throughout the new Christian territories in the Holy Land, both to provide visual expression of their power and to protect trade routes.*

16

17

but pledged to fight in defense of the Holy Land. The military orders secured considerable donations, and they commissioned numerous small chapels throughout Europe. The chapels were invariably based on a central plan, recalling Constantine's Church of the Holy Sepulchre; their decoration reflected the military role of the order and inspired similar imagery in other churches.

The Second and Third Crusades were less than successful, and the West finally lost Jerusalem at the hands of Saladin in 1187. The Fourth Crusade never arrived. Through the machinations of the Venetians, who had made an alliance with the claimant to the Byzantine throne, the Crusaders were persuaded to provide assistance in return for monetary and military support. But the support did not materialize, and the Crusaders sacked Constantinople (1204). Western rulers acquired new relics looted from that city. Louis IX of France obtained Christ's crown of thorns and built Sainte-Chapelle in Paris to house it. Pope Innocent III was especially proud of his relic of the True Cross, which he put on display at the Fourth Lateran Council (1215). Venice, which had consistently acted in its own interest, made a handsome profit out of the sack of Constantinople and strengthened its economic ties with the East. Its booty was publicly displayed on the façade of Saint Mark's Basilica; among the items were the now-familiar four bronze horses and porphyry statues of the Tetrarchs.

18. Soldiers fighting. *Basilica, crypt, Aquileia. Fresco. Ca. 1200. Painted on the dado beneath a scene of the Deposition of Christ, these images of soldiers reflected the new military role of the Church.*

19. Tetrarchs. *Saint Mark's Square, Venice. Porphyry. Early fourth century. The façade of Saint Mark's acquired some of its most memorable details from the sack of Constantinople in 1204. Like the four bronze horses, this late-imperial statue of the Emperor Diocletian and his co-regents (285–305) was a trophy displayed as a symbol of imperial ower.*

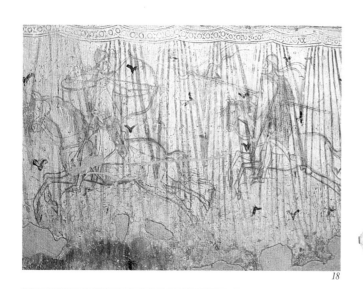

18

19

THE REVIVAL OF TRADE IN ELEVENTH-century Europe stimulated the growth of urban populations. This led to a redistribution of wealth in favor of secular power that benefited the new middle classes and the monarchies in France and England. Money and power moved from the monastery to the town. Cathedral schools in cities such as Paris and Chartres replaced monastic libraries as centers of intellectual life. The growing power and wealth of northern Europe was expressed in the emergence of a new architectural style. The impetus for its development came from an abbey,

CHAPTER 17

THE GOTHIC CATHEDRAL

Technology and Style

but one closely associated with royal power. Saint-Denis, just outside Paris, had long been the burial place of the French kings and contained the relics of Saint-Denis, the patron saint of France. Suger was appointed abbot of Saint-Denis (1122) by King Louis VI (r. 1108–1137) and acted as chief adviser to both him and his successor, Louis VII (r. 1137–1180). The decision to rebuild the old Carolingian basilica, with funds provided by Louis VII, was a deliberate attempt to enhance the political ambitions of the French monarchy by association with the power of the Church. A landmark in the history

1

of architecture, the new building established a style that profoundly affected the development of European art.

Abbot Suger and Saint-Denis

Suger's project for Saint-Denis involved the addition of a narthex (begun 1137) and a new choir with ambulatory and radiating chapels, similar in plan to the pattern established in the pilgrimage churches. According to his account of the new building, the expansion of the east end was intended to cope with increasing numbers of pilgrims. But its scale and grandeur suggest more material considerations. The pointed arches and buttressing, popularized by their use at Cluny III, were used to support rib vaults, which had been introduced by the Normans at Durham and Saint-Etienne in Caen. The rib vaults were a technical improvement over the structure of Cluny III, requiring less wood support (centering) during construction and thereby reducing cost and time. Suger's use of this innovation reflected his desire for unprecedented splendor, which he achieved by adopting the most elaborate and novel features from other stylistic traditions. The combination of pointed arches, rib vaults, and flying buttresses was revolutionary, as was the decision to open up the ambulatory chapels. Suger's embellishment of the church consistently emphasized its royal context, reinforcing the ambitions of the French crown. Alongside traditional Benedictine imagery, the stained glass windows told stories of the First Crusade, reflecting Louis VII's fervent interest in that endeavor. Suger's own window of the *Tree of Jesse* delineated Christ's descent from the kings of Judah. The same kings appeared as statues on the portal

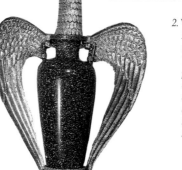

1. Notre Dame, east end. *Paris. Begun 1163. Flying buttresses, an essential element of the Gothic structural system, were developed to counter the thrusts of the pointed vaults inside.*

2. Vase. *Louvre, Paris. From the Treasury of Saint-Denis. Ca. 1140. This silver and gold porphyry vase, in the form of an eagle, was one of the many precious objects commissioned by Abbot Suger for Saint-Denis.*

2

3. Abbey Church of Saint-Denis, choir. *Paris. Begun ca. 1137. Suger's rebuilding of the east end of Saint-Denis inaugurated a dramatic change in architectural construction and style.*

4. Suger's window. *Abbey church of Saint-Denis, ambulatory, Paris. Ca. 1140. According to Suger, elaborate and expensive decoration reaffirmed the spiritual power of the Church.*

3

4

as a parallel to the tombs of Louis VII's ancestors inside, which Suger restored. The new style emphasized structural innovation and bourgeois extravagance to create a more secular interpretation of monastic architecture.

Gothic Architecture

The essential feature of Gothic architecture was the combination of pointed arches, rib vaults, and flying buttresses. These features created a structure with the capacity to carry the weight of a Gothic cathedral, acting in the same way as a modern steel frame.

Cathedral designers exploited the potential of this system to give the building vertical thrust, reflecting the enthusiasm of the new bourgeois culture. The 120-foot (37-m) nave of Chartres was soon overtaken by that of Amiens (139 feet, 42 m) and others; overambition and technical errors at Beauvais (157 feet, 48 m) resulted in the collapse of the vaulting. The new Gothic system allowed for greater window area, as the burden of support shifted from the walls to the structural members. The wall space given to stained glass was relatively small at first but increased as designers gained experience and

confidence. Greater height initially was achieved by the addition of another level in the elevation of the nave, as at Laon, with its arcade, gallery, triforium, and clerestory. But these horizontal divisions, derived from Roman architecture, soon gave way to a more vertical emphasis. As at Chartres, the gallery was omitted in favor of greater concentration on the nave arcade and clerestory. The small triforium at Chartres illustrated a decisive break with the Roman tradition of proportional relationships between levels. Columns became decorative and were grouped

THE GOTHIC CATHEDRAL

5. Cathedral, nave. *Amiens. Begun 1218. This nave reached a height of about 139 feet (42 m).*

6. Cathedral, nave. *Chartres. Begun 1194. Vertical supports dominated the horizontal divisions, giving visual emphasis to the height of the structure.*

7. Cathedral, south transept. *Reims. Ca. 1200. Early Gothic designers began to take advantage of the new method of construction, which freed walls from their load-bearing function, by opening up long lancet and circular rose windows.*

5

6

7

STAINED GLASS

The structural innovations that formed the basis of Gothic architecture freed walls from their traditional load-bearing function and allowed for the development of huge areas of fenestration. The practical value of light needs no explanation, but during the Middle Ages it also played a symbolic role. Christ as the Light of the World was an image that appeared regularly in medieval painting and literature. It was particularly important to Abbot Suger, whose patronage of the abbey of Saint-Denis not only introduced the new Gothic architecture but also included a number of stained glass windows.

Stained glass was not new. It had been used on a small scale in Carolingian buildings, and Theophilus, the author of an early twelfth-century treatise on the arts, had described its manufacture and use. Now, however, with advances in structural engineering, it became an essential feature in church design. Essentially transparent mosaics, stained glass windows were composed of pieces of glass held together by strips of lead. The window was painstakingly assembled over a design drawn in advance and held in its final position by iron bars.

Early Gothic windows can be distinguished by the use of deep colors, especially red and blue, that were fired into the glass. With the development of stone tracery patterns in mid-thirteenth-century windows, the colors became lighter and were painted directly onto the glass. Like other medieval patrons, Abbot Suger was exceptionally proud of his stained glass. Praising it for both its material cost and its skilled execution, Suger justified the splendor and extravagance as a reflection of his personal devotion to the power of Christianity.

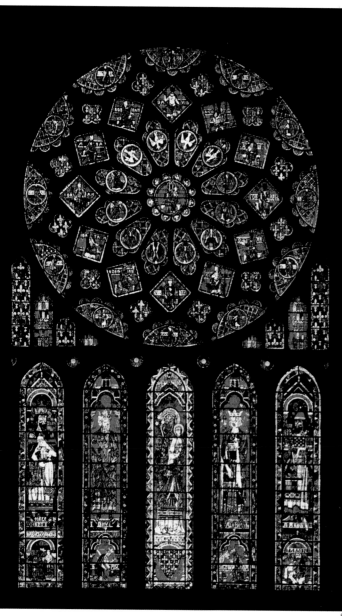

8

9

8. Cathedral, north transept. *Chartres. Ca. 1225. As cathedral designers became more confident, larger areas were devoted to stained glass, and the divisions between them became narrower. As a result, rose windows began to merge with the lancets beneath them.*

9. Cathedral, nave to east. *Laon. Begun ca. 1165. In an attempt to achieve greater height, the designers at Laon added an extra level so that the nave elevation was divided into arcade, gallery, triforium, and clerestory.*

10. *Cross-section of a Gothic nave showing rib vaults, with their diagonal and transverse ribs, resting on pointed arches and supported on each side by flying buttresses.*

10

around a central core (compound pier), their elongation reinforcing the vertical emphasis of the building. The capitals were uniform in design, in contrast to the variety of Romanesque types, but adopted simple leaf carving that bore little relationship to Roman prototypes.

The new style spread rapidly throughout northern Europe. When Canterbury Cathedral burned down in 1174, the monks took the opportunity to incorporate a shrine in the new cathedral to house the relics of Saint Thomas Becket (martyred 1170). Their decision to hire William of Sens as the master mason in charge of construction indicated their intention of adopting the new French style. English cathedrals soon developed their own characteristics, however, rejecting sculptured portals in favor of screen façades and emphasizing elaborate vaulting patterns over the verticality so valued by the French.

Gothic Sculpture

Sculptural decoration reinforced the new message. Increasingly extravagant portals expressed the growth of urban wealth at the expense of the monasteries. Whereas one sculpted door in the west façade had sufficed for most of the pilgrimage churches, now there were three, and portals were added to the transepts as well. Costly figure sculpture replaced the cheaper columns that had supported Romanesque tympana. The style of these figures became markedly more naturalistic. Variety of facial features, poses, and drapery contributed to the individuality of each image, reflecting a new interest in the human aspect of biblical personalities. The human origins of the Virgin Mary made her an approachable intercessor, and her growing popularity was reflected in a surprising number of French cathedrals dedicated

11. Cathedral, choir. *Canterbury. Begun 1175. Rebuilt after a disastrous fire (1174), this choir was the first example of the new French style in England. The monks at Canterbury deliberately employed a French mason, William of Sens, for this purpose.*

12. Cathedral, nave vault. *Lincoln. Ca. 1240–1250. English Gothic cathedrals never reached the height of their French counterparts, as designers concentrated on developing elaborate vaulting patterns. Only the main diagonal and transverse ribs here are functional. The others, called tiercerons, are purely decorative.*

13. Cathedral, west front. *Wells. Begun ca. 1220. English Gothic cathedrals developed distinctive characteristics, including a screen façade that carried a monumental program of sculpture.*

to Notre Dame ("Our Lady"): in Paris, Chartres, Amiens, Laon, and elsewhere. Images of the Virgin enthroned or being crowned became standard decoration for portals on the prestigious west façade, second in importance only to Christ himself. The depiction of events from everyday life was further evidence of the secularization of Christian culture. Whereas Romanesque sculpture had emphasized the coming of Judgment Day, Gothic sculpture reflected the new importance of temporal authority with images that emphasized respect and obedience.

The Building Industry

The cathedrals were not commissioned by the bishop but by the cathedral chapter, an administrative body composed of local clergy (canons). Funding was generated by taxes on mercantile wealth, supplemented by a form of "spiritual persuasion": the right to be buried within the cathedral precinct in exchange for payment and the granting of indulgences for voluntary contributions. Sometimes, to raise more money, the canons took cathedral relics on tour.

The new Gothic style required expertise on a level unknown since the fall of the

Roman Empire. With the growth of towns, building became an urban occupation. Craftsmen were organized under trade guilds, which controlled the apprenticeship of members. The chapter employed a master mason, whose technical ability was considerable, to supervise the work of skilled and unskilled laborers. At York Minster, for example, the laborers worked twelve hours each day in the summer and eight hours per day in the winter, with fourteen days off at Christmas and shorter holidays for other Church feasts. Monks involved in the construction of the pilgrimage churches may have worked for the glory of God, but these

14

16

14. Cathedral, west portals. *Chartres. Ca. 1145–1170. This ambitious sculptural program was devised by cathedral authorities and includes statues of the kings and queens of Judah (flanking the portals), scenes from the life of Christ (on the capitals), the Ascension, Christ with the apocalyptic symbols of the Evangelists, and the Virgin and Child (in the tympana). It was extravagance on this scale that provoked criticism from those who believed the Church should return to the life of poverty espoused by Christ and the Apostles.*

15

15. Notre Dame, west front. *Paris. Begun ca. 1220. Patterns of increasing elaboration were reflected in the Gothic use of three sculptured portals on major façades, compared with only one in Romanesque churches.*

16. Virgin enthroned. *Cathedral, west front, south portal tympanum, Chartres. Ca. 1145–1170. The growing popularity of the cult of the Virgin was reflected in her inclusion on the prestigious west front at Chartres. As in other cities, the church itself was dedicated to her.*

17

urban workers were paid for their efforts. Thus, cost became an important factor in cathedral design, and the more mercantile approach to money was not without consequences at the stylistic level.

It was probably no accident that the uniform capitals and moldings of Gothic architecture were quicker and cheaper to produce than the variety of Romanesque details. Suger's statement that the craftsmanship at Saint-Denis surpassed the materials was not only a comment on the skill involved but also on how much it had cost. The assessment of a craftsman's contribution in terms of monetary value was a reflection of the new mercantile culture and an important step in reviving the concept of the artist that had been lost with the fall of the Roman Empire.

Symbolism and Extravagance

The immensity of the new cathedrals, which could accommodate entire civic populations, came to symbolize the power of the Church within the urban community. Imitating the metaphoric language of the New Testament, contemporary writers reinforced this image by describing the buildings in symbolic terms. Suger wrote that the choir at Saint-Denis was built with twelve supports to signify the twelve Apostles. Other writers identified the pillars with the bishops and doctors of the Church. Metaphors such as these were applied throughout the cathedral, making it a symbol of heaven and providing an image of a highly ordered society.

The reality was inevitably more prosaic. Gothic cathedrals represented an enormous financial undertaking. Although they created employment and stimulated expansion of the building trades, they were not productive in a material sense. Continual demands for funding, which translated

THE GOTHIC CATHEDRAL

17. Aristotle and Pythagoras. *Cathedral, west front, Chartres. Ca. 1145–1170. The inclusion of pagan philosophers on a Christian building reflected the growing importance attached to learning. Pythagoras and Aristotle represented Music and Dialectic, two of the seven liberal arts that formed the basis of a classical education.*

18. Saints. *Cathedral, north portal, Chartres. Ca. 1200. Elegant and individualized, these figures show a greater interest in detail than Romanesque sculpture.*

19. Annunciation and Visitation. *Cathedral, west front, Reims. Ca. 1220. These jamb figures from the portal of the Virgin illustrate two of the scenes from her life. Their style suggests a knowledge of classical sculpture.*

18

19

into higher taxes for local residents, created civic unrest and forced some towns into bankruptcy, as in the case of Amiens. Such extravagance was inevitably the object of criticism. Suger responded to his critics by saying that the size of the expenditure reflected the value placed on the object by its patron. He told the story of how he had planned a modest altar for Saint-Denis but that the Holy Martyrs miraculously intervened to help him acquire the gold and stones necessary to satisfy their wish for lavish adornment. Suger's written account of the rebuilding of Saint-Denis provides a fascinating insight into medieval attitudes toward the arts. He makes no reference to any individual artist, architect, or sculptor, clearly seeing himself as the creative force of the entire project—no doubt the case. The inscriptions in the building, which he quotes in his text, are requests for intercession on his own behalf, placed on what he considered the most important parts of the building: the sculpted façade, bronze doors, royal tombs, and gold altar frontal.

20. *Jan van Eyck*, Saint Barbara. *Musée des Beaux Arts, Antwerp. 1437. It is easy to forget the enormity of the undertaking, and the problems associated with it, to build the great cathedrals without the use of modern machinery.*

21. May. *Cathedral, west front, Amiens. Ca. 1220. One of a series of scenes depicting the Labors of the Months, a common secular theme for decorative detail on Gothic cathedrals.*

20

21

CHAPTER 18

THE REVIVAL OF THE PAPACY

Art in Medieval Italy

T HE UNITY OF THE ITALIAN PENINSULA had disintegrated with the collapse of the Roman Empire, and medieval Italy was politically divided. A succession of invaders, including the Goths, the Byzantine emperors, Charlemagne, and the Normans, had attempted to establish their authority in Italy. Their ultimate goal was Rome, and control of the spiritual leadership of Christian Europe. Rome proved remarkably resilient, but Italy was subject to a number of different cultural influences. These were reflected in a variety of regional artistic styles, which, at the same time, had many characteristics in common.

Romanesque Style in Northern Italy

The introduction of the pointed arch by Abbot Desiderius at Montecassino and Sant'Angelo in southern Italy had a crucial impact on monastic architecture in France. The Normans in Sicily had made use of the pointed arch (see chapter 16), but it had little immediate influence in northern Italy, where feudal lords and bishops owed their allegiance to the German emperors. In Milan, as in other northern Italian cities that had been important centers in the Roman Empire, early Christian traditions persisted.

The original church of Saint Ambrose, consecrated by Saint Ambrose himself (386), was rebuilt from the ninth century onward as befitted the coronation church of the German emperors. The old wooden-roofed nave was replaced during the twelfth century by a more expensive stone-ribbed groin vault. But stone vaults were relatively rare in Italy before 1200, and the old tradition of wooden roofs predominated. To display their relics, Lombard monasteries developed a different solution from that of the French pilgrimage churches, raising the choir above a crypt and retaining the early Christian basilical plan.

Decorative schemes concentrated on imagery that reinforced faith through tradition. They also reflected the new spirit of independence, fostered by the growing wealth of northern Italian cities. Venice, for one, had consistently asserted its independence from imperial control. By basing the design of Saint Mark's Basilica on the Church of the Holy Apostles in Constantinople, the Venetians gave visual expression to their economic and cultural links with that city. Tuscany had easy access to marble, and a distinctive style of decoration emerged there for structures that were essentially early Christian. In Florence,

both the Baptistery of San Giovanni and San Miniato are associated with the patronage of Countess Mathilda (1046–1115), whose alliance with the papacy further weakened imperial power in northern Italy.

Papal Ambition

Charlemagne's coronation in 800 had established a division between temporal and spiritual power in Europe. There was little dispute over papal spiritual authority, but the idea that it extended to ecclesiastical appointments became a major bone of contention during the twelfth century

1. Pope Innocent III showing his Bull for Subiaco. *Sacro Speco, lower church, Subiaco. Early thirteenth century. Innocent III's efforts to reform church abuses included the requirement that all archbishops visit Rome after their appointment and that the crucifix become an essential feature on all altars.*

2. Cathedral, nave. *Modena. Begun 1099 (vault, fifteenth century). Lombard church designers developed a distinctive solution to the position of the crypt, placing it under a raised choir.*

3. San Zeno, portal. *Verona. Ca. 1138. The scene of San Zeno handing the standard of Verona to its citizens, an image of civic power, appears in the lunette and occupies the primary position on the portal. The portal was flanked by reliefs depicting scenes from the Hebrew Bible (right) and New Testament (left).*

4. Wiligelmo, Daniel and Zacharias. *Cathedral, Modena. Stone. Ca. 1100. The figures and reliefs carved by Wiligelmo (active ca. 1099–1110) at Modena are distinctive for their solidity of form and their expressive poses and gestures at a time when French Romanesque sculptors were developing a more decorative and idealized style.*

2

3

4

between the popes and Charlemagne's successors, the German emperors. Imperial rights were countered by an increasingly confident papacy, which asserted its independence through clerical and monastic reforms aimed at separating Church institutions from secular interference. These included a new system of papal election that excluded the traditional rights of the emperor; selection was put in the hands of a small group of top clerics, mainly papal appointees, which formed the basis of the College of Cardinals. But spiritual independence was not enough; temporal power was needed to guarantee it. Papal ambitions in this arena changed the character of the papal court, which increasingly resembled its secular rivals. A successful pope needed to be worldly and politically astute, like Innocent III (1198–1216), who established the papacy as an independent force in European politics, emphasizing its role as a disinterested referee in temporal disputes. Innocent's successors became more directly involved.

The revival of the papacy during the course of the twelfth and thirteenth centuries established Rome as an important administrative, legal, and diplomatic center, attracting educated clerics to transact the new business of the Curia. These intellectuals promoted the new role of the papacy and reinforced its status through propaganda. The most powerful piece of propaganda at hand was the *Donation of Constantine*, putatively written by the Roman emperor himself in 313, which gave historical validity not only to the papal claim to spiritual primacy in the Church but also to temporal authority in Italy. The document, later exposed as an eighth-century forgery, purported to be Constantine's reward to Pope Silvester I for the emperor's miraculous recovery from leprosy. This wholly

5. Sant'Angelo in Formis. *Santa Maria Capua Vetere. Finished ca. 1075. Directly influenced by the Benedictine monastery at Montecassino, this façade was another example of the early use of the pointed arch in the Christian West.*

5

6. Saint Ambrose's, nave. *Milan. Twelfth century. The persistence of Roman features in Italian Romanesque architecture reflected the continuity of tradition.*

6

7. Baptistery. *Florence. Eleventh to thirteenth centuries. Consecrated in 1059, the baptistery was octagonal in design and based on a much older structure. The elegant round arches supported on classical columns and inlaid marble decoration were distinctive features of Tuscan Romanesque style and provided prototypes for later development.*

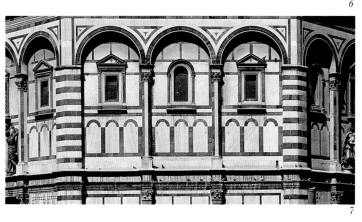
7

8. Saint Mark's. *Venice. Begun 1093. Basing the design of their major church on Byzantine prototypes, the Venetians consistently emphasized their economic and cultural links with Constantinople.*

8

apocryphal story provided a potent image for papal power. The continuity of temporal authority from Constantine to the papacy was further reinforced by a collection of ancient statues in front of the Lateran Palace in Rome (the papal residence in the Middle Ages), which included an equestrian monument of Marcus Aurelius thought to be Constantine (erroneously).

The Revival of Rome

But the most dramatic expression of the new power of the papacy was the revival of Rome itself. Barbarian invasions and the fall of the

---

THE DONATION OF CONSTANTINE

The spiritual authority of the pope as the successor to Saint Peter was not seriously challenged during the Middle Ages, but it proved difficult to enforce without the backing of temporal power. The *Donation of Constantine*, a document dated 313 C.E. but in reality an eighth-century forgery, provided the papacy with such a claim. The myth on which the *Donation* was based centered around Constantine's miraculous recovery from leprosy. Advised by pagan doctors to wash in the blood of innocent children, Constantine dreamed that Saint Peter and Saint Paul told him that Pope Silvester would provide a cure. The pope came to see him, bringing portraits of the two saints, which Constantine immediately recognized. Healed by baptism, the emperor granted the pope primacy in the Church and temporal power in Italy. The fifteenth-century Italian humanist Lorenzo Valla exposed the document as a forgery in his famous pamphlet *De falso credita et ementita Constantini donatione*, published in 1440. The episode illustrates the power invested in visual imagery as a representation of reality. Constantine's recognition of the two saints from their portraits reaffirmed the truth of the fresco itself, underlining the crucial role played by art in the politics of the Middle Ages.

10

9. Triumph of the Cross. *San Clemente, Rome. Apse mosaic. Ca. 1130. The use of mosaics revived another early Christian tradition, and its links with late imperial Rome were reinforced by the acanthus leaf scrolls dominating the apse.*

10. Pope Silvester I showing images of Saint Peter and Saint Paul to Constantine. *Basilica, San Piero a Grado (Pisa). Fresco. Eleventh century.*

9

11

11. San Clemente, interior. *Rome. Before 1130. Although much altered, San Clemente still has its schola cantorum and pavement. Made from old marble fragments and inspired by classical Roman examples, these opus alexandrinum pavements were an important feature of the twelfth-century revival of early Christian Rome.*

empire had left Rome a small rural town, set amid the ruins of past glory—hardly an appropriate image for the revival of power. In parallel with religious reforms, therefore, the papacy made efforts to restore the visual appearance of Rome as well. At the same time that Abbot Suger was introducing an innovative architectural style in northern Europe, the popes in Rome were reviving Constantinian church design and decoration. The contrast was marked. While being far from unadventurous, the papacy was consciously stressing its temporal and spiritual authority through a revival of its imperial past. San Clemente was typical of churches of this period. In plan and elevation it followed the standard early Christian basilica, an association strengthened by its *opus alexandrinum* pavement and by a mosaic in the apse. In a Roman context, the Byzantine imagery of the apse mosaic corroborated the papal claim of being the sole successor to both Saint Peter and the emperors in the West.

Imperial imagery was carried a step further at Santa Maria in Trastevere, where the apse mosaic depicted the *Coronation of the Virgin.* In Saint Peter's, Innocent III emphasized the spiritual supremacy of the papacy by replacing the old apse mosaic with one (now destroyed) showing him not as the donor but as the personification of the papal institution. The inscription referred to Saint Peter's as the mother of all churches, a title previously reserved for the traditional seat of the pope, San Giovanni Laterano. By shifting the focus to Saint Peter's, Innocent III was deliberately emphasizing the link between the modern papacy and the first pope, Saint Peter.

Rome in the Late Thirteenth Century

By the end of the thirteenth century, the independence of the papacy was once

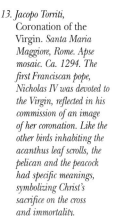

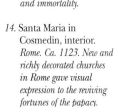

12. Coronation of the Virgin. *Santa Maria in Trastevere, Rome. Apse mosaic. Ca. 1140. Lambs were traditional Christian symbols for the Apostles, with the Lamb of God in the center. But Christ and the Virgin enthroned in heaven were a more direct reminder of their supreme authority on earth.*

13. *Jacopo Torriti,* Coronation of the Virgin. *Santa Maria Maggiore, Rome. Apse mosaic. Ca. 1294. The first Franciscan pope, Nicholas IV was devoted to the Virgin, reflected in his commission of an image of her coronation. Like the other birds inhabiting the acanthus leaf scrolls, the pelican and the peacock had specific meanings, symbolizing Christ's sacrifice on the cross and immortality.*

14. Santa Maria in Cosmedin, interior. *Rome. Ca. 1123. New and richly decorated churches in Rome gave visual expression to the reviving fortunes of the papacy.*

15. San Lorenzo fuori le Mura, nave. *Rome. Begun ca. 1200. Concentrating on enlarging this church, Pope Honorius III (1216–1227) added the nave, which was built with classical columns taken from Roman ruins nearby.*

again under threat. At a time when papal fortunes were exceptionally low, a succession of Italian popes set out to give Rome another facelift, promoting an image of wealth and power in an attempt to hide the economic and political realities of the time. The patronage of these popes and their cardinals reached heights of ostentation and extravagance not seen since the fall of the Roman Empire. Once again the papacy turned back to its roots for an appropriate theme. Late antique sources in Rome provided the model for Pope Nicholas IV (1288–1292) and his decoration of the apses at San Giovanni Laterano

and Santa Maria Maggiore. Nicholas IV was the first Franciscan pope, and his adoption of the imperial style of early Christian Rome in preference for the simplicity espoused by his fellow friars (see chapter 19) was indicative of the importance he attached to temporal power. The image of the coronation of the Virgin had been popularized in Rome during the twelfth century, but Nicholas's version was considerably more ostentatious in its use of gold and its quantity of figures. A blue mandorla, studded with gold stars, emphasized the heavenly context of the scene. The inclusion of the Franciscan saints,

Francis and Anthony of Padua, reflected its modernity.

Boniface VIII

In an attempt to replenish the depleted papal coffers and to reassert the spiritual authority of the Church, Pope Boniface VIII (1294–1303) announced the first Holy Year (1300), giving special dispensation to pilgrims who visited Rome. Boniface concentrated on direct images of papal power and revived the antique tradition of large-scale bronze statuary, commissioning a new Benediction Loggia at the Lateran

16. Arnolfo di Cambio, Ciborium. *Santa Cecilia in Trastevere, Rome. Marble. 1293. Trained in Florence as a stone mason, Arnolfo di Cambio (ca. 1245–1302) found ready employment in Rome. His classically inspired style also included Gothic details, reflecting the cosmopolitan nature of the papal court.*

17. Cavallini (Pietro de' Cerroni), Birth of the Virgin. *Santa Maria in Trastevere, Rome. Mosaic. Early 1290s. In contrast to earlier medieval mosaicists, Cavallini (active 1273–1321) attempted to create a more naturalistic style for his figures and settings.*

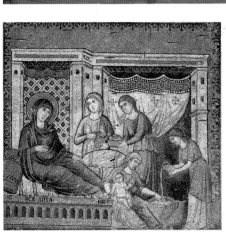

18

16

17

and a bronze statue of Saint Peter by Arnolfo di Cambio. He also insisted that statues of himself be erected to commemorate his achievements. Boniface's cardinals added to the ostentation of his court. His nephew, Cardinal Jacopo Stefaneschi, commissioned works for Saint Peter's that including Giotto's *Navicella* mosaic and an altarpiece for the High Altar. The latter depicted Saint Peter in full papal regalia and was a clear reminder of the supreme authority of the Petrine tradition. His brother, Bertoldo Stefaneschi, commissioned a series of mosaics for Santa Maria in Trastevere that demonstrated a growing interest in the methods of pictorial composition and naturalism used by late antique mosaicists in Rome. Foreign cardinals, like Jean Cholet, stimulated the introduction of Gothic details into otherwise traditional works.

Despite these efforts in the architectural and artistic realm, the political and economic realities of the papacy soon became apparent. Papal interference in the quarrels between France and England seriously damaged its authority. The involvement of the papacy in the European political arena and its repeated attempts to subject temporal rulers to spiritual authority inevitably provoked dispute. In Rome, factional feuds between cardinals of different political allegiances forced Pope Clement V (1305–1314) to establish his court at Avignon (1309; see chapter 20). By the mid-fourteenth century, the papacy was dominated by the French monarchy and Rome once again fell into decline.

THE REVIVAL OF THE PAPACY

19

21. Arnolfo di Cambio, Saint Peter. *Vatican. Bronze. Ca. 1296. Reviving the classical tradition of bronze commemorative statues, the solidity, facial features, and drapery style were also inspired by the sculptural remains of Ancient Rome.*

18. and 19. Giotto (attrib.), Stefaneschi altarpiece. *Pinacoteca, Vatican. Panel. Late 1320s. This double-sided altarpiece was designed to be seen both by the congregation in Saint Peter's and by the papal court behind in the apse. The patron, Cardinal Jacopo Stefaneschi, is shown offering his painting to Saint Peter, whose papal regalia is a clear reminder of the authority of the Petrine tradition.*

20. Arnolfo di Cambio, Boniface VIII. *Museo dell'Opera del Duomo, Florence. Marble. Ca. 1300. Rigid and imposing, this image was designed to reinforce papal authority.*

20

21

THE MIDDLE AGES: NEW HORIZONS

The birth of new religious orders between the twelfth and thirteenth centuries played a determining role in the spread of new figurative and architectural languages in Western Christianity.

Around the middle of the twelfth century in the churches of northern France (see preceding timeline and chapter 17), the first signs of what is generally known as Gothic Art were already visible. Actually, the term "Gothic Art" was coined during the Renaissance and had a negative connotation. The new building

techniques used in France spread beyond the Alps at the beginning of the thirteenth century. One of the main bearers was the Cistercian Order. Its spiritual message, based on the thought of its founder, St. Bernard of Clairvaux, was based on simplicity and renewed rigor in contrast with the laxness of the Cluniac Order whose leader had been Suger, the abbot of Saint-Denis.

In Italy, where Gothic architecture never attained the daring and boldness that it did in northern Europe, the birth

of two mendicant orders, the Franciscans and Dominicans, had a major impact. The Franciscan basilica in Assisi became an extraordinary site where artists such as Lorenzetti and Martini of Siena and Cimabue and Giotto of Florence gathered along with hosts of helpers.

Then a new impulse in building and decoration reached Italy thanks to the initiatives of the free city-states and the great trading families, while in fourteenth-century France and England an elegant and decorative courtly style flourished.

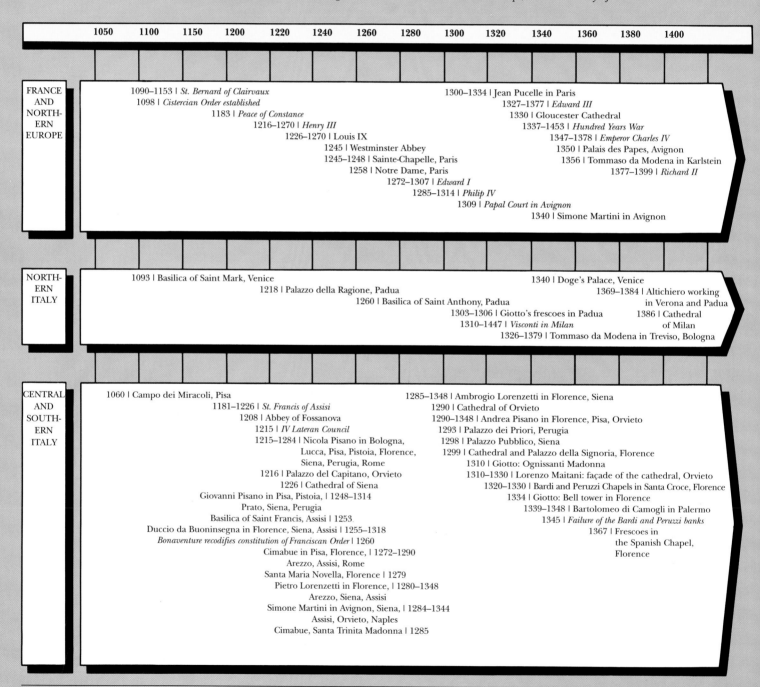

| 1050 | 1100 | 1150 | 1200 | 1220 | 1240 | 1260 | 1280 | 1300 | 1320 | 1340 | 1360 | 1380 | 1400 |

FRANCE AND NORTHERN EUROPE

1090–1153 | *St. Bernard of Clairvaux*
1098 | *Cistercian Order established*
1183 | *Peace of Constance*
1216–1270 | *Henry III*
1226–1270 | Louis IX
1245 | Westminster Abbey
1245–1248 | Sainte-Chapelle, Paris
1258 | Notre Dame, Paris
1272–1307 | *Edward I*
1285–1314 | *Philip IV*
1309 | *Papal Court in Avignon*
1340 | Simone Martini in Avignon

1300–1334 | Jean Pucelle in Paris
1327–1377 | *Edward III*
1330 | Gloucester Cathedral
1337–1453 | *Hundred Years War*
1347–1378 | *Emperor Charles IV*
1350 | Palais des Papes, Avignon
1356 | Tommaso da Modena in Karlstein
1377–1399 | *Richard II*

NORTHERN ITALY

1093 | Basilica of Saint Mark, Venice
1218 | Palazzo della Ragione, Padua
1260 | Basilica of Saint Anthony, Padua
1303–1306 | Giotto's frescoes in Padua
1310–1447 | *Visconti in Milan*
1326–1379 | Tommaso da Modena in Treviso, Bologna

1340 | Doge's Palace, Venice
1369–1384 | Altichiero working in Verona and Padua
1386 | Cathedral of Milan

CENTRAL AND SOUTHERN ITALY

1060 | Campo dei Miracoli, Pisa
1181–1226 | *St. Francis of Assisi*
1208 | Abbey of Fossanova
1215 | *IV Lateran Council*
1215–1284 | Nicola Pisano in Bologna, Lucca, Pisa, Pistoia, Florence, Siena, Perugia, Rome
1216 | Palazzo del Capitano, Orvieto
1226 | Cathedral of Siena
Giovanni Pisano in Pisa, Pistoia, | 1248–1314
Prato, Siena, Perugia
Basilica of Saint Francis, Assisi | 1253
Duccio da Buoninsegna in Florence, Siena, Assisi | 1255–1318
Bonaventure recodifies constitution of Franciscan Order | 1260
Cimabue in Pisa, Florence, | 1272–1290
Arezzo, Assisi, Rome
Santa Maria Novella, Florence | 1279
Pietro Lorenzetti in Florence, | 1280–1348
Arezzo, Siena, Assisi
Simone Martini in Avignon, Siena, | 1284–1344
Assisi, Orvieto, Naples
Cimabue, Santa Trinita Madonna | 1285

1285–1348 | Ambrogio Lorenzetti in Florence, Siena
1290 | Cathedral of Orvieto
1290–1348 | Andrea Pisano in Florence, Pisa, Orvieto
1293 | Palazzo dei Priori, Perugia
1298 | Palazzo Pubblico, Siena
1299 | Cathedral and Palazzo della Signoria, Florence
1310 | Giotto: Ognissanti Madonna
1310–1330 | Lorenzo Maitani: façade of the cathedral, Orvieto
1320–1330 | Bardi and Peruzzi Chapels in Santa Croce, Florence
1334 | Giotto: Bell tower in Florence
1339–1348 | Bartolomeo di Camogli in Palermo
1345 | *Failure of the Bardi and Peruzzi banks*
1367 | Frescoes in the Spanish Chapel, Florence

THE PROSPERITY AND INCREASING secularization of the Church during the twelfth century stood in marked contrast to the poverty and spirituality of Christ and his Apostles as portrayed in the New Testament. Monastic reformers sought purity in new communities that were closer imitations of the *vita apostolica*. Foremost among these were the Cistercians, an order founded (1098) in reaction to the extravagance of Cluny. To escape the temptations of society, they built monasteries in remote areas and bred sheep to provide basic necessities: milk, cheese, mutton, wool, parchment, and manure.

Under the influence of Saint Bernard of Clairvaux (ca. 1090–1153), a contemporary of Abbot Suger, they became a powerful force in the Church and politics of the twelfth century. Cistercian monasteries were under the direct authority of their mother-house at Cîteaux, and each abbot was expected to attend the triennial General Chapter (legislative assembly). This innovative system of centralized control proved so effective in maintaining standards that it became the model for the reorganization of all religious orders imposed by the Fourth Lateran Council (1215).

1

Saint Bernard spearheaded the attack on monastic excess. He condemned the trade that had developed in valuable relics, the commercial aspects of pilgrimage, and the extravagant display of wealth in the structure and decoration of monastic architecture. Cistercian abbots rejected luxury and grandeur, adopting simple Latin Cross plans with square east ends and no ambulatories for relics. Façades and portals deliberately avoided elaborate sculptured decoration. The Cistercians adopted the pointed arch, which had been popularized by its use in Cluny III, but used it to articulate simple elevations, often without a triforium or gallery. The uniformity of these interiors left little scope for competition and reflected the highly organized structure of the order. A conscious effort to express a return to the purity and spirituality of early Christianity, Cistercian architecture eschewed the images of scale and extravagance used in the Gothic cathedrals. This provided an influential model for later followers of the *vita apostolica*.

Cistercian Influence

Cistercian reform was aimed at monastic life, but the appeal of the *vita apostolica* affected all levels of society and inspired the growth of lay religious movements such as the Cathars and Humiliati. Their transgression of the ban on lay preaching and their message of poverty posed a threat to papal authority, and they were excommunicated as heretics (1184). But the lay spiritual revival was too powerful and soon found its champions in Saint Francis (ca. 1181–1226) and Saint Dominic (1170–1221). The son of a wealthy Assisi merchant, Saint Francis with his followers rejected both personal and communal property in favor of an evangelical life of poverty, preaching,

2. Abbey church, nave. *Fossanova. Consecrated 1208. Cistercian architecture deliberately avoided sculptural decoration and adopted simple elevations articulated with pointed arches.*

3. Abbey church. *Fossanova. Consecrated 1208. The Cistercian reformer Saint Bernard of Clairvaux was a leading critic of the extravagant displays of wealth that characterized contemporary monastic architecture.*

1. Basilica of Saint Francis, interior of upper church. *Assisi. Founded 1228. Epitomizing Franciscan design and decoration, this interior gave visual expression to the ideals of the new monastic order.*

4. Santa Maria Novella, nave. *Florence. Begun by 1279. Neither the Franciscans nor the Dominicans in Italy showed any interest in developing the structural potential of the pointed arch as contemporary designers were doing in France.*

5. Santa Croce, nave. *Florence. Founded 1294–1295. The great popularity of the Franciscans and Dominicans in Italy stimulated a building boom.*

and charity. Official approval for their way of life was granted by Pope Innocent III (1210), who insisted on their submission to papal authority. The Dominicans also renounced material wealth, obtaining papal approval for their order (1216), organized for the conversion of the Cathars in France. Papal support for the mendicant (begging) orders identified the Church with the growth of lay spirituality. Both orders aimed at making religion more comprehensible. The Dominicans supported that aim by stressing the importance of education. Through Saint Thomas Aquinas and other theologians, their impact on the intellectual life of the thirteenth century was enormous. The Franciscans were also intellectually active, but their message, which emphasized the humanity of Christ, had a more popular appeal. The order grew dramatically: by 1380 there were 1,500 houses with 90,000 friars in Europe. The issue of communal ownership of property was never a problem for the Dominicans, but it was a dilemma for the Franciscans. After the death of Saint Francis, the ban on communal ownership of property was relaxed, splitting the movement between the majority Conventuals, who accepted communal property, and the minority Spirituals, who rejected it in favor of a more rigorous interpretation of Franciscan privation.

Mendicant Churches

The new orders needed a new image. The Cistercians had withdrawn from worldly temptation, but the mendicant churches were located in town centers, and their message was aimed directly at the new urban populations. Nevertheless, the friars faced

6. Basilica of Saint Francis. *Assisi. Founded 1228, consecrated 1253. Following the Cistercian example, the new mendicant orders avoided elaboration and excess. Saint Francis himself had rejected both personal and communal ownership of property, but this ideal proved impractical with the establishment of the Franciscan order.*

7. *Plans of Franciscan and Dominican churches in Italy, from left to right: Lower Church, basilica of Saint Francis, Assisi; Upper Church, basilica of Saint Francis, Assisi; Santa Maria Novella, Florence; Santa Croce, Florence.*

6

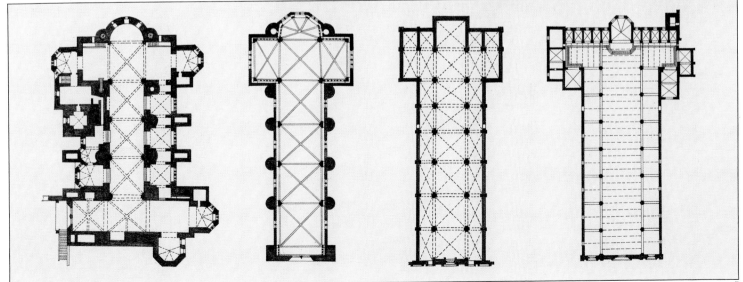

7

the same problem as the Cistercians: how to design a building to reflect their power and to avoid the extravagance of the lifestyle they had renounced. The solution was large and simple. They rejected both the elaborate Romanesque current in Italy and the complications of contemporary Gothic architecture in northern Europe. Following the Cistercian example, they adopted uncomplicated Latin Cross plans with square-headed or angular chapels. Even when ritual function called for more elaborate plans, as with the ambulatory in the pilgrimage church of Saint Anthony's in Padua, their goal was simplicity. Like the Cistercians,

they avoided elaborately sculpted portals, and from Cistercian architecture they borrowed such stylistic features as plain façades, pointed arches, two-story interior elevations, ribbed vaults, and lancet windows.

Thus the distinction was drawn between the simple spiritual architecture of Cistercian, Franciscan, or Dominican churches and the images of wealth and power embodied in cathedrals. The use of the pointed arch in Italy is usually described as Gothic, and the friars had no interest in exploiting its structural potential. The vertical emphasis of French Gothic is similarly lacking in mendicant architecture,

echoing Saint Bernard's criticism of excessive height. The Franciscan statutes of 1260 banned stone vaults except over the main altar. Although both orders used features of Cistercian architecture, they did not adopt its uniformity. The use of local building materials and adherence to local traditions was important to these urban-based orders, whose success depended on their popular appeal. The church of Saint Francis in Bologna, like many local churches, was built of brick; the domes of Saint Anthony's in Padua derived from Venetian architecture. The architectural similarity of Franciscan and Dominican churches

8. Saint Francis. *Bologna. Begun 1236. A rare example of the use of flying buttresses in Italy, this brick exterior was distinctive for its austerity and simplicity.*

9. Saint Anthony. *Padua. Begun ca. 1260. Inspired by the domed architecture of nearby Venice, the designers of Saint Anthony's adopted a locally recognizable image of power.*

10. The Ministry of Christ. *Basilica of Saint Francis, upper church, Assisi. Apse. Ca. 1275. Stained glass windows continued the themes frescoed on the walls.*

8

9

10

reflected their common spiritual ideals, while the difference in the aims and methods of the two orders were expressed in their distinctive decorative programs.

The Basilica of Saint Francis, Assisi

The basilica of Saint Francis in Assisi, commissioned by the minister-general and paid for by donations, was decorated with frescoes (painted in the 1280s and after). The choice of fresco rather than mosaic is yet another example of the mendicant desire to avoid extravagance. The decorative schemes, conceived by the Order itself, set a precedent for Franciscan art both in imagery and in interpretation. Tradition and innovation were combined to project an image that emphasized the new message and reinforced the continuity of belief.

Biblical scenes were standard for nave decoration, but scenes from the life of Saint Francis occupied the most prominent position in the nave of the upper church. Francis's desire to imitate the life of Christ was stressed by the juxtaposition of the Crucifixion with the scene of his own death. The pointed arch was the architectural symbol of the new reformed religion. Its importance to the Franciscans was reinforced by the scenes in which Saint Francis meets the pope. In the first, set in round arches, he asks Innocent III to approve his way of life. In the second, set in pointed arches, he preaches before Honorius III as the founder of an officially recognized order. The new Franciscan style had replaced the old architecture, which, with its round arches, carried associations of both pagan antiquity and contemporary wealth. The importance of building Christian and moral architecture was further reinforced in the Apocalyptic scenes at the east end of the upper church, including *The Fall of Babylon*.

11

12

12. *Giotto*, Saint Francis before Honorius III. *Basilica of Saint Francis, upper church, Assisi. Fresco. 1290s. The use of pointed arches and star-studded vaults deliberately reflected the architecture and decoration of the basilica itself.*

11. Bay of decoration in upper church. *Basilica of Saint Francis, Assisi. Fresco. 1290s (?). Top: Expulsion and Labors of Adam and Eve (destroyed); Middle: Isaac and Jacob and Isaac and Esau; Bottom: Confirmation of Franciscan Rule, Vision of the Fiery Chariot, and Vision of Fra' Leone. The walls of the upper church nave were divided into three levels for decoration. The upper two levels were devoted to the Hebrew Bible and New Testament, which, following custom, faced each other across the nave. In the most visible position were scenes of the life of Saint Francis.*

The Bible is full of accounts of God's wrath directed at extravagant architecture, the image of immorality, and material wealth. The reality of this threat was clearly spelled out in the ruins of Ancient Rome.

Franciscan Imagery

The Franciscan message was reinforced by the use of traditional Christian themes that had special significance for the order. The altar vault in the lower church displayed personifications of Poverty, Chastity, and Obedience, the standard monastic vows. It was Saint Francis's unwavering adherence to these vows that had inspired his followers, of which they were reminded by the three knots in their girdles. Other saints, like Saint Martin, who had also renounced material wealth, or Saint Lawrence and Saint Stephen, who had distributed the wealth of the Church to the poor, were obvious exemplars of earlier attempts to pursue the *vita apostolica* and often associated with Franciscan decorative schemes. Biographers of Saint Francis stressed his devotion to the Virgin, and the apse of the upper church at Assisi was decorated with scenes from her life. The Franciscans strongly supported the controversial doctrine that she was conceived without sin, an idea denied just as strongly by the Dominicans. Her Immaculate Conception was declared a Franciscan feast at the General Chapter of Pisa (1263), but it did not become official Catholic dogma until 1854. The event is typically represented in Franciscan art as the meeting at the Golden Gate, a symbolic kiss between Joachim and Anna, the parents of the Virgin.

Giotto's *Meeting at the Golden Gate* was commissioned by the Paduan banker Enrico Scrovegni, a member of a lay charitable organization associated with the Franciscans.

13

13. *Cimabue,* The Fall of Babylon. *Basilica of Saint Francis, upper church, Assisi. Fresco. Ca. 1280s. Cimabue (active 1272–1302) was one of a number of painters who worked on the decoration of the upper church. His move from Rome to Assisi after the 1270s reflected a desire on the part of the Franciscans to commission established artists for their prestigious project.*

14. *Taddeo Gaddi,* Meeting at the Golden Gate. *Santa Croce, Baroncelli Chapel, Florence. Fresco. 1332–1338. The importance of the meeting of Anna and Joachim was reinforced by the intensity of their expressions.*

15. *Maestro delle Vele,* Allegory of Poverty. *Basilica of Saint Francis, lower church, Assisi. Fresco. Early fourteenth century. Saint Francis's decision to reject material wealth in favor of the asceticism and spirituality of the lives of Christ and his Apostles was given visual expression by his 'marriage' to Lady Poverty.*

15

14

16

The fresco formed part of a cycle of the lives of Christ and the Virgin that decorated Scrovegni's private chapel. Giotto specialized in fresco cycles for the wealthy middle class, and most are associated with the Franciscans, whose churches attracted considerable funds from the urban rich. Giotto's Bardi and Peruzzi chapels at Santa Croce in Florence were commissioned by two of the city's leading banking families and reflect Franciscan ideas about religion. The Franciscans sought to make all religious concepts comprehensible and exhorted people to visualize biblical stories in order to understand Christ's message.

This was the principal basis of their appeal to the masses.

Rejecting the complex symbolic imagery of earlier periods, the Franciscans needed art that communicated directly and was easily understood. Giotto and other painters did precisely this. Their aim was to depict scenes that looked real, and paint provided a much better medium than mosaic. The narrative clarity of Giotto's *Dance of Salomè* is very different from the frontality and stylization of Byzantine or Romanesque art. The figures are solid and positioned naturally rather than artificially. The table, set at an angle with figures seated behind it,

gives depth to the architectural setting and illustrates the efforts made to paint a convincing three-dimensional space.

Dominican Imagery

The growing divergence between the Franciscans and the Dominicans, reflected in the location of their churches on opposite sides of towns, became increasingly obvious as they took opposing sides in theological debates. Although both orders had been founded in response to the growth of lay spirituality, their methods were very different. Whereas the Franciscan message appealed

17. Arena Chapel, interior. *Padua. Begun 1303. Built to expiate the sin of usury, the Arena Chapel was decorated to reinforce its patron's devotion to the Virgin.*

16. Simone Martini, Saint Martin lays down his arms. *Basilica of Saint Francis, lower church, Assisi. Fresco. Ca. 1320–1330. Already established in Siena, Simone Martini (ca. 1284–1344) had also received commissions from the king of Naples. His frescoes of the life of Saint Martin are notable for their precise attention to detail.*

17

GIOTTO

Giotto (ca. 1267–1337) has long occupied a preeminent position in the history of Italian art. Judged the founder of the Renaissance by the sixteenth-century art theorist Giorgio Vasari, his reputation as the leading figure in the development of naturalism in art has never really been questioned.

Although his authorship of the Saint Francis cycle in Assisi has been decisively rejected, his major verifiable works were produced for patrons with strong Franciscan links: the Arena Chapel in Padua for Enrico Scrovegni (1303–1306), a member of a lay order associated with the Franciscans; and two chapels in the Florentine Franciscan church of Santa Croce for the Bardi and Peruzzi families (mid-1320s). Giotto's stylistic innovations provided visual images that reflected, par excellence, the aims of the Franciscan preachers, who encouraged their audiences to visualize the life of Christ and other biblical events as an aid to understanding. Giotto did precisely the same on church walls. Solid figures set in realistic three-dimensional spaces illustrated his rejection of the formal, frontal, and flat images of Byzantine and Romanesque art.

By positioning his figures carefully within the fictive architectural frame, Giotto enhanced the narrative clarity of the story. Replacing symbolism with factual detail, his images became more easily intelligible by ordinary, and mainly illiterate, people.

Perhaps his major achievement was the introduction of a new language based on realistic gestures and facial expressions to convey the complete range of human emotions to the observer—from pain and sadness to joy and excitement—that give meaning to the mysteries of religious belief.

18. *Giotto*, Meeting at the Golden Gate. *Arena Chapel, Padua. Fresco. 1303–1306. Convincing architectural settings, solid figures, and natural gestures combined to present a scene of human tenderness that would have been easily understood by the viewer.*

19. *Giotto*, Adoration of the Magi. *Arena Chapel, Padua. Fresco. 1303–1306. The appearance of Halley's Comet in 1301 inspired Giotto to include it as the star that guided the Three Kings to Bethlehem.*

20. *Giotto*, Dance of Salomè. *Santa Croce, Peruzzi Chapel, Florence. Fresco. Mid-1320s.*

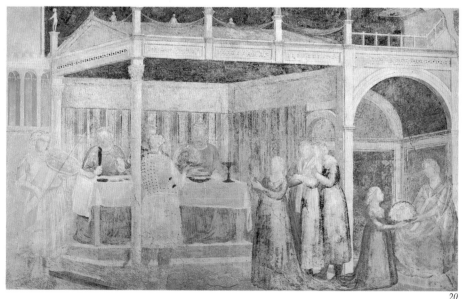

to popular piety through emotion, the Dominicans sought to restore doctrinal purity through reform at the intellectual level. The Franciscan order soon abandoned Saint Francis's strict adherence to poverty, preferring a less austere life in conventual buildings. The Franciscans' need to recall and reassert their origins was therefore greater than that of the Dominicans, who had changed little. Life cycles of Saint Dominic were rare, while the Dominican saint most commonly depicted was Saint Thomas Aquinas. Canonized in 1323, his fame rested on his *Summa Theologiae* (1267–1273). A synthesis of moral and political philosophy, his treatise succeeded in reconciling the differences between the pagan Greek philosophers and Christian theologians, thereby stemming the growing threat posed by free debate. The apotheosis of Saint Thomas was a popular theme in Dominican art, which celebrated his intellectual achievement. The sources of his inspiration and knowledge (Jesus, Moses, Saint Paul, the Evangelists, Plato, and Aristotle) direct their texts at Saint Thomas, the links emphasized by rays that connect to his brain and his own text. Each figure is distinguished in importance by relative level and size.

This mathematically precise imagery was typical of the Dominicans, whose belief in rigid social stratification ordained by God was reflected in the pyramidal construction of the image. Clear and didactic, it defies misreading.

The Dominicans also received large donations from the wealthy middle class.

21. Andrea da Firenze, The Church Militant. *Santa Maria Novella, Spanish Chapel, Florence. Fresco. Begun 1365. The only element of informality in this carefully arranged and precisely detailed work is the little piebald dogs, a visual pun on* Domini canes, *or hounds of the Lord. The church on the left is based on the newly approved design (1367) for the cupola of Florence's cathedral.*

22. Francesco Traini (?), The Apotheosis of Saint Thomas Aquinas. *Santa Caterina, Pisa. Panel. 1363. The Dominican order emphasized intellectual reform, and its doctrinal purity was reflected in formal, clear compositions.*

23. Tommaso da Modena, Saint Albertus Magnus. *San Nicolò, Treviso. Fresco. 1352. The lined forehead of Albertus Magnus and his ink pot and quill pen illustrate the importance of detail in Dominican art.*

The Spanish Chapel was paid for by Buonamico Guidalotti, who left funds in his will (1355) for a chapter house that would contain his tomb. The building, based on Cistercian prototypes, was decorated with images chosen by the monks to communicate the Dominican message. The order had been founded to combat heresy and placed considerable emphasis on the preservation of the institutions of the Church. The physical image of its power was represented by the new cathedral of Florence, then under construction. Beneath is a formal arrangement of Church leaders, reflecting the Dominican emphasis on the authoritarian structure of ecclesiastical power. The scampering piebald dogs, known as *Domini canes*, or "the hounds of the Lord," are a punning reinforcement of Dominican control.

The institutionalization of the Cistercians, Franciscans, and Dominicans by the papacy was a clever move that served to avoid open conflict. It led to the reform of religious life in monasteries, in intellectual circles, and among the common people. New ideas require vehicles of dissemination, and the reform movement was expressed in visual and interpretive innovations that had important implications for the history of art.

24

24. Andrea da Firenze, Triumph of Saint Thomas Aquinas. *Santa Maria Novella, Spanish Chapel, Florence. Fresco. Begun 1365. Clarity, simplicity, and rigidity were the hallmarks of Dominican art. Enthroned between* the doctors of the Church, Thomas Aquinas presided over fourteen female personifications of the Arts and Sciences; each sits under her own Gothic canopy, with the leading historical figures in each field seated beneath.

25. Nardo di Cione, Paradise. *Santa Maria Novella, Strozzi Chapel, Florence. Fresco. Mid-1350s. This hierarchic image of paradise under the authority of Christ and the Virgin Mary reflected the ordered ideal of the Dominican worldview.*

25

CHAPTER 20

ROYAL AND PAPAL COURTS

Gothic as a Decorative Style

THE THIRTEENTH AND FOURTEENTH centuries in northern Europe saw the rise of powerful secular rulers who claimed supreme authority within their domains. Monarchic rule became increasingly institutionalized, as assemblies of prelates, nobles, and civic representatives were established to regulate sovereign power. Laymen replaced clerics in the administrative bodies that administered royal finances and justice. The ambiguous relationship between ecclesiastical and secular power was decisively resolved by the French and English kings, who resisted papal efforts to dictate Church appointments and exercised their growing power over the papacy (finally forcing it to leave Rome and settle in Avignon in 1309). By the mid-fourteenth century the papacy was controlled by the French monarchy. Royal coffers were opened to promote new national images and encourage the growth of secular culture. New styles developed in response to the change in patronage. The builders of the Gothic cathedrals had concentrated on the structural potential of their new building method (see chapter 17). Under the stimulus of royal patronage, designers explored its decorative possibilities, masking the structure beneath a profusion

1

of detail dominated by refined tracery patterns and stained glass.

Louis IX and the Sainte-Chapelle

The long reign of Louis IX (1226–1270) consolidated royal power in France and established a new image for the French monarchy. His crusades against Cathar heretics in southern France and against Muslims in Egypt and Palestine brought political advantages and earned him a reputation for piety; they also led to his death. His expenditure on tombs to house the remains of his ancestors in the royal mausoleums at Royaumont and Saint-Denis (mostly destroyed during the French Revolution) reinforced the continuity of monarchic authority.

The defining image of Louis's reign was his palace chapel in Paris, the Sainte-Chapelle, built to house his collection of relics, notably Christ's Crown of Thorns from Constantinople. Structural support was kept to the barest minimum. Wealth and power were celebrated in the proliferation of detail and in the unprecedented richness of the gilded decoration, sculpture, and stained glass. Designed for use by the court, the upper chapel emphasizes its connections with royal power, from the gold fleur-de-lis in the vaults to the ornate statues of the Apostles on the walls. The association of beauty and goodness is indelibly impressed on all those who enter. The spiritual perfection of the religious figures is reflected in their physical beauty, expensive materials, and exquisite clothing. Louis drew a direct parallel between his own richly clad court and the court of heaven, emphasizing the authority of the French monarchy. The association of royal with spiritual power was further reinforced by the canonization of Louis IX (1297), an overtly political act resulting from French

1. Window, detail. *Sainte-Chapelle, Paris. Stained glass. Ca. 1250. Carefully painted facial details, elaborate clothing, and the royal fleur-de-lis reinforced the courtly setting of the Sainte-Chapelle.*

2. Apostle. *Sainte-Chapelle, Paris. Stone. Ca. 1250. The physical beauty of the Apostles that decorated the shafts of Sainte-Chapelle were a deliberate reflection of their spiritual perfection.*

3. Sainte-Chapelle, interior. *Paris. Ca. 1245–1248. Reducing Gothic architecture to its structural members allowed the development of huge stained glass windows.*

4. Notre Dame, south transept. *Paris. Begun 1258. The radiating patterns of tracery in rose windows gave this style its French name,* Rayonnant. *Small-scale, intricate, and elaborate, it emerged above all under the influence of court patronage.*

pressure on Pope Boniface VIII; Louis's successors had actively promoted him as a saint. Some of Louis's relics were added to those already in the Sainte-Chapelle, and others were distributed to members of the French aristocracy, who built their own imitations of Sainte-Chapelle to house them. As both a king and saint, Louis IX personified the new nationalist image exploited by the monarchy to reinforce its power. The patronage of Louis IX established Paris as the cultural center of northern Europe.

The Fourth Lateran Council (1215), meanwhile, had decided that education in the basic articles of Christian faith should be extended to everyone and not restricted to monks and clerics. This decision was a major stimulus for the production of psalters, Books of Hours, and other forms of devotional literature for the lay public. Louis IX was notable for his patronage in this field as well, commissioning numerous manuscripts for his personal library; those who could afford to followed his example. Under his successors, Paris became a major center for the production of manuscripts, setting standards that were emulated throughout Europe. Royal and noble patrons expressed their wealth through expensive materials and the use of elegant, sinuous figures, reflecting the courtly images of saints and apostles in the Sainte-Chapelle.

Religion and Kingship in England

The image of kingship created by Louis IX was imitated at secular courts throughout Europe. Henry III (r. 1216–1272) deliberately set out to revive the prestige of the English monarchy by promoting his ancestor, Edward the Confessor, in the role of saintly monarch. Canonized in 1161, Edward the Confessor had been the last king before the Norman invasion (1066) and provided an ideal focus

5. Virgin and Child. *Louvre, Paris. Silver gilt. 1399. Commissioned by Jeanne d'Evreux, the wife of Charles IV of France (1322–1328), as a gift to the royal abbey of Saint-Denis, this statuette presented a courtly image of the Virgin with its sinuous pose, elegant clothes, and jeweled fleur-de-lis, the emblem of French monarchy.*

6. Sainte-Chapelle. *Paris. Ca. 1245–1248. Built by Louis IX of France to house his relic of the Crown of Thorns, this elegant chapel was originally part of his palace complex. (The present rose window dates from the fifteenth century).*

4

5

6

The decision of the Fourth Lateran Council (1215) that laypeople should be educated in the basics of Christian faith acted as a major stimulus to the development of manuscript illumination. Part of a wider attempt to curb the power of the monasteries, it encouraged the production of manuscripts by lay artists outside the monastic scriptoria. The style established by King Louis IX of France (r. 1226–1270) and his artists was continued by his successors. Exquisite and refined, the miniatures emphasized courtly elegance. But the growing desire for more realistic religious imagery, which found expression in the major stylistic innovations of artists like Giotto in Italy, was also reflected in developments in miniature painting at the French court. Master Honoré, who worked for King Philip IV (r. 1285–1314), adopted a bulkier figure style, emphasizing solidity. His successor, Jean Pucelle (active ca. 1300–1334), developed three-dimensional architectural settings and a realistic use of light to enhance the reality of his scenes. His illuminated manuscripts were commissioned by Jeanne de Belleville and by King Charles IV. Lay patrons not only commissioned devotional texts, such as psalters and Books of Hours, but also epic poems, romances, and chronicles inspired by the chivalric ideal. The increasing secularization of courtly culture was given visual expression in a proliferation of precisely rendered marginal details that bore little relevance to the religious text. These images of the secular world included birds, animals, flowers, peasant and idyllic scenes, and heraldic devices, reflecting the love of ornament, embellishment, and display so characteristic of the medieval courts throughout Europe.

7. *Jean Pucelle,* Page from Belleville Breviary. *Bibliothèque Nationale, Paris. MS Lat. 10483, f. 31. 1323–1326.*

8. Cathedral, choir. *Gloucester. After 1330. A veneer of tracery hides the solid Romanesque piers behind an elegant, detailed façade. The huge east window was commissioned to commemorate the Battle of Crécy (1346), a major English success in the Hundred Years' War against the French.*

9. Tomb of Edward the Confessor. *Westminster Abbey, London. Marble. 1269. Commissioned by Henry III, who employed Roman marble workers specifically for the project, this tomb of the beatified English King Edward the Confessor established the tradition of Westminster Abbey as a royal mausoleum.*

for English nationalism. Henry chose the name Edward for his eldest son, and it was no accident that his major architectural project was the rebuilding of Edward the Confessor's church, Westminster Abbey, to house an elaborate and costly shrine for the remains of the saint. Henry imported marble workers from Rome to carve the shrine and introduced French architectural ideas to reflect the authority and prestige of the monarchy. The east end of the church was built with flying buttresses and an apse, both unusual in England. Henry's desire to emulate French achievements was evidenced as well in tracery patterns and other details derived from buildings such as the Sainte-Chapelle and Reims Cathedral.

Edward the Confessor's tomb established Westminster Abbey as the royal mausoleum. Henry's son Edward I (r. 1272–1307) embellished the church with tombs for other members of the royal family, notably his wife, Eleanor of Castile. Eleanor had died near Lincoln, and Edward erected crosses where her funeral cortege had rested on its journey to London. In what almost amounted to canonization, Eleanor's remains were distributed as relics, thus reinforcing secular authority by spiritual association.

Like the relics of Louis IX and Edward the Confessor, Eleanor's bowels in Lincoln Cathedral and her bones in Westminster Abbey were royal counterparts to older religious relics and provided an added attraction for pilgrims.

The English Style

The fourteenth century in England was a period of nationalism and expansionism. Edward III (r. 1327–1377) reestablished monarchic authority after the disastrous reign of his father, Edward II (r. 1307–1327). He laid claim to the French crown and

8

9

10. Torel, Tomb of Eleanor of Castile. Westminster Abbey, London. Gilt brass. 1291. For the wife of Edward I, this was one of the first royal tombs set up in Westminster Abbey; it presented a stylized, expensive image of monarchic power.

10

started the so-called Hundred Years' War (1337–1453). English replaced French as the language of the court. Chaucer, whose *Canterbury Tales* (1388) was written in English, enjoyed the patronage of one of Edward III's sons, John of Gaunt. These developments were reflected in the architecture of the period. The decorative excesses of Henry III's French style were rejected in favor of a flat veneer of stylized tracery panels and repetitive ornament. Emphasis on the decorative potential of tracery was typical of late Gothic throughout Europe, but this variant was peculiarly English. Established as the court style with the palace chapel at Westminster (Saint Stephen's Chapel, since destroyed), it was adopted for the rebuilding of the east end of Gloucester Cathedral to house the tomb of Edward II. Unlike the French, the English had already evolved complex vaulting patterns, which became increasingly elaborate with the addition of *tierceron* (intermediate) and *lierne* (secondary) ribs. The development of fan vaults allowed the tracery veneer to extend over walls and ceiling, completely masking the structure of the vaults (see Figure 15). This concern for decoration was also extended to wood roofs. When Richard II (1377–1399) remodeled the hall of the royal palace at Westminster, he commissioned an ambitious and elaborate hammerbeam roof to crown this new setting for court ceremonial in a distinctively English way.

Chivalry

Fighting was endemic in the Middle Ages. The education of royal and noble children in the arts of war and chivalric ideals was very different from the more practical education of the mercantile classes. The cult of knighthood was central to court society throughout Europe.

11. Neville screen. *Cathedral, Durham. Stone. Completed 1379. One of many costly gifts given by John, Lord Neville, to Durham Cathedral, this screen was made in London and transported to Durham by sea. (The 107 alabaster statues that originally adorned it are now lost).*

12

12. Mirror case. *Museo Civico, Bologna. Ivory. Fourteenth century. This French ivory was decorated with scenes from the legend of Gawain, nephew of King Arthur. An ideal of knightly honor, brave in love and in war, Gawain was a popular image in the cult of chivalry.*

11

13

Tournaments were an integral part of royal ceremony and provided an institutionalized arena for settling factional disputes. Military heroes such as Alexander the Great, Charlemagne, King Arthur, and Tristan were the subjects of romances and epics of courtly love and chivalric ideals. The Arthurian legends in particular provided themes for the decoration of furnishings in royal palaces and inspired the foundation of chivalric associations such as the Knights of the Garter, founded by Edward III (1344) in direct imitation of King Arthur and the Knights of the Round Table.

Images of Power in Avignon and Milan

The style established by the French kings was developed in courts throughout Europe. When the Holy Roman Emperor Charles IV (r. 1346–1378) made Prague his new capital, he imported the French mason Mathias of Arras to supervise the construction of a new cathedral as his family mausoleum. Even the papacy adapted French innovations to provide a new image for its change of residence. The move of the papacy from Rome to Avignon was given visual permanence in the construction and decoration of a new papal palace by three

French popes, Benedict XII (1334–1342), Clement VI (1342–1352), and Innocent VI (1352–1362). The secularization of the papal court was reinforced by the adoption of the courtly style for religious imagery established by Louis IX. This was a marked contrast to papal patronage in the twelfth and thirteenth centuries, which had consistently emphasized its Roman heritage and made no attempt to imitate the current styles in northern Europe (see chapter 18).

One of the few places in Italy to adopt French standards was the Visconti court in Milan. The largest city in fourteenth-century Europe, Milan had been an important center

13. Westminster Hall, interior. *1394–1401. Designed by the royal carpenter Henry Herland, this hammerbeam roof spanned about 69 feet (21m). The hall was the setting for royal ceremonial and originally designed to hold statues of the thirteen English kings from Edward the Confessor to its patron, Richard II.*

14

15

16

14. *Matteo Giovannetti,* Job and Solomon. *Palais des Papes, Avignon. Fresco. Ca. 1350. Elegant, richly dressed, and highly stylized, these images of courtly wealth and power decorated the audience chamber in the papal palace.*

16. Hawking. *Palais des Papes, Avignon. Fresco. Ca. 1350. Scenes of hunting were typical of secular palace decoration and continued traditional themes. Their use in this context emphasized the secularization of papal power.*

15. Cathedral, cloisters. *Gloucester. 1377–1412. The development of fan vaults allowed the ceiling as well as the walls to be covered in a veneer of elegant tracery that disguised the structure beneath.*

since the Roman Empire. The newly established Visconti dynasty (1310–1447) expressed its political aspirations by strategic marriages with northern European rulers. A feast in 1368 to celebrate the wedding of Violante Visconti to Lionel, son of Edward III of England, reputedly included among its guests Petrarch, Jean Froissart, and Chaucer, all key figures in the development of the new secular culture. Milan's cathedral, begun by Gian Galeazzo Visconti (r. 1378–1402) adapted current French Gothic styles to create an image that was markedly different from contemporary architecture in the Italian city-states (see chapter 21).

The Visconti library included Books of Hours, a type of devotional literature unusual in Italy. Their illuminations reflect the influence of French court and illustrate a conscious attempt on the part of the Viscontis to imitate the images of royal power developed in northern Europe.

17. *Giovannino de' Grassi,* Marriage of the Virgin. *Biblioteca Nazionale, Florence. BR 397, f. 90. Ca. 1370. From a book commissioned by Gian Galeazzo Visconti, this miniature reflected the courtly style of French manuscript illumination.*

18. Cathedral. *Milan. Begun 1386. Despite the later addition of window pediments, this rare example of late Gothic architecture in Italy gave visual expression to the Visconti court's economic and cultural links with northern Europe.*

19. *Bonino da Campione,* Monument to Bernabò Visconti. *Castello Sforzesco, Milan. Marble. Ca. 1360. The equestrian monument was a popular means of commemorating an individual ruler's temporal power in northern Italy. It was inspired by ancient Roman examples, most notably the statue of Marcus Aurelius then outside the Lateran in Rome.*

18

19

ITALIAN MERCHANTS TOOK ADVANTAGE OF THE increasing demand for luxury goods in twelfth-century Europe. Trade between Christian northern Europe, the Byzantine Empire, and the Muslim East flourished. Urban populations grew, especially in Italy. By 1300, Milan and Venice could boast populations of more than 120,000, and seven other Italian cities had more than 30,000 inhabitants. Lack of centralized authority in northern Italy had allowed these towns to benefit from the power struggle between the papacy and the Holy Roman Empire, with their independent status officially recognized by the Peace of Constance (1183).

CHAPTER 21

THE RISE OF CIVIC POWER

Art in the Italian City-States

If hegemony initially lay in the hands of the old aristocracy, the new power of money began to challenge traditional structures of authority. Mercantile wealth replaced inheritance as the basis of power. In many communes, membership in a guild, which was essential for the practice of business, also entitled a citizen to vote and to hold political office. Citizens were elected to serve on the main governing council, as well as subsidiary committees appointed to manage such specific areas as finance or defense, and the bodies were reconstituted regularly to avoid factional control. Internal feuds were controlled by the appointment of a *podestà*,

1

a magistrate from outside the city-state who served a fixed term. This network of checks and balances mirrored the complexities of mercantile exchange, developed in response to the growth of banking, currency dealings, and marine insurance. Taxes on wealth provided state funds that financed a spectacular building boom in thirteenth- and fourteenth-century Italy, as a direct response to the new communal freedom and prosperity.

Civic Cathedrals

The most prestigious building in these new city-states was the cathedral, and civic achievement often provided the impetus for construction. Pisa's cathedral was begun soon after a major naval victory over the Arabs in Sicily; its nave was built with classical columns looted from a mosque in Palermo. St. Mark's in Venice was likewise decorated with symbols of the city's conquests, in this case spoils from the sack of Constantinople (1204). In Florence, as in many other city-states, the new cathedral was started shortly after the expulsion of the old nobility. The importance that the new mercantile rulers placed on the acquisition of material wealth was reflected in the extravagance of their cathedrals.

Competition among the city-states encouraged highly individual images and a tendency toward increasing elaboration. The cathedral in Siena would have been even grander if plans for its enlargement had not been abruptly halted by the Black Death (1348). That catastrophe also interrupted ornamentation of the façade, and the richer upper level was not added until the 1370s. The civic cathedrals were rarely innovative in style, preferring to emphasize the wealth of the city in grander and more elaborate versions of established formats. The multicolored marble facings of the cathedrals of Pisa, Florence, Siena, and Orvieto were

1. Panorama of Siena. *Vast, imposing, and designed to be seen from a distance, the marble cathedral gave visual expression to the power and wealth of the city-state of Siena.*

2. Cathedral complex. *Pisa. Cathedral begun 1060; façade ca. 1200; baptistery ca. 1153; campanile ca. 1174. Typically, the religious centers of the Italian city-states included not only the cathedral but also a separate baptistery and bell tower.*

3. Cathedral, nave. *Pisa. Begun 1060. These antique columns, taken by the Pisans from a mosque in Palermo, were a deliberate reminder of their victory over the Arabs (1063).*

4. Plan of Siena's cathedral *and its projected enlargement. The plan would have made the existing nave and choir into the transepts of the new building. Part of the walls of the new nave still stand as a reminder of the havoc caused by the Black Death.*

5. Cathedral. *Siena. Begun before 1226, façade ca. 1280–1320. The city-states expressed their new wealth through elaboration and extravagance, but did not develop new forms for their religious architecture.*

2

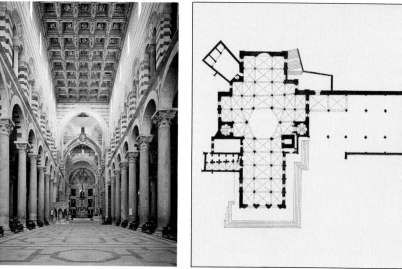

3

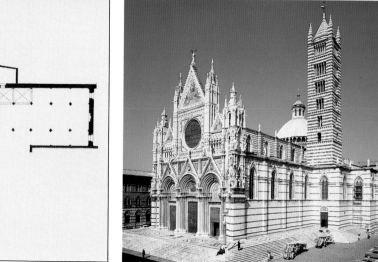

4

5

typical of earlier Tuscan architecture. The designers of the civic cathedrals showed little interest in the structural achievements of northern Europe, preferring the ribbed groin vaults of Romanesque Italy, but some did adopt the Gothic features popularized by the Franciscans and Dominicans, most notably the pointed arch.

Decision-Making and Design

The fact that responsibility for commissioning and financing the construction of these cathedrals lay in the hands of local government and not the Church indicates the power of the new communes. It also explains the importance of the buildings as a reflection of pride in the new civic identity. For Florence, the thirteenth century was a period of economic expansion. The city had minted its own gold florin in 1252, and Florentine bankers came to dominate the European credit market. The final expulsion of the old nobility in the 1250s provided the impetus for the construction of the cathedral and the Palazzo della Signoria, both begun in 1299. With regard to the cathedral and its campanile (bell tower), construction was financed by city funds and by contributions from the Arte della Lana, or wool guild, whose prestige was enhanced by its involvement. The composition of the Opera, or Board of Works, directly reflected the dual sources, with two members of the guild serving alongside four prominent citizens. The Opera was responsible for the day-to-day running of the cathedral as well as for its construction and sculptural embellishment. It appointed both the organist and the master mason, organized the supply of building materials, employed the workforce, and commissioned independent sculptors to carve statues for the elaborate façades. Like the committees elected to deal with political issues, the Opera had ample, but not

6. St. Mark's Horses. *St. Marks's, façade, Venice. Begun 1093. The four bronze horses above the main door, as well as many of the columns below, were looted during the sack of Constantinople (1204) by the Venetians and the Crusader armies. Their new position reinforced Venetian power.*

7. Cathedral, nave. *Arezzo. Begun before 1277. Arezzo was one of the few civic cathedrals to adopt the new pointed arches introduced from northern Europe by the Franciscans and Dominicans.*

8. Cathedral, nave. *Orvieto. Founded 1290. Uninterested in the new Gothic styles developed in northern Europe, the Italian city-states preferred their own Romanesque traditions.*

9. Cathedral complex. *Florence. Cathedral begun 1299; campanile begun 1334; baptistery eleventh century (?). Expensive white marble from Carrara contrasted with local red and green stones to create this distinctive image of Florentine prestige.*

unlimited, autonomy. The most important questions required a broader consensus. Decisions that would significantly affect the visual appearance of the cathedral were made by a wider cross section of Florentine citizens.

The design came about in stages. Although construction had begun in 1299, it was only in 1367 that the final decisions were made concerning the design of the dome. The decision-makers without technical expertise, in this case the Opera and a large proportion of the voting public, were advised on the ramifications of the various options by hands-on experts, mainly stone masons, painters, and goldsmiths. The winning design was incorporated in a contemporary Florentine fresco cycle in the Spanish Chapel at Santa Maria Novella, but the dome itself was not constructed until the fifteenth century. This system was common throughout Europe, differing only in the inclinations of the voting body. The determining voices were the people with political power, which in Florence and the other city-states meant the rich mercantile class.

Religious Images

The extravagant exteriors of the civic cathedrals were matched by the expensive altarpieces, pulpits, tombs, and other furnishings of their interiors. These provided an important forum for the development of new imagery. The Tuscan fashion for elaborate marble pulpits gave Nicola Pisano and his son, Giovanni, the opportunity to experiment with figure styles inspired by classical sculpture. To represent the figure of Prudence, for example, Giovanni copied the pose of an antique Venus. His translation of a pagan figure into a Christian context was typical of medieval attitudes toward antiquity. It also reflected the revived interest in naturalistic portrayal and the increasing rejection of traditional hierarchic

10

13

10. Nicola Pisano, pulpit. Baptistery, Pisa. Marble. Ca. 1260. Inspired by antique sarcophagi and other classical reliefs, Nicola Pisano (ca. 1220– ca. 1284) also worked for Emperor Frederick II in southern Italy, whose revival of the culture of Imperial Rome was deliberate propaganda for his reign.

11

11. Giovanni Pisano, Fortitude and Prudence. Duomo, from pulpit, Pisa. Marble. 1302–1310. Inspired by the antique statues of Venus Pudica, the pose of this classical nude was deliberately adopted to convey modesty.

12

12. Andrea Pisano, Building. Museo dell'Opera del Duomo, Florence. Stone. Ca. 1334–1337. The importance of the building industry to the Florentine economy and its contribution to state propaganda were reflected in this relief of masons at work.

Active during a period of exceptional prosperity in Siena, Duccio di Buoninsegna (ca. 1255–1318) obtained many important commissions, the most prestigious being his *Maestà* for the high altar in the city's cathedral (1308). The work took nearly three years to complete. The front of the altarpiece showed the Virgin enthroned as Queen of Heaven, surrounded by her court of angels and saints. Rigidly symmetrical, the combinations of frontal and

DUCCIO'S *MAESTÀ*

three-quarter faces were exactly mirrored on either side of the throne. The back was decorated with twenty-six scenes of Christ's Passion, from his *Entry into Jerusalem* (bottom left) to the *Appearance at Emmaus* (top right). The truth of the events was reinforced by Duccio's careful attention to biblical details, like the tax man Zacchaeus, who climbed a tree

to get a better view of Christ's entry into Jerusalem, or the sandals removed while Christ washed the apostles' feet. The scenes were didactic, providing visual images for the illiterate. Duccio's inclusion of a staircase linking the scenes of Peter's *First Denial* and *Christ Before Annas* (bottom right), emphasized by the figure of a maid carrying a pitcher, was evidence of a growing interest in incidental details, added to enhance the illusion of reality.

imagery in a culture dominated by the middle class. Duccio's *Maestà*, commissioned for the high altar of Siena's cathedral, was a forceful expression of wealth in its use of gold as well as its scale, detail, and profusion of figures, all of which added to the cost of a painting. Rather than reinforcing the power of religion, however, the work commemorated the city's devotion to the Virgin. The image was deliberately Sienese. It is the patron saints of the city who kneel in front of the angels and saints surrounding the Virgin; the theme is reinforced by an inscription at the base of the throne requesting peace for Siena (and a long life for Duccio).

THE RISE OF CIVIC POWER

14

16

13. *Duccio,* Maestà, *rear view. Museo dell'Opera Metropolitana, Siena. Panel. 1308–1311.*

14. *Duccio,* Maestà, *front view. Museo dell'Opera Metropolitana, Siena. Panel. 1308–1311.*

15. Palazzo del Capitano. *Orvieto. Begun 1216. Solid and imposing, this fortified palace was typical of the new type of government buildings required by the Italian city-states.*

16. Palazzo Pubblico. *Siena. Begun 1298. A more elegant government office block than the Palazzo della Signoria in Florence, this building should be considered in its relationship to the other public works in Siena.*

17. Palazzo della Signoria (now Palazzo Vecchio). *Florence. Begun 1299. Rough blocks of local stone contrasted with the more expensive imported marble of the cathedral. It promoted an image of morality and strength for the new city government.*

15

17

Images of Political Power

If the wealth of the city-states was expressed in their cathedrals, government buildings created an image of their political power. At a functional level, these buildings reflected the structure of government itself. They were conspicuously less expensive than the civic cathedrals, since the new political regime needed to project a more responsible, less extravagant image than could be justified in a religious context. The local stone and lack of decoration on Florence's Palazzo della Signoria, for example, provided a marked contrast to the costly decoration of the cathedral. The location of the Palazzo, in a broad open space where the palaces of the old nobility had stood, was a conscious expression of the power of the new regime.

In the hilltop city of Siena, the distinction between the cathedral and the Palazzo Pubblico was reinforced by their relative positions. The plain brick Palazzo Pubblico was built below the marble cathedral, and, unlike the cathedral, faced a large square, itself designed as a kind of civic center. Even before construction began on the Palazzo Pubblico, restrictions were placed on the design of windows on other buildings in the square to ensure visual uniformity. The scale of the square in contrast to the narrowness of the surrounding streets consciously reinforced the authority of city government and demonstrated an acute awareness on its part of the value of architecture as propaganda.

In Venice, meanwhile, the relationship among the civic buildings reflected a different system of government. The figurehead of the state was the doge, a Venetian appointed for life whose power was limited by the other members of the ducal council. The proximity of St. Mark's to the Doge's Palace emphasized the fact that the church was essentially the doge's private chapel—a direct imitation of the relationship between

18

19

21

18. Palazzo Ducale. Venice. 1340 onward. Constructed of white Istrian limestone with details of red Verona marble, the decorative features of Venice's government offices emphasized the city's close links with the Middle East.

19. Palazzo della Ragione. Padua. Begun 1218. Continuing the function of the ancient Roman basilicas as law courts, these buildings were common in northern Italian city-states and reflected the growing importance of rational urban law in contrast to unreasonable, arbitrary feudal law.

20. Palazzo dei Priori, Fontana Maggiore. Perugia. Begun 1293–1297. Finished 1278. Civic power and prestige, combined with a refreshing coolness, provided a fitting image for the Perugian city-state.

20

the Byzantine emperor and the Hagia Sofia in Constantinople. It was no accident that the Hagia Sophia provided one of the models for St. Mark's. As in the government palaces in Florence and Siena, the patterned stone exterior of the Doge's Palace is noticeably less extravagant than the gilded mosaics of St. Mark's. But the government buildings in the three cities could hardly be more dissimilar in style. The elaborate sculptural decoration on the Doge's Palace has little in common with the austere façade of Florence's Palazzo della Signoria. This can be partly explained by the use of local stone, which was considerably easier to carve in Venice. It also

reflects the individual characters and diverse traditions of the two city-states.

Decoration and Propaganda

For each city-state, the decorative schemes for government palaces provided an opportunity to project an image of its choosing. The cathedrals were restricted by Christian traditions, but secular buildings could experiment with different imagery. The close relationship between Church and State in Venice was reflected in the choice of religious themes for the capitals of the Doge's Palace. While Venice had always been a

Christian city, this was not true of many of the other city-states, whose origins were often earlier. Perugia had been a Roman town (and before that Etruscan), and its long history was commemorated in twenty-four statues decorating the upper basin of a monumental fountain in the main square. Alongside patron saints, religious leaders, and personifications of Perugia and Rome stood heroes of Perugian history, including its mythical founder. More recent achievements were commemorated in the figures of the Capitano del Popolo and the *podestà* in power in 1278. This deliberate statement of political power was typical of the new city-states. Like the Romans, the Perugian

22

23

22. *Simone Martini,* Guidoriccio da Fogliano. *Palazzo Pubblico, Siena. Fresco. Ca. 1330. Despite modern controversy over the dating of this work, there seems little doubt that it was originally painted in the eleventh century to commemorate the military achievements of the Sienese army under its commander, Guidoriccio.*

21. Palazzo della Ragione, interior. *Padua. Mid-fourteenth century. Within a fictive architectural framework, individual scenes included religious subjects, the patron saints of the city, the Doctors of the Church, and astrological signs.*

23. *Simone Martini,* Maestà. *Palazzo Pubblico, Siena. Dated 1315. Simone Martini (ca. 1284–1344) was a pupil of Duccio, and this painting was the civic version of Duccio's* Maestà *in the cathedral. Less complex and less extravagant, it provided a more appropriate image for moral government.*

authorities recognized that the survival of the city depended on an adequate water supply. Perugia had no river, and the importance of the fountain was emphasized in the cost of its elaborate decoration.

The Palazzo Pubblico, Siena

Pride in civic achievement also formed the basis for the decoration of the interior of the Palazzo Pubblico in Siena. In the main council chamber two images faced each other, both painted by Simone Martini: the *Maestà* and *Guidoriccio da Fogliano*, the mercenary leader of the Sienese troops whose victories helped to establish Sienese rule in Tuscany. The inclusion of such a potent image was intended to reflect the military strength of the regime. The frescoes in the adjoining chamber, where political decisions were made, conveyed a more direct message. Rather than resorting to religious or historical imagery, this room emphasized the functions and responsibilities of political power, contrasting good and evil in the context of government. In the *Allegory of Good Government*, a personification of the Commune of Siena, holding an orb and scepter as symbols of temporal power, is guided by Faith, Hope, and Charity; she sits in consultation with the Virtues necessary for the proper administration of power, such as Peace, Justice, and Magnanimity. In the *Allegory of Bad Government*, by contrast, the personification of Tyranny is guided by Greed, Pride, and Boastfulness and takes counsel from Cruelty, Deceit, and Discord. The paintings provided a constant reminder and exhortation to the decision-making council that convened in the chamber. The message was reinforced by scenes that spelled out the economic implications of good and bad decisions for the town and the entire country, providing a moral justification for material success and reflecting the importance of mercantile wealth to the new city-states.

24

25

24. and 25. Ambrogio Lorenzetti, The Effects of Good Government in the City and Country. *Palazzo Pubblico, Siena. Fresco. 1338–1339. Lorenzetti's townscape did not include distinctive Sienese buildings, but the* style of the architecture certainly implied a Sienese context. Neat fields, hard-working laborers, and leisure for the wealthy provided an interesting comment on the ideal to which the Sienese government aspired.

26. Ambrogio Lorenzetti, Allegory of Good Government. *Palazzo Pubblico, Siena. Fresco. 1338–1339. The growth of civic power stimulated a demand for new themes to promote the morality of government. Ambrogio Lorenzetti's cycle in Siena was one of the most ambitious.*

27. Ambrogio Lorenzetti, Allegory of Bad Government. *Palazzo Pubblico, Siena. Fresco. 1338–1339. The need to avoid political immorality was reinforced by Lorenzetti's realistic images of ugliness and abnormality as personifications of sin.*

26

27

CHAPTER 22

PERCEPTION AND REALITY

Italian Art in the Fourteenth Century

THE EMERGENCE OF A MIDDLE CLASS whose wealth derived from trade had important implications for the development of European society. Mercantile culture questioned established institutions. A more rational, urban system of law replaced the arbitrary feudal law. The measurement of time in canonical hours, which varied according to the season and divided daylight into flexible units for monastic worship, gave way to a more logical division into twenty-four equal-hour days. Clocks replaced church bells for indicating the time. Giovanni Dondi's clock in Padua (1344) also predicted eclipses and included a perpetual calendar for dating Easter and other holidays. Medieval Latin, the administrative and liturgical language of Christianity, was rejected by such writers and poets as Dante, Boccaccio, and Petrarch in Italy, Jean Froissart in France, and Geoffrey Chaucer in England, all of whom preferred to write in the vernacular. Education, previously in the hands of the Church, soon became more widely available. Merchants had many good reasons for wanting to be literate and numerate.

1

The Growth of Mercantile Wealth

Mercantile wealth brought a new type of patron onto the scene. To create images that reflected their new economic and political power, merchants imitated established patterns of patronage, commissioning family chapels and large houses. The interior decoration of their residences was an uncomplicated expression of material wealth. But their chapels were also a reflection of guilt and fear. Only a few merchants went as far as St. Francis and renounced their material heritage in preference for a life of poverty, but most donated some percentage of their wealth to religious institutions as a kind of insurance policy against damnation.

Usury, the lending of money for excessive profit, was banned by the Church. St. Thomas Aquinas had accepted the concept of interest on the basis of "just price," defined as reasonable compensation for services rendered, but the vast fortunes amassed by Italian banking families were based on more extortionate rates. Few merchants were rich enough to commission entire chapels, but one of these was Enrico Scrovegni. The decoration of his chapel in Padua, which he intended as his tomb, was commissioned to the great Giotto and included a direct message to the Virgin. Scrovegni had himself painted in the middle of the scene of the *Last Judgment*, offering the chapel to the Virgin in return for her intercession on his behalf.

Fourteenth-century Europe experienced a series of major disasters. It was a period of general economic decline, precipitated by harvest failures and the crash of the Bardi and Peruzzi banks (ca. 1345). The situation was worsened by the Black Death, or bubonic plague, which arrived in Italy from the East in 1347 and spread rapidly throughout Europe. Estimates vary, but it is likely that

1. Palazzo Davanzati, bedroom. *Florence. Fresco decoration. Mid-fourteenth century. Fictive architecture, framing scenes from a courtly French romance above fake marble paneling and tapestry, provided the setting for wealthy Florentine mercantile families.*

2. Palazzo Spini-Feroni. *Florence. Mid-fourteenth century (restored). Vast and imposing, this mercantile palace gave visual expression to wealth and power through its decorative use of fortified details.*

3. Bardi and Peruzzi Chapels. *Santa Croce, Florence. 1320s. Mercantile profits financed the decoration of these chapels by Giotto; they reflected the stigma attached to commercial profits in the eyes of the Church.*

4. Buffalmacco (?), Hell. *Camposanto, Pisa. Fresco. Early 1350s. During the Middle Ages, hell had a very real meaning, reinforced not only by the lurid descriptions of preachers but also by visual images notable for their minute attention to the details of torture.*

the population of Europe was reduced by about one-third in only a few years. Cities were hit especially hard because of the density of urban populations. Explanations of every kind were advanced, but the disaster was widely viewed as an expression of God's anger at the growing corruption and greed on Earth. There were certainly biblical precedents for such an explanation, by which cities were destroyed as punishment for the accumulation of material wealth. Ironically, the prevalence of this belief had a significant effect on the patronage of art. Donations to religious institutions and mercantile expenditures on art increased dramatically.

A New Approach to Christian Art

Franciscan preachers directed their message at urban populations. In an attempt to communicate the essential truths of Christianity, they encouraged listeners to imagine the reality of Christ's life and suffering. It was not the language of blind obedience but of logic and persuasion, a method more appropriate to the increasingly sophisticated middle classes. The new approach found expression in Franciscan art, to be sure, but it had a much broader appeal. Christian art, which had begun by rejecting the physical and

naturalistic aspects of classical style in favor of more mystical and spiritual imagery, now turned back to the material world as a more comprehensible and convincing setting for this new attitude toward religious belief.

Stylistic Change

One of the engines of this stylistic transformation was precisely the patronage of the urban middle class. Cimabue's *Santa Trinita Madonna* and Giotto's *Ognissanti Madonna* were created only thirty years apart,

6

7

8

9

5. Giotto, Enrico Scrovegni Offers His Chapel to the Virgin. *Arena Chapel, Padua. Fresco. 1303-1306. Scrovegni's desire to expiate the sin of usury lay behind his patronage of the Arena Chapel with its remarkable fresco cycle by Giotto.*

6. Cimabue, Santa Trinita Madonna. *Uffizi, Florence. Panel. Early 1280s (?).*

7. Giotto, Ognissanti Madonna. *Uffizi, Florence. Panel. Ca. 1310–1315. Ethereal beauty was gradually replaced by more prosaic images that reinforced the human reality of religious events.*

8. Ambrogio Lorenzetti, Madonna del Latte. *St. Francis's, Siena. Panel. Mid-1320s (?). The image of a mother feeding her child was as immediately recognizable in the fourteenth century as it is today, reinforcing the humanity of Christ and the Virgin.*

9. Bartolomeo di Camogli, Madonna of Humility. *Museo Nazionale, Palermo. Panel. 1346. Images of the Virgin seated on the ground first became popular in fourteenth-century Italy and expressed a very different ideal from the traditional representation of the Virgin enthroned as the Queen of Heaven.*

but the differences between them well illustrate the evolution then under way. Cimabue emphasized the heavenly context with an ethereal Virgin, supported on her throne by hovering angels. Giotto's Virgin is solid, and his angels stand or kneel on firm ground. The latter image reflects the growing interest in the naturalistic depiction of human forms that developed during the fourteenth century. The frontality and formality of imperial or hierarchic imagery gradually gave way to an emphasis on the actual or material aspects of the human body. This was reflected in a change of attitude toward the figure of the Virgin. The image of the Queen of Heaven was replaced by that of the Madonna of Humility, seated on the ground without a throne. Other interpretations stressed her maternal role. In Ambrogio Lorenzetti's *Madonna del Latte*, she affectionately cradles her baby in her arms; the infant Christ does not raise his hand in a gesture of benediction but merely feeds. Earlier images of Christ had stressed his divine nature by depicting him as a miniature man. The emphasis on his humanity was more easily understood by ordinary citizens.

Similar changes were reflected in the settings of religious scenes. Pietro Lorenzetti placed his *Birth of the Virgin* in a middle-class domestic interior. His attention to the details of everyday domestic items (clothes, curtains, blankets, and rugs) indicates a conscious effort to depict a recognizable scene; the linear patterns on the floor and bed give it a greater sense of depth and verisimilitude. The interest in perspective and convincing use of an architectural setting served to enhance the illusion of reality. Altichiero used crowds in his Crucifixion for the same purpose. The people gathered around the Cross include not only the key persons in the narrative—the grieving Marys and the soldiers throwing

10. *Lorenzo Maitani,* Expulsion. *Duomo, façade, Orvieto. Ca. 1310–1330. Maitani's scenes from Genesis on the façade of Orvieto's cathedral stressed the reality of Biblical events with drama, movement, and expression.*

11. *Giotto,* Perspective panel. *Arena Chapel, Padua. Fresco. 1303–1306. Experiments with perspective were an essential element in the development of convincing architectural settings and provided decorative details for the Arena Chapel that reflected Giotto's skill in this field.*

12. *Pietro Lorenzetti,* Birth of the Virgin. *Museo dell'Opera Metropolitana, Siena. Panel. 1342. A convincing architectural definition of space, solid figures, and, above all, carefully detailed objects of everyday use make it easy for the viewer to identify with this scene.*

10

11

12

Set beside the Franciscan church of St. Anthony's, the Oratory of St. George in Padua was commissioned as a funeral chapel by Raimondino Lupi di Soragna and finished after his death (1379) by his heir, Bonifacio.

Documentary evidence shows that Raimondino commissioned Altichiero to decorate the interior of the chapel and that this appointment was confirmed by Bonifacio, who also employed Altichiero on his own chapel in St. Anthony's. Another painter, Jacopo Avan-

zo, has also been associated with the oratory frescoes, but he is not mentioned in the documents, and the extent of his contribution remains controversial.

An important center of early humanism, Padua was responsive to the stylistic innovations in religious art that emerged at the beginning of the fourteenth century with Giotto's fresco cycle

in the Arena Chapel. Illustrating scenes from the lives of Christ, St. George, St. Catherine, and St. Lucy, Altichiero's paintings in the Oratory of St. George show the development of these new ideas, above all in the use of architectural frameworks to provide convincing settings for the stories.

According to her legend, St. Lucy endured various forms of torture aimed

at forcing her to renounce her faith. Her breasts were cut off and her eyes gouged out before she was killed with a dagger. Altichiero's *Martyrdom of St. Lucy* depicted only two tortures with her death. His solid figures of the soldier shielding his eyes from the flames and of the industrious bellows worker reinforce the appearance of reality. The three scenes are united by a Gothic framework that includes intricate and recognizable details, such as plants growing in a window box.

PERCEPTION AND REALITY

13

13. Altichiero,
The Martyrdom
of St. Lucy. *Oratory
of St. George, Padua.
Fresco. 1379–1384.*

14. Altichiero, Crucifixion.
*Oratory of St. George,
Padua. Fresco. 1379–
1384. Following
tradition, the Good
Thief is represented
on Christ's right and
the Bad Thief on his
left; they are further
distinguished by their
different attitudes
to death.*

15. Altichiero, Crucifixion,
detail (left).
*St. Anthony's, San Felice
Chapel, Padua. Fresco.
1379. The little dog
on the far left and other
incidental details,
together with the variety
of people in the crowd,
reinforce the reality
of the event.*

14

15

dice for Christ's tunic—but many incidental figures presented in a variety of types, poses, and clothes to reinforce the reality of the event. Perhaps the most humanizing element of the new style was the introduction of emotion to scenes previously depicted as devoid of human feeling. In his *Lamentation*, for example, Giotto not only illustrated the profound grief of bystanders at the suffering of Christ, but he shows the same emotion in the angels as well. Facial expressions, elaborated by gestures, were a simple but effective method of directing the response of the viewer. The message of the *Triumph of Death* is clear. The futility of material riches in the face of inevitable death is expressed in the horrified response of three richly dressed riders at the sight of rotting corpses, presented in three stages of decay. The solution is illustrated in the upper part of the painting, in which the simplicity of poverty and purity of a religious life provide a marked contrast. Also common, not surprisingly in this time of calamity, are representations of the damned in hell and the Day of Judgment.

Religious Tradition and Classical Culture

Economic power had challenged the old structures of political authority in Italy with startling success. In the intellectual realm as well, traditional beliefs and institutions were questioned. Classical texts, which had been declared heretical in the fourth century, had become increasingly available, in particular through trade with the Arab world. The growth of free debate, fostered by the new urban centers of learning, was perceived by the Dominicans as a threat to the authority of the Church. St. Thomas Aquinas attempted to institutionalize this

16. *Giotto,* Lamentation. *Arena Chapel, Padua. Fresco. 1303–1306. Emphasizing the sadness of the event by the use of gestures, poses, and facial expressions for Christ's earthly mourners, Giotto reinforced the emotion by depicting grieving angels as well.*

17. *Buffalmacco (?),* Triumph of Death. *Camposanto, Pisa. Fresco. Early 1350s (?). The horror and inescapability of death were given particular emphasis by images of the Black Death. The disease raged through Europe (1347–1349), killing about one-third of the population.*

16

17

threat by reconciling Plato and Aristotle with Christian theology. In the new city-states of Italy, this position was countered by a growing interest in civic ideology and classical precedents for representative government. Petrarch is generally credited with reviving the classical concept of factual history, emphatically rejecting the Christian version of historical events as interpreted through the Bible. Like other early Italian humanists, Petrarch studied classical literature, writing treatises of his own in classical Latin. It is known that he found a copy of Cicero's letters in Verona and that he owned a copy of works by Virgil with a frontispiece illustrated by Simone Martini.

Other humanists collected antique inscriptions. The study of these texts revived interest in the classical concept of beauty. Petrarch, like Boccaccio, defined the beauty of Giotto's paintings as something that could be appreciated only by the cultured few and was lost on the ignorant masses. This understanding represented an important step in the rise of the artist's status and the recognition of a difference between creativity and craft. It is well to remember that already in this period a teacher like Giotto had come to be called an "illustrious painter" by followers who were less illustrious and less well-known in Florentine circles. The growing interest in the dignity of the artist, and with it the cultural heritage of the classical world, set the scene for the complex artistic-cultural phenomenon known as the Renaissance (see chapters 23–27).

18

19

18. *Giovannino de' Grassi,* Page from a notebook. *Biblioteca Civica, Bergamo. MS D.VII.14. Late fourteenth century. A new desire for realistic representation led to careful studies, like these birds.*

19. *Simone Martini,* Frontispiece to Servius's Commentary of Virgil. *Biblioteca Ambrosiana, Milan. Between 1340 and 1344. This frontispiece to Petrarch's copy of Virgil reflected the growing importance of classical culture that was to become such an essential feature of the fifteenth century.*

THE FIFTEENTH CENTURY

Humankind developed a new awareness of itself and its surroundings (humanism). This led to a renewed interest in classical civilizations and, in brief, the basis for what would become a decisive turning point in culture and art. While humanistic studies of ancient philosophy and literature expanded, enthusiastic collectors competed to gather testimonies of Greek and Roman traditions (codices, rare gems, sculptures, curiosities). The artists of the early thirteenth century carefully studied the architectural ruins and sculptures of Ancient Rome and from them drew a new and vital lymph that was never manifested in shoddy imitations.

In Florence, the experiments of masters such as Brunelleschi, Donatello, and Masaccio would serve as models for future generations–a new way of seeing humanity in space and hence a rigorous application of carefully studied perspective. People also developed a new attitude toward God; it was no longer in the purely mystical sense of the Middle Ages. An awareness of human ability made headway and affirmed the concept of the individual. The master who had only the ancient world as a model acquired new dignity. The "artisan" became an "artist" and could be a sculptor, architect, painter, and even theoretician all at the same time. In parallel with Renaissance studies and research in Italy, in Flanders artists such as Jan van Eyck or Rogier van der Weyden began experimenting with oil paints and developed an extraordinary eye for detail in figures and landscapes. This trend was well received and partly assimilated by the Italian masters.

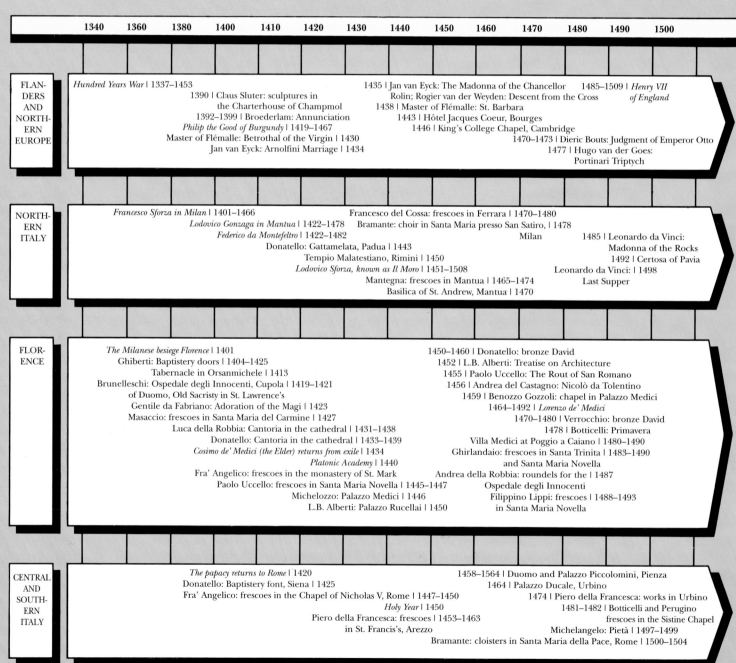

1340 1360 1380 1400 1410 1420 1430 1440 1450 1460 1470 1480 1490 1500

FLANDERS AND NORTHERN EUROPE

Hundred Years War | 1337–1453
1390 | Claus Sluter: sculptures in the Charterhouse of Champmol
1392–1399 | Broederlam: Annunciation
Philip the Good of Burgundy | 1419–1467
Master of Flémalle: Betrothal of the Virgin | 1430
Jan van Eyck: Arnolfini Marriage | 1434
1435 | Jan van Eyck: The Madonna of the Chancellor Rolin; Rogier van der Weyden: Descent from the Cross
1438 | Master of Flémalle: St. Barbara
1443 | Hôtel Jacques Coeur, Bourges
1446 | King's College Chapel, Cambridge
1470–1473 | Dieric Bouts: Judgment of Emperor Otto
1477 | Hugo van der Goes: Portinari Triptych
1485–1509 | Henry VII of England

NORTHERN ITALY

Francesco Sforza in Milan | 1401–1466
Lodovico Gonzaga in Mantua | 1422–1478
Federico da Montefeltro | 1422–1482
Donatello: Gattamelata, Padua | 1443
Tempio Malatestiano, Rimini | 1450
Lodovico Sforza, known as Il Moro | 1451–1508
Mantegna: frescoes in Mantua | 1465–1474
Basilica of St. Andrew, Mantua | 1470
Francesco del Cossa: frescoes in Ferrara | 1470–1480
Bramante: choir in Santa Maria presso San Satiro, | 1478 Milan
1485 | Leonardo da Vinci: Madonna of the Rocks
1492 | Certosa of Pavia
Leonardo da Vinci: | 1498 Last Supper

FLORENCE

The Milanese besiege Florence | 1401
Ghiberti: Baptistery doors | 1404–1425
Tabernacle in Orsanmichele | 1413
Brunelleschi: Ospedale degli Innocenti, Cupola | 1419–1421 of Duomo, Old Sacristy in St. Lawrence's
Gentile da Fabriano: Adoration of the Magi | 1423
Masaccio: frescoes in Santa Maria del Carmine | 1427
Luca della Robbia: Cantoria in the cathedral | 1431–1438
Donatello: Cantoria in the cathedral | 1433–1439
Cosimo de' Medici (the Elder) returns from exile | 1434
Platonic Academy | 1440
Fra' Angelico: frescoes in the monastery of St. Mark
Paolo Uccello: frescoes in Santa Maria Novella | 1445–1447
Michelozzo: Palazzo Medici | 1446
L.B. Alberti: Palazzo Rucellai | 1450
1450–1460 | Donatello: bronze David
1452 | L.B. Alberti: Treatise on Architecture
1455 | Paolo Uccello: The Rout of San Romano
1456 | Andrea del Castagno: Nicolò da Tolentino
1459 | Benozzo Gozzoli: chapel in Palazzo Medici
1464–1492 | Lorenzo de' Medici
1470–1480 | Verrocchio: bronze David
1478 | Botticelli: Primavera
Villa Medici at Poggio a Caiano | 1480–1490
Ghirlandaio: frescoes in Santa Trinita | 1483–1490 and Santa Maria Novella
Andrea della Robbia: roundels for the | 1487 Ospedale degli Innocenti
Filippino Lippi: frescoes | 1488–1493 in Santa Maria Novella

CENTRAL AND SOUTHERN ITALY

The papacy returns to Rome | 1420
Donatello: Baptistery font, Siena | 1425
Fra' Angelico: frescoes in the Chapel of Nicholas V, Rome | 1447–1450
Holy Year | 1450
Piero della Francesca: frescoes | 1453–1463 in St. Francis's, Arezzo
1458–1564 | Duomo and Palazzo Piccolomini, Pienza
1464 | Palazzo Ducale, Urbino
1474 | Piero della Francesca: works in Urbino
1481–1482 | Botticelli and Perugino frescoes in the Sistine Chapel
Michelangelo: Pietà | 1497–1499
Bramante: cloisters in Santa Maria della Pace, Rome | 1500–1504

FLORENCE WAS A CITY DOMINATED by merchants and bankers. Its businessmen were organized into guilds that controlled commercial transactions. Guild membership not only was required to practice a trade or profession, but also conferred eligibility for political office. The members of the seven major guilds (among them judges and notaries, bankers, doctors, wool and silk merchants, and clothiers) contributed more to the wealth of the city and thus occupied a greater share of government positions than the fourteen minor guilds (such as linen

CHAPTER 23

GUILDS AND MERCHANTS IN FLORENCE

The Early Renaissance

drapers, stone masons, armorers, and butchers). Independent and prosperous, Florence was the third largest city in Italy after Milan and Venice, but its independence was threatened by the growing power of Milan. In 1401 the Milanese army laid siege on Florence, which avoided almost certain defeat by the timely death of the Milanese leader. The narrow escape was celebrated in a burst of artistic patronage, as the guilds and their members created images to express the renewed prestige of their city.

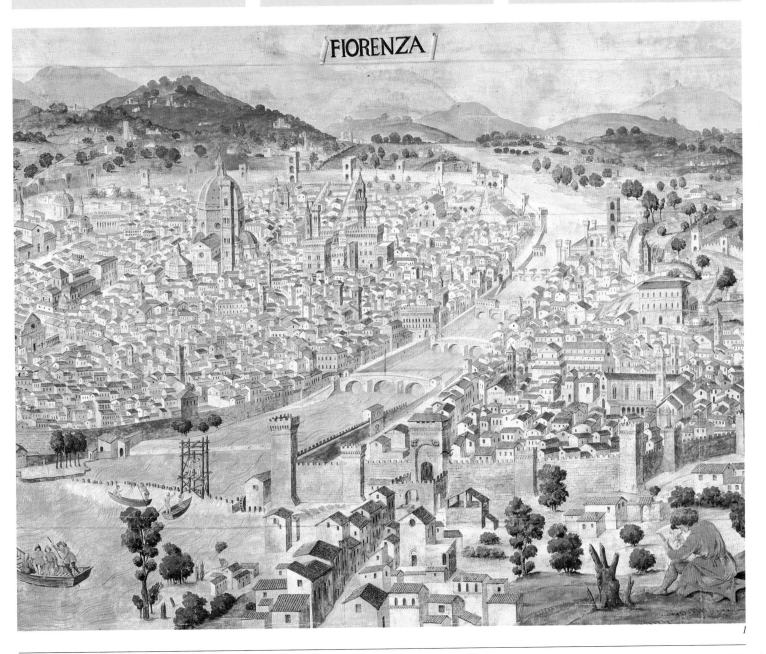

1

Baptistery and Cathedral

The Baptistery in Florence was given a facelift. In 1401, its patron, the Calimala, or cloth merchants' guild, announced a competition for a new set of bronze doors, which was won by Ghiberti. A second set of doors soon followed (1425), and these panels established Ghiberti as the leading sculptor in Florence. Work on the unfinished cathedral (begun 1299) was resumed in a major effort to complete the crucial image of civic power by its patron, the Arte della Lana, or wool merchants' guild. A competition was held in 1418 to find a way of constructing the ambitious dome, whose design had been finalized in 1367. Filippo Brunelleschi won the competition despite considerable opposition to his unorthodox scheme for a double-shelled structure.

A National Architectural Style

The sense of national identity that followed the defeat of the Milanese found expression in the development of a national culture. Belief in the superiority of Florentine traditions was reflected in a proliferation of literature extolling the virtues of the Florentine language, history, and heroes, especially Dante. The sentiment was expressed visually in the construction of the Ospedale degli Innocenti, a charitable orphan institution commissioned by the Arte della Seta, or silk guild. Eschewing the decorative, pointed-arched style of late fourteenth-century Gothic, the guild approved a design by Brunelleschi based on the elegant round-arched architecture of Tuscan Romanesque buildings, such as the Baptistery and San Miniato. Gothic, with all its foreign associations, was rejected in favor of a distinctive local style.

1. *Stefano Buonsignori,* View of Florence. *Museo di Firenze com'era, Florence. 1584. Florence was a city dominated by artisans, tradesmen, and bankers. The prime images of its power and prestige were the cathedral and government offices, the Palazzo della Signoria.*

2. *Lorenzo Ghiberti,* Joseph in Egypt. *Baptistery, Florence. Panel from Paradise Doors. Bronze. Begun 1425. Starting with Joseph being abandoned by his brothers in a well (top right), Ghiberti condensed the other major events in Joseph's life into this simple panel while still managing to create a unified image.*

3. *Lorenzo Ghiberti,* North Doors. *Baptistery, Florence. Bronze. 1403–1424. Elegant decorative style and the use of gilded bronze for these scenes from the New Testament expressed the prosperity of mercantile Florence and established Ghiberti (1378–1455) as the leading sculptor of his generation.*

4. *Lorenzo Ghiberti,* East (Paradise) Doors. *Baptistery, Florence. Bronze. Begun 1425. Replacing the decorative quatrefoil frames of the earlier doors with simple square panels, Ghiberti's second set of doors presented a clear and concise account of events from the Hebrew Bible.*

3

4

Orsanmichele

The importance of artistic patronage was given the force of law. External niches on the church of Orsanmichele had been allocated to individual guilds in 1360, but by 1406 only four of them had been filled. The government threatened confiscation and reallocation, which acted as a spur. Orsanmichele soon became a competitive arena for guild patronage and an expression of their individual power. The wealthiest guilds could afford to commission Ghiberti, arguably the most prestigious sculptor of the time. His *St. John the Baptist* (1412–1416) was commissioned by the cloth merchants, his *St. Matthew* (1419–1422) by the bankers, and his *St. Stephen* (1425–1428) by the wool merchants. These idealized and accomplished images reflected the power of the guilds, their wealth reinforced by the use of bronze, the most expensive material available. The poorer guilds commissioned less expensive marble statues by less well-known sculptors, such as Donatello. His statues at Orsanmichele were very different from Ghiberti's more traditional expressions of wealth and power. Donatello's *St. George* (1415–1417) for the armorers' guild was far from a stylized image of political or material success. The figure of St. George is simple and unassuming, and the emphasis on human personality provided a novel image for a less important guild. With the benefit of hindsight, it is easy to see how Donatello established an important foundation for the development of figurative style, and we tend to relegate Ghiberti to a lower level of creativity. Contemporaries, however, had different opinions about the two sculptors. It is highly unlikely that the richest guilds would deliberately commission images they perceived as second-rate.

GUILDS AND MERCHANTS IN FLORENCE

5. Filippo Brunelleschi, Cupola of Duomo. *Florence. Designed 1367, construction begun 1420. The technical achievement of Brunelleschi (1377–1446) in working out a method for constructing this dome was a vital step in the application of intellect to architecture. Previously dominated by the skill of craftsmen and the funds of patrons, this development had important implications for the growing status of the architect.*

6. Filippo Brunelleschi, Ospedale degli Innocenti. *Florence. Begun 1419. Elegant round arches carried on columns, triangular pedimented windows, and a gray and white color scheme were essential features of Tuscan Romanesque architecture and provided a national language to express the renewal of Florentine prestige in this century.*

7. Andrea della Robbia, roundel. *Ospedale degli Innocenti, Florence. Glazed terracotta. Ca. 1487. Inexpensive and informative, these roundels depicting children were a suitable choice for the decoration of a charitable institution for orphans.*

The Cost of Art

Every society based on a mercantile economy places a high value on the acquisition of wealth. Different levels of wealth typically generate different forms of patronage. The ability to commission architectural works is obviously reserved to the very rich, which explains why most of the major architectural and sculptural works of the early Renaissance were financed by guilds. Bronze was more expensive than marble, but painting cost less than sculpture. The Ospedale degli Innocenti had cost 30,000 florins, while Ghiberti's *St. Matthew* came to cost 945 florins, more than half of which went to materials. Fra' Angelico's *Linaiuoli Madonna* for the linen drapers' guild cost only 190 florins, of which 85 florins was spent on the frame. Because this painting used a lot of gold, it still cost more than a simple fresco like Castagno's *Niccolò da Tolentino*, which cost only 24 florins, despite being considerably larger. Nevertheless, art patronage at even the lowest levels was restricted to the upper echelons of Florentine society; a skilled craftsman earned only about 45 florins a year.

Masaccio and Perspective

In commissioning an *Adoration of the Magi* for his private chapel in Santa Trinita, Palla Strozzi, perhaps the richest Florentine in the 1420s, expressed his wealth and status through the choice an elaborate design, expensive materials, and an established artist, Gentile da Fabriano. His son-in-law, Felice Brancacci, took a different approach, commissioning a fresco cycle for his family chapel from a comparatively unknown artist, Masaccio. The reasons for his choice are unclear, but Masaccio was the herald of a new style. Like Brunelleschi and Donatello,

8. *Lorenzo Ghiberti, St. Matthew. Orsanmichele, Florence. Bronze. 1419–1422. The idealization of this figure is reflected in the stylized facial feature and carefully arranged drapery folds that form a decorative curving pattern.*

9. *Luca della Robbia, Cantoria. Museo dell'Opera del Duomo, Florence. Marble. 1431–1438. Commissioned by cathedral authorities, Luca della Robbia (1400–1482) illustrated Psalm 150 with words and visual images. His figure style owed much to the study of antique sculpture.*

10. *Donatello, St. George. Museo Nazionale del Bargello, Florence. Marble. 1415–1417. An important early work by Donatello (ca. 1386–1466), this statue from the armorers' niche on Orsanmichele presented Florentines with a more naturalistic and less decorative sculptural style, which soon replaced Ghiberti's stylized images of prestige.*

8

10

9

11

he rejected the old courtly image in favor of simplicity, rationality, and solidity. Mercantile wealth and power found a new means of expression in the use of perspective. Brunelleschi is generally credited with the invention of a mathematical framework for projecting a three-dimensional space onto a flat plane. But it is unlikely that his invention would have been possible without the mathematical mentality necessitated by a mercantile system, which was also expressed in the development of double-entry bookkeeping and formulas for the calculation of exchange rates and the volume of solid materials.

Morality and the Display of Wealth

The patronage of a single merchant, intended as a display of personal wealth, was regulated by a moral code quite different from the one applied to the corporate patronage of guilds. Throughout the Middle Ages, the sin of usury had been a powerful weapon against the acquisition of mercantile fortunes. Bankers were technically forbidden to charge interest above the basic cost of a loan, but they developed a system whereby bills were payable in another currency, thereby taking advantage of exchange rates.

The great quantity of fifteenth-century literature condemning this practice shows that the moral argument still carried enormous weight. Individuals could atone for their sins by giving a third of their wealth to the Church. Patronage in a religious context was encouraged by the Church, but the sheer quantity of altarpieces, fresco cycles, and family chapels that made explicit references to the patrons themselves suggests that the motive was not entirely spiritual. In theory, individual excesses were controlled by sumptuary laws, a reflection of a political system designed to avoid domination

11. Donatello, Cantoria. Museo dell'Opera del Duomo, Florence. Marble. 1433–1439. Donatello's Cantoria was commissioned to complement Luca della Robbia's, but it was very different. His use of colored stones set in the columns and background provided a contrast with the plain marble figures, creating a sense of space enhanced by movement.

13

14

12

12. Gentile da Fabriano, Adoration of the Magi. Uffizi, Florence. Panel. Finished 1423. One of the leading painters in early fifteenth-century Florence, Gentile da Fabriano (ca. 1370–1427) used an ornate and decorative style much favored by the prosperous mercantile community in Florence.

13. Masaccio and Masolino, The Raising of Tabitha (detail). Santa Maria del Carmine, Florence. Fresco. Ca. 1427. Masaccio (1401–1428) and Masolino (ca. 1383–1440) were commissioned by Felice Brancacci to decorate his family chapel in Santa Maria del Carmine. They rejected the courtly image favored by their contemporaries in favor of local settings and a new solid approach to figure style.

14. Masaccio, The Tribute Money. Santa Maria del Carmine, Florence. Fresco. Ca. 1427. The issue of paying taxes was especially topical in 1427, when they were first levied on the property and income of Florentine citizens. Masaccio's composition was based on a perspective scheme with its vanishing point behind Christ's head, emphasizing his central importance in the scene.

UCCELLO'S *ROUT OF SAN ROMANO*

Not commissioned by the Medicis, as had long been believed, this panel was one of three that decorated a room in the Florentine palace of the wealthy Bartolini family. The other two are now at the Louvre in Paris and the National Gallery in London.

The scenes commemorated a major Florentine victory over the Sienese at San Romano (1432). Expressing national pride rather than religious belief, the commission reflected a growing interest in historical themes on the part of humanist patrons. The panels also reflected the new theories of art current in Florence. Uccello displays his skill at applying the new rules of mathematical perspective to create a convincing pictorial space. Carefully positioned lances form the basic lines of the scheme, and the sense of space is enhanced by the foreshortened figures of dead soldiers and horses on the ground.

Uccello's picture also reflected other contemporary ideas on pictorial composition, codified by Alberti in his treatise on painting (1435). The colors, gestures, and poses of the men and animals were deliberately contrasted. Pitching and rearing horses presented in profile and from behind enhance the drama of the scene. This is reinforced by the main event, the overthrow of the central horseman, presumed to be the leader of the Sienese troops. The application of theory to painting was inspired by the growing knowledge of classical culture. Awareness of pictorial composition marked a major event in the history of art. The lack of gold and other expensive colors in Uccello's panels reinforced this change.

As the fifteenth century progressed, intellect began to replace materials as the most costly and prestigious component of a work of art.

16. *Paolo Uccello*, The Rout of San Romano. *Uffizi, Florence. Panel. 1455.*

16

15. *Andrea del Castagno*, Niccolò da Tolentino. *Duomo, Florence. Fresco, transferred to canvas. 1456. The custom of honoring military leaders with equestrian monuments was popular in Ancient Rome, best known from the bronze statue of Marcus Aurelius that stood outside the Lateran during the Middle Ages. The mercenary soldier Niccolò da Tolentino was made captain general of the Florentine armies in 1431.*

15

17. *Fra' Angelico*, Linaiuoli Madonna. *Museo di San Marco, Florence. Panel. 1433. A Dominican friar, Fra' Angelico (ca. 1395–1455) worked in Florence, but his reputation was such that popes Eugenius IV and Nicholas V commissioned him to decorate chapels in the Vatican.*

17

by individuals. Both the laws and the system, however, were open to abuse.

Cosimo de' Medici

The emergence of the banker Cosimo de' Medici as the de facto ruler of Florence by 1440 was made possible by his enormous wealth, his charismatic personality, and his ability to control the government through the manipulation of its elected representatives. His political power rivaled that of the guilds, and he competed with them in the field of art patronage as well. Cosimo

de' Medici was already experienced in corporate projects; as a member of the bankers' guild he had been on the committee that commissioned Ghiberti's *St. Matthew*. But his vision extended beyond the city walls. In addition to religious and secular buildings in and around Florence, his personal patronage included projects in Milan, Venice, and even Jerusalem, where he built a hostel for pilgrims.

For a private citizen, patronage on this scale was unprecedented and had important repercussions. In Florence, the construction of parish churches was traditionally a

responsibility of the commune, with the support of prominent local families. Cosimo's father had been involved with his parish church of St. Lawrence and had commissioned its sacristy. But when Cosimo took over sole responsibility for the construction of the east end of St. Lawrence in 1442, insisting that the Medici coat of arms be displayed in the choir, his disregard of custom caused considerable offense. The abbot of the Badia at Fiesole (another of Cosimo's projects) defended the scale of Cosimo's patronage on the basis of Aristotle's concept of *magnificentia*, according to which large-scale expenditures

GUILDS AND MERCHANTS IN FLORENCE

18

20

18. Fra' Angelico, Annunciation. *Museo di San Marco, Florence. Fresco. Ca. 1440. Simple, direct images with careful attention to detail were typical of Fra' Angelico's frescoes that decorated the monastery of St. Mark.*

19. Filippo Brunelleschi, Donatello, and others, St. Lawrence, Old Sacristy, *Florence. Begun 1421. Following the same format as the thirteenth-century Baptistery in Padua, this simple square building was crowned by a hemispherical dome; the same format was repeated on a smaller scale on the altar niche. The interior was decorated with classically inspired*

pilasters and roundels, dominated by the Medici coat of arms.

20. Michelozzo, St. Mark Library, *Florence. Ca. 1440. The use of Ionic capitals in the rebuilding of the monastery complex of St. Mark, designed by Michelozzo (1396–1472) and financed by Cosimo de' Medici, was inspired by local traditional styles.*

21. Donatello, The Feast of Herod. *Baptistery, font, Siena. Bronze. Ca. 1425. Donatello created a convincing sense of pictorial space by deliberately ordering the architecture, background figures, and foreshortened steps on the right.*

19

21

of this type are a moral obligation of the very rich. Pope Eugenius IV took a somewhat different view, encouraging Cosimo to finance an enlargement and decoration of the monastery of St. Mark. Cosimo's patronage was largely religious, with the notable exception of his family palace. As befitted Cosimo's new position in Florentine society, the Medici Palace was a much larger version of an established format. The heavy cornice, inspired by classical architecture, was an expression of the growing interest in the culture of Ancient Rome.

Cosimo was the first private citizen to finance building projects on a large scale, but other Florentine families soon began to follow his example. By mid-century, successful Florentine bankers became involved in the patronage of major works of art and architecture as actively as they took part in the political life of the city. As the initiative shifted from the guilds to individuals, self-glorification was no longer considered morally reprehensible. Giovanni Rucellai's expenditure on Santa Maria Novella, for example, was explicitly commemorated in the proliferation of family emblems and a huge inscription

on the façade. In his memoirs, Rucellai explained that his patronage had three motives: to glorify God, honor his city, and commemorate himself. He also allowed that the two greatest pleasures a man could have in life are to make money and to spend money—but that he could not decide which he preferred.

22

24

22. *Benozzo Gozzoli,* Procession of the Magi. *Palazzo Medici, Chapel, Florence. Fresco. 1459. The importance of Medici wealth as the basis of their power was given visual expression both in the choice of subject matter and in the highly decorative style of these frescoes in the family chapel. Cosimo appears on the left, on a horse with gilded harness.*

23. Palazzo Medici. *Florence. Begun 1446. According to Cosimo's grandson, Lorenzo de' Medici, the family account books showed that they spent the immense sum of 663,755 florins on buildings, charities, and taxes. The bulk of the money went to Cosimo's architectural projects.*

24. *Alberti,* Façade. Santa Maria Novella, Florence. *Begun twelfth century, completed 1470. Usually attributed to Leon Battista Alberti (1406–1472), the design of the façade of this prestigious church followed Florentine tradition in its use of multicolored marble. It included classical details such as the Corinthian columns and the Roman letters for displaying the patron's name.*

23

CHAPTER 24

THE HUMANIST IMAGE IN FLORENCE

The Revival of Antiquity

FIFTEENTH-CENTURY FLORENCE PROMOTED an image of cultural superiority. One of its central themes was the rediscovery of classical antiquity. The myth that Florence was solely responsible for this revival has proved remarkably enduring. But the Renaissance had its roots in the mercantile city-states of northern Italy, where fourteenth-century humanists such as Petrarch had developed an interest in the culture of Ancient Rome (see chapter 22). Many of these city-states lost their independence as a result of territorial expansion by Venice and Milan. But Florence successfully resisted Milanese domination in 1401 and became the center of classical studies under the leadership of its humanist chancellor and friend of Petrarch, Coluccio Salutati.

The term "humanist" refers to someone who studied and wrote about the literature of Ancient Greece and Rome, using classical Latin and Greek. Their emphasis on the use of correct Latin, rather than its debased medieval form, acted as a spur to eager Florentines, who continued the search for literary texts in monastic libraries. Collected by wealthy merchants, these texts provided new models for artistic patronage.

1

221

The styles of Ancient Rome could be seen in architectural and sculptural remains throughout Italy. But Renaissance patrons and artists were not interested in slavish imitation. They lived in a Christian society and adapted an essentially pagan style to suit it.

Pagan Images in a Christian Context

Medieval artists had translated pagan images into a Christian context, and this practice increased dramatically in Florence as a reflection of the growing interest in classical culture after 1401. Brunelleschi's *Sacrifice of Isaac* quoted the antique statue of the *Spinario*, which had long stood outside San Giovanni Laterano in Rome. Brunelleschi's version of this figure is an almost direct copy and, as a pagan symbol, diverges from the biblical story. Such specific references to Ancient Rome marked an important turning point in the *quality* of interest in antiquity—a difference that distinguishes the Renaissance from the Middle Ages. But there were problems inherent in using pagan prototypes for Christian images. More common was Nanni di Banco's use of antique models for his Four Crowned Martyrs, which had the advantage of being historically appropriate for saints martyred by the Emperor Diocletian in 306 B.C.E. Classical details were copied and used for architectural backgrounds. Masaccio's use of a coffered barrel vault supported on Ionic columns and flanked by fluted Corinthian pilasters in his *Trinità* fresco was a decisive change from the foliage capitals and pointed arches of medieval architecture.

Art and Intellect

Under the influence of humanism, the arts slowly acquired an intellectual content.

1. *Filippo Brunelleschi,* Sacrifice of Isaac. *Museo Nazionale del Bargello, Florence. Bronze. 1401. Commissioned to design a competition piece for the first set of baptistery doors, Brunelleschi included an incidental figure copied from the antique statue of the Spinario, an example of the growing interest in classical culture.*

2. Spinario. *Uffizi, Florence. Marble copy of Roman bronze, itself a copy from a Hellenistic original, second century B.C.E. The Spinario, or thorn-drawer, was one of a number of antique Roman bronzes that stood outside the church of San Giovanni Laterano in Rome during the Middle Ages.*

3. *Nanni di Banco,* Four Crowned Martyrs. *Orsanmichele, Florence. Marble. Ca. 1413. Made for the Guild of Stonemasons and Woodworkers, this group of patron saints by Nanni di Banco (ca. 1384–1421) reflects the study of antique sculpture in the treatment of the hair, faces, and drapery.*

4. *Paolo Uccello,* The Flood. *Santa Maria Novella, Chiostro Verde, Florence. Fresco. Ca. 1445–1447. Using perspective to create an illusion of depth, Uccello (1397–1475) represented the dramatic forces of nature with powerful effect.*

5. *Masaccio,* Trinità. *Santa Maria Novella, Florence. Fresco. Ca. 1427. The classical setting of this traditional theme was a decisive break from contemporary preferences for ornate and decorative Gothic details.*

This aspect soon replaced the use of gold and other expensive materials as an expression of status. Mathematical acumen had been used by Brunelleschi, Masaccio, and Donatello in the development of perspective (see chapter 23), and their followers exploited its potential by experimenting with the construction of different types of pictorial space. Artists also applied rational rules to pictorial composition, emphasizing balance and symmetry in the use of color and gesture, as well as in the age and sex of figures. Appropriate movements and gestures emphasized narrative clarity.

Alberti's formalization of these contemporary ideas into a theory of painting in 1436 was directly inspired by classical literature. His discussion of an intellectual formula for pictorial composition was radically different from medieval texts on art, which had concentrated on practical advice to the craftsman, such as methods for mixing colors.

Donatello and the Equestrian Monument

The majority of the art produced in fifteenth-century Florence was religious. The importance of Christian belief and its role in generating patronage cannot be overestimated. Although pagan prototypes posed problems within a Christian context, this was not the case with secular images, and the growing interest in antiquity inevitably revived old art forms. The Romans had commemorated their military successes with equestrian monuments, which had become popular again during the fourteenth century on the tombs of military leaders in northern Italian cities. But Donatello's statue of Erasmo da Narni, Gattamelata, the mercenary leader of the Venetian troops, broke new ground. His use of bronze and the decision to place it outside in

6. *Piero della Francesca,* The Queen of Sheba Worshipping the Wood. *St. Francis's, Arezzo. Fresco. Ca. 1453–1464. In this scene from the story of the True Cross, Piero della Francesca (ca. 1415–1492) developed Alberti's rules for pictorial composition. Piero's interest in perspective was evident in his own treatise on painting, "De prospectiva pingendi."*

7

7. *Fra' Filippo Lippi,* The Feast of Herod. *Duomo, Prato. Fresco. 1452–1466. Using perspective to create an illusion of broad space allowed Filippo Lippi (ca. 1406–1469) to include three separate scenes around Herod's banquet table.*

6

8

8. *Fra' Angelico,* Altarpiece. *St. Mark's, Florence. Panel. Ca. 1440. The new ideas in Florentine art, codified into a treatise by Alberti, were evident in the works of Fra' Angelico (ca. 1395–1455).*

a prominent public place, rather than incorporate it in a tomb, made a clear reference to the equestrian monument of Marcus Aurelius, one of the antique bronzes outside San Giovanni Laterano, Rome. Donatello's interpretation of the theme relies far more on the antique prototype than on medieval derivatives.

Portrait Busts

Another example of antique revival was the portrait bust, which gained considerable popularity in the humanist circles of Florence. Unlike their classical prototypes, which had been primarily commemorative, Florentine busts were invariably of the living. Following the realistic tradition of Roman Republican portraiture, citizens like the humanist Matteo Palmieri commissioned lifelike images of themselves, often based on life masks. Piero de' Medici preferred a more stylized image to reflect his role as the de facto leader of Florence, a position he inherited from his father, Cosimo.

Antiquity and the Medici

Like other wealthy Florentine merchants, Cosimo, Piero, and his son, Lorenzo, spent considerable sums on lavishly decorated manuscripts of classical texts and amassed a substantial collection of antique gems, cameos, coins, and other precious objects. Copies of the cameos were made for the roundels in the courtyard of the Medici palace. The centerpiece of the palace was Donatello's bronze *David*, the first male nude since antiquity. David's victory over Goliath symbolized freedom from oppression, and it was a popular image of Florentine Republicanism. Dante had recognized a parallel to his achievement in the mythical *Labors of Hercules*. This was another subject popular with the Medici, who, despite their

9

10

12

11

13

9. Donatello, Gattamelata. Piazza del Santo, Padua. Bronze. Commissioned 1443. The use of equestrian monuments to commemorate military achievement was well established in the Veneto region of Italy. What was new about Donatello's statue was the use of bronze and emulation of antique prototypes.

10. Mino da Fiesole, Piero de' Medici. Museo Nazionale del Bargello, Florence. Marble. 1453. More stylized than Rossellino's bust of Palmieri, this image reflected Piero's preeminent position in Florentine politics and commerce.

11. Donatello, David. Museo Nazionale del Bargello, Florence. Bronze. 1450s (?). The first male nude since antiquity, Donatello's statue of David emphasized the extreme youth of the shepherd boy, who was too young to join his brothers in the battle against the Philistines.

dominant position in Florentine politics, promoted an image as supporters of the Republic. But classical subjects were not common in fifteenth-century Florentine art. A group of them were commissioned from Botticelli by a member of another branch of the Medici family, Lorenzo di Pierfrancesco, to decorate his town house; among these were *The Birth of Venus* and *Primavera*. The elements of these paintings were worked out by humanists in the Medici circle, and their meaning is much debated, but they clearly reflect a flourishing interest in the literary legacy of antiquity.

Religious Art

Mercantile patronage in the fourteenth century had stimulated the development of religious images translated into the context of modern life (see chapter 22). The trend continued in fifteenth-century Florence. Patrons commissioned painted and sculpted versions of the Virgin and the infant Christ, typically portrayed in a simple and direct manner as mother and child—images with which ordinary people could easily identify. The same idea was extended to portraits of real people. Ghirlandaio's cycle of the life of St. Francis, deliberately

chosen by Francesco Sassetti to decorate his chapel, included not only the customary donor portraits but also images of contemporary Florentines, notably Lorenzo de' Medici.

Palaces and Villas

Fifteenth-century Florence also saw a remarkable building boom. Apart from chapels, churches, and public buildings, more than seventy palaces were constructed as monuments of mercantile wealth. Contemporary chroniclers listed them with considerable pride. Despite the proliferation

12. Antonio Rossellino, Matteo Palmieri. Museo Nazionale del Bargello, Florence. Marble. 1468. This bust of the prominent Florentine humanist was intended to rest above the front door of his house.

13. Verrocchio, David. Museo Nazionale del Bargello, Florence. Bronze. 1470s (?). Also commissioned by the Medici family, this statue of David by Verrocchio (ca. 1435–1488) illustrates the young shepherd boy strong and proud in his moment of triumph.

14. Frontispiece to Johannes Argiropolous's Commentary on Aristotle's "De Physica." Biblioteca Laurenziana, Florence. Mid-fifteenth century. A key figure in the revival of Greek learning in Florence, this Byzantine scholar gave public lectures on Aristotle and dedicated this text to Piero de' Medici. The frontispiece was elaborately decorated with old-style motifs and the Medici coat of arms.

14

15

15. Antonio del Pollaiuolo, Hercules and Antaeus. Uffizi, Florence. Panel. Ca. 1460. Detailed study of human anatomy enabled Pollaiuolo (ca. 1432–1498) to create a convincing representation of the physical struggle between Hercules and the giant Antaeus.

of classical details, Florentine architecture was slow to respond to the growing interest in antiquity, since Florentine merchants generally preferred traditional forms. Giovanni Rucellai was the only patron to adopt the classical orders as decorative veneer for the façade of his palace. But it was customary to emphasize the *piano nobile*, or first floor, where the most important rooms were located, by making it the most decorative. Designers, therefore, generally rejected the classical custom of placing the most decorative order at the top. Other classical details included an incised diamond pattern at the base of the palace, derived from a type of Roman brickwork called *opus reticulatum*.

The innovations in the Palazzo Rucellai reflect a familiarity with the architectural remains of Ancient Rome. For this reason its design is usually attributed to Alberti, whose treatises on painting, sculpture, and architecture had established him as a leading authority on the arts of antiquity. Alberti encouraged young architects to study Roman ruins, and in 1471 he gave Lorenzo de' Medici a personal tour of Rome. In remodeling his villa at Poggio a Caiano, Lorenzo included what was probably the first example of a classical temple front used on a secular building. This break with tradition was an important prototype for the development of the villa in the sixteenth century.

The Status of the Artist

Florentine artists responded to the new demands of their patrons. Direct knowledge of the remains of Ancient Rome increased in importance as the century progressed. By 1470 a biographer of Brunelleschi (probably Antonio Manetti) enhanced the status of his subject by claiming that he had gotten his ideas from the study

16. *Sandro Botticelli*, Primavera. *Uffizi, Florence. Panel. Ca. 1478. The precise meaning of this famous painting is not known, but it reflected the Neo-Platonic ideas of the Medici circle. The three dancing girls on the left were derived from antique statues of the Three Graces.*

17. *Sandro Botticelli*, Portrait with a Medal. *Uffizi, Florence. Panel. 1470s. Secular patronage stimulated the development of portraiture. The young man depicted has not been identified, but he holds a medal of Cosimo de' Medici.*

16

17

18. *Desiderio da Settignano*, Virgin and Child. *Galleria Sabauda, Turin. Marble. Ca. 1460. One of the major sculptors in mid-fifteenth-century Florence, Desiderio da Settignano (ca. 1430–1464) specialized in the use of low relief, or* rilievo stiacciato, *for his maternal images of the Virgin.*

18

19

226

The idea of the Renaissance—a rebirth of culture in fifteenth-century Italy after a millennium of darkness following the fall of the Roman Empire—became popular in the sixteenth century and formed an essential element in the image of cultural superiority promoted in Italy. But the term "Renaissance" is misleading. Interest in antiquity had not "died" during the Middle Ages. To isolate the fifteenth century from its medieval past or to deny the period a classical heritage is mistaken. The major source of unity in both medieval and Renaissance European society was the Catholic Church, which had its origins in Ancient Rome. What did change during the fifteenth century was the attitude to the *remains* of Ancient Rome. Rome attracted many visitors: political leaders paid their respects to the pope, pilgrims visited holy shrines, and artists were imported to work at the papal court. Before 1450 there is little evidence of a serious interest in the visual remains of antiquity, but this soon changed. The humanist architect Leon Battista Alberti took the Florentines Lorenzo de' Medici and Bernardo Rucellai on a guided tour of the ruins while they were in Rome to meet Pope Sixtus IV (1471). Alberti was probably the author of a book on measuring antique monuments, and in his treatise on architecture he encouraged designers to draw directly from classical remains. Giuliano da Sangallo was one of a number of artists whose sketchbooks included drawings of temple façades, capitals, and other antique details. Raphael wrote a report to Pope Leo X (1527) on the condition of the ruins, which were continually pillaged for marble and rapidly deteriorating. His concern was symptomatic not only of a growing desire to preserve the past, but of a cultural and artistic perspective in which archaeological remains were a vital element.

THE HUMANIST IMAGE IN FLORENCE

20

22

23

19. Domenico Ghirlandaio, Birth of the Virgin. *Santa Maria Novella, Tornabuoni Chapel, Florence. Fresco. 1485–1490. Setting the scene in a Florentine interior, Ghirlandaio (1449–1494) included not only an old-style frieze and inscription but also portraits of the Tornabuoni household.*

20. Giuliano da Sangallo, Villa Medici. *Poggio a Caiano (near Florence). 1480s. The use of a classical temple façade for this villa was a major artistic development.*

21. Domenico Ghirlandaio, Confirmation of the Rule of St. Francis. *Santa Trinita, Sassetti Chapel, Florence. Fresco. 1483–1486. The Florentine context of this fresco was reinforced by the presence of the Palazzo della Signoria in the background and Lorenzo de' Medici on the right, standing between Antonio Pucci and the patron of the chapel, Francesco Sassetti, with his son.*

22. Leon Battista Alberti, Palazzo Rucellai. *Florence. Ca. 1450. The use of the classical orders on this façade, together with the diamond pattern on the basement that derived from Ancient Roman opus reticulatum, reflected a keen interest in the architectural language of antiquity.*

23. Giuliano da Sangallo, View of Rome. *Biblioteca, Vatican. MS Barb. lat. 4424, f. 36v. Ca. 1480.*

of Roman architecture. In response to the demand for realistic portrayal, painters and sculptors studied the human form. Leonardo da Vinci was among those who analyzed human anatomy and musculature in an attempt to understand its composition and structure, developing theories about the ideal proportions among the different parts of the body. The new intellectual content of painting inevitably affected the status of the artist as well as art itself. The contribution of the artist was no longer confined to manual skill. The idea of artistic creativity as distinct from craftsmanship slowly gained momentum during the late fifteenth century and set the scene for an elevation in the status of artists during the sixteenth.

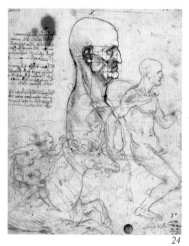

24. Leonardo da Vinci, Studies of the Human Face. *Accademia, Venice. Ca. 1490. Leonardo da Vinci (1452–1519) made many important contributions to the history of art. His analysis of the human form reflected a desire to understand its structure.*

24

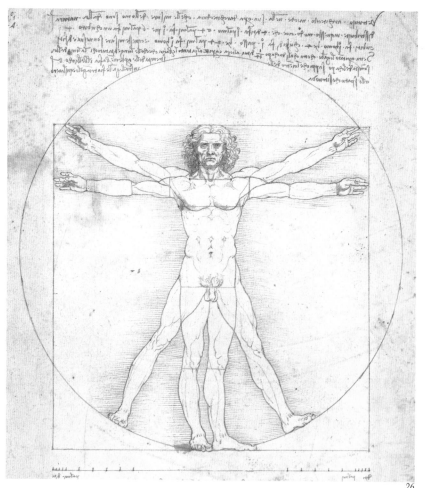

26

25

25. Verrocchio, Head of an Angel. *Gabinetto Disegni e Stampe degli Uffizi, Florence. 1470s. During the Renaissance studies and designs were an important part of the creative* process for artists concerned with verisimilitude.

26. Leonardo da Vinci, Vitruvian Man. *Accademia, Venice. Ca. 1485–1490. Relating the human* body to the ideal shapes of the square and the circle, Leonardo proposed both the groin and the navel as the centers of the male body.

FIFTEENTH-CENTURY ITALY WAS DOMINATED by five major powers: Milan, Venice, Naples, Florence, and the papacy. Within this structure a series of smaller states flourished under the leadership of their ruling families, including the d'Este in Ferrara, the Malatesta in Rimini, the Gonzaga in Mantua, and the Montefeltro in Urbino. An uneasy balance of power was maintained through alliances and counter-alliances. Subtle manipulation of influence replaced brute force, diplomacy superseded war, and culture became a powerful tool of state propaganda. A growing interest in antiquity during the fifteenth century played a crucial part

CHAPTER 25

ANTIQUITY AT THE ITALIAN COURTS

Classical Images of Prestige

in the creation of their artistic images. At the same time, economic and political rivalries were reflected in a lack of uniformity among the different centers of patronage. Absolute rulers could exploit the imperial image of Ancient Rome in ways that would have been inappropriate in Florence, with its representative government. Mercantile patronage in Florence was restricted by the size of personal fortunes. Ostentation, frowned upon in Florence, was an important element in the display of absolute power, and the scope of a ruler's patronage was considerably broader. Taxes were used to pay for roads, bridges, churches,

1

fortifications, hunting lodges, and stables. Above all, they paid for palaces. Court artists were employed to decorate their interiors as well as to design furnishings, tapestries, gold plate, and even clothes. These images of power visually dominated each city and added luster to the names of their rulers.

Alberti and the Revival of Classical Architectural Style

One of the major figures in the dissemination of classical culture was the Florentine humanist Leon Battista Alberti (1404–1472). His treatise on architecture (1452) owed much to the writings of the Roman architect Vitruvius. Written in Latin and aimed at patrons and the educated elite, it emphasized the value of classical architecture in the creation of an image of power. The work established Alberti as a leading authority on the subject, and he became involved in the design of monuments at the courts in Ferrara, Rimini, and Mantua. These buildings were conspicuously more classical than those attributed to him in Florence. Sigismondo Malatesta commissioned Alberti to design a new exterior for St. Francis's to reflect its new role as his mausoleum.

The side niches were intended as tombs for humanists, a variation on the medieval practice of collecting the relics of saints. Alberti's use of Composite capitals, Roman lettering for the inscription, and triumphal arch adaptation for the façade, as well as the Roman convention of carrying arches on piers and supporting architraves on columns, were all conspicuously antique. But pagan architecture was inappropriate for Christian worship, and each of the Composite capitals was decorated with cherubim to remind the visitor that this was a Christian building.

1. *Andrea Mantegna, Ceiling oculus. Palazzo Ducale, Camera degli Sposi, Mantua. Fresco. 1465–1474. Fictive architecture and figures were deliberately designed to amuse and impress.*

3. *Pisanello, Leonello d'Este. Museo dell'Accademia Etrusca, Cortona. 1444. The most popular of the classical portrait types was the commemorative medal with its distinctive profile image. Pisanello (ca. 1395–1456) made medals of the Gonzaga, d'Este, and Malatesta families, as well as humanists such as Vittorino da Feltre, the resident tutor at the Gonzaga court.*

3

4

2. *Leon Battista Alberti, St. Andrew's. Mantua. Begun 1470. Designed by Alberti (1406–1472) on a scale to recall the monuments of Ancient Rome, the combination of triumphal arch and temple façade was a direct reference to antiquity.*

4. *Leon Battista Alberti, St. Francis's (Tempio Malatestiano). Rimini. Begun 1450. According to an inscription on one side of the façade, Sigismondo Malatesta dedicated his mausoleum to God and the city of Rimini. The pervasiveness of his personal insignia suggests other motivations.*

5. *Leon Battista Alberti, St. Andrew's, interior. Mantua. Begun 1470. The use of a coffered barrel vault reflected Alberti's belief, expressed in his treatise on architecture, that designers should study the remains of Ancient Rome.*

2

5

Lodovico Gonzaga and Alberti in Mantua

Alberti's major buildings were designed for Lodovico Gonzaga, the second marquis of Mantua (1422–1478). The city of Mantua was effectively an island, surrounded on three sides by mosquito-infested swamps. Its position on the border between the expanding powers of Milan and Venice guaranteed independence. Through strategic marital alliances and judicious political support for rulers in Italy and northern Europe, Lodovico and his successors achieved a level of prestige for Mantua out of proportion to its size. Their success owed in part to the image of wealth and power promoted at the Mantuan court, which helped transform an insignificant and unhealthy city into one of the most important cultural centers of the Renaissance. Lodovico had persuaded the pope to hold a congress in Mantua (1459–1460), which provided the impetus for a major program of restoration and urban renewal. Lodovico's education under the humanist Vittorino da Feltre made him receptive to Alberti's ideas on architecture, and he consciously promoted classical culture as an appropriate image for the Mantuan court; the city was, among other things, the birthplace of the Roman poet Virgil. Alberti's two churches in Mantua, dedicated to St. Sebastian and St. Andrew, were designed on a scale that recalled the monumentality of Ancient Rome, and they exploited the use of classical forms and motifs in a Christian context. The façade of St. Andrew's was derived from a triumphal arch, its pediment suggesting a temple front. Alberti modeled the interior on the three apses of the Basilica of Maxentius in Rome, which had been completed by the first Christian emperor, Constantine. The articulation of the nave repeated the form of the façade in scale and decoration. This reflected Alberti's theories on the unity of design and marked a decisive break with

---

ANTIQUITY AT THE ITALIAN COURTS

---

6. *Andrea Mantegna,* The Gonzaga Court. *Palazzo Ducale, Camera degli Sposi, Mantua. Fresco. 1465–1474. Lodovico Gonzaga and his wife, Barbara of Brandenburg, surrounded by their family, courtiers, and a dwarf, were meticulously portrayed by Mantegna (ca. 1431–1506) in an architectural setting full of old-style motifs.*

7. *Gian Cristoforo Romano,* Francesco Gonzaga. *Museo del Palazzo Ducale, Mantua. Terracotta. Ca. 1498. Decorated with classical motifs and the family insignia, Francesco Gonzaga's breastplate also reinforced his image as a military leader.*

8. *Francesco del Cossa,* April. *Palazzo Schifanoia, Sala dei Mesi, Ferrara. Fresco. 1470s. Alive with old-style motifs, such as Venus's boat drawn by two swans, this fresco cycle provided the context for court ceremonials.*

6

7

8

the medieval practice of designing the façade as a separate unit.

Mantegna at the Gonzaga Court

Lodovico's appointment of Mantegna as his court artist (1460) was another conscious step in the realization of a classical image. Mantegna's passion for antiquity had already established his reputation in humanist circles in Padua. His major work for Lodovico was the decoration of the so-called *Camera degli Sposi*. The vaulted ceiling was decorated with a *trompe l'oeil* painting that simulated a series of stucco roundels with portraits of Roman emperors. Mantegna's ability to exploit the potential of perspective was fully displayed in the central oculus, with its illusion of open air. The walls were painted with scenes of court life, including portraits of the Gonzaga family, their courtiers, dogs, dwarfs, and visiting dignitaries. Dynastic and imperial, the room provided an effective instrument of propaganda for the Gonzaga court. Francesco, the fourth Marquis, continued the classical theme, but his military preoccupations encouraged the revival of other aspects of Roman culture. A portrait bust that portrayed him in armor had a curved base, markedly different from the horizontal line popular in Florence that directly recalled the imperial busts of Ancient Rome. Mantegna continued to work for Lodovico's successors, and his *Madonna della Vittoria* commemorated Francesco's victory over the French (1495); the figure of Francesco with two oversized warrior-saints, Michael and George, emphasized the military theme.

Francesco's wife, Isabella d'Este, promoted a very different image. To decorate her studio, which contained an impressive collection of antique gems, coins, and statuettes, she commissioned Mantegna to paint *Parnassus*. Isabella and her humanist advisors devised the iconographic program themselves.

9. *Andrea Mantegna,* Madonna of the Victories. *Louvre, Paris. Canvas. 1496. Mantegna's knowledge of classical remains was reflected in the decorative details of this altarpiece, commemorating Francesco Gonzaga's victory over the French.*

10. *Andrea Mantegna,* Parnassus. *Louvre, Paris. Canvas. 1496–1497. Commissioned by Francesco Gonzaga's wife, Isabella d'Este, this painting of the Roman deities celebrated classical culture and provided an appropriate context for her collection of antiquities.*

11. *L'Antico,* Cupid. *Museo Nazionale del Bargello, Florence. Bronze and gilt. Ca. 1496. Better known by his nickname, L'Antico was born Pier Alari Bonacolsi (ca. 1460–1528). He established a reputation at the Mantuan court for his copies of antique sculpture.*

11

9

10

As in the case of many mythological paintings of the Renaissance, the precise meaning of this work is not entirely clear. Mars, the god of war, is presented as Venus's lover, not as a military figure. Beneath them dance the Muses, goddesses of artistic creativity—certainly a fitting image for the flourishing culture of the Mantuan court.

Federico da Montefeltro and Urbino

Urbino was another small state that benefited from the aspirations of its ruler to create an important cultural center as an expression of his own power. Federico da Montefeltro (1422–1482) was a mercenary whose services to the papacy earned him the title of duke (1474). His military success also made him exceptionally rich. In the service of the king of Naples, his salary was 8,000 ducats per month, cut to 6,000 ducats during peacetime. The Venetians once offered him 80,000 ducats not to fight. By way of comparison, the annual profits of the Medici bank never exceeded 20,000 ducats. Federico used his wealth to set up what were arguably the most brilliant of the Renaissance courts. Like Lodovico Gonzaga, he was educated by Vittorino da Feltre, but his interests leaned heavily toward the scientific disciplines. He encouraged such mathematical talents as Piero della Francesca, whose treatises on perspective and geometry were found in the palace library alongside Alberti's treatise on architecture, classical texts, and works on military strategy. Federico's decision to acquire a library was an important element in the creation of his image; more than half of its 1,000 works were acquired from the Florentine dealer, Vespasiano.

Federico spent most of his money on architecture, however, and he embarked on an ambitious building program that included fortresses designed by the Sienese architecture theorist Francesco di Giorgio.

12. and 13. Piero della Francesca, Battista Sforza and Federico da Montefeltro. Uffizi, Florence. Panel. After 1474. This pair of portraits, painted by Piero della Francesca (ca. 1415–1492), expressed Federico's enormous wealth in his wife's jewelry and intricate hairstyle.

12

13

14. Piero della Francesca, Flagellation. Galleria Nazionale delle Marche, Urbino. Panel. Ca. 1455. Both the dating and precise interpretation of this work are much disputed, but it certainly illustrates Piero's interest in the architectural language of antiquity and his use of perspective in pictorial composition.

14

The centerpiece of his program was the palace in Urbino. Externally fortified, the palace presented a very different image in the interior. A classical inspiration was evident in its composite columns, courtyard inscription, and antique motifs carved on marble doorframes and fireplaces. Federico's private study, the Studiolo, was decorated with portraits (now lost) of celebrated figures from classical and modern times. The decoration was dominated, however, by elaborate and expensive intarsia; the panels fully exploited the potential of perspective, creating an illusion of open cupboards filled with scientific instruments

and classical texts as an expression of the intellectual atmosphere of the Urbino court.

The Sforza Court in Milan

Milan was the largest city in fifteenth-century Italy. An important urban center since the Roman Empire, it achieved enormous prosperity during the late fourteenth century under the Visconti dukes. The battle over succession to Filippo Maria, the last member in the family's ducal branch, was won by a mercenary captain named Francesco Sforza (1401–1466). The scale and prestige of the Sforza court offered

considerable opportunities for artists and attracted talents from all over Italy.

Leonardo and Bramante

Foremost among those employed by Lodovico Sforza (1451–1508) were two painters, Bramante and Leonardo da Vinci. Bramante came from Urbino. In one of his first commissions in Milan, Santa Maria presso San Satiro, he demonstrated how the potential of perspective could be exploited on a grand scale; the structure allowed no space for a choir, but Bramante was able to paint a perfect illusion. Leonardo, meanwhile, in a letter

15

15. View of Urbino. *Dominated by the Palazzo Ducale with its two austere towers enclosing more elaborate arched openings, the external image of Urbino was deliberately fortified.*

16. Palazzo Ducale, courtyard. *Urbino. Ca. 1464. The Roman Composite capitals and lettering in the inscription gave visual expression to the image of classical culture promoted at the Urbino court.*

16

17

17. Palazzo Ducale, Studiolo. *Urbino. Ca. 1475. Expensive intarsia woodwork was cunningly contrived to create an illusion of open fretwork doors and cupboards filled with books and scientific instruments.*

to Lodovico (1482), expressed his desire to move from Florence and gain regular employment at the Milanese court. In the letter, Leonardo emphasized his talents as a military engineer, adding that he was also trained as a designer of buildings, a sculptor, and a painter. This was no false modesty. His creative talents in the technical field were far more valuable to Lodovico than his artistic abilities. A great patron, Lodovico concentrated on large-scale architectural projects in both Milan and other important centers in the state, notably the Certosa at Pavia. In scale, complexity, and materials, his projects conveyed the wealth and power of the Milanese court. Lodovico commissioned Leonardo to design a giant equestrian statue of his father, Francesco. Leonardo made a terracotta model of the monument, but the final bronze casting was never realized. As a court artist, Leonardo was involved in the design of military machinery as well as costumes and scenery for court masques, altarpieces, and portraits of Lodovico's courtiers.

Lodovico's major project, an enlargement of the monastery of Santa Maria delle Grazie, involved the talents of both Leonardo and Bramante. Intending it as the new Sforza mausoleum, Lodovico commissioned Bramante to design a new east end and cloisters, and Leonardo to paint a fresco of the *Last Supper* in the refectory. The image of the *Last Supper* was customary for a refectory, but this interpretation was new. Traditionally, the scene had emphasized the institution of the Eucharist and the designation of Judas as Christ's betrayer. By contrast, Leonardo's work depicted the preceding moment in the story, in which Christ announces only that someone would betray him. This choice of a more dramatic image reflected a need to reinforce the Christian message at a time when the institutions of the Church were increasingly

18. Certosa, façade. *Pavia. Begun 1492. Highly elaborate and decorative, this façade reflected the love of ornament and display that gave visual expression to the prestige of the Sforza court in Milan.*

18

19

19. Bramante, Choir. *Santa Maria presso San Satiro, Milan. Begun 1478. False architectural elements create the illusion of a choir whose physical construction behind the altar would have been impossible.*

20. Leonardo da Vinci, Church plans. *Institut de France, Paris. 1488–1489. Leonardo's notebooks contain many fascinating inventions, including bird's-eye views of these designs for churches.*

20

Commissioned by Lodovico Sforza for the refectory of Santa Maria delle Grazie in Milan, Leonardo's *Last Supper* has long been considered a masterpiece. His unsuccessful experiments in fresco technique caused it to decay rapidly, no doubt enhancing its mystique. His innovations in composition and interpretation, however, were part of wider changes in art that developed around 1500, a period known as the High Renaissance. Leonardo's use of perspective

LEONARDO'S
LAST SUPPER

to create the illusion of extended space in the refectory itself summed up the achievements of the fifteenth century. Earlier examples of the *Last Supper* had stressed horizontality by setting the scene in front of a flat wall. But Leonardo's use of depth reinforced the central position of Christ. His depiction of the dramatic moment, when Christ announces that one of those present would betray him, differed from earlier interpretations; previous renditions invariably recorded Christ's blessing of the bread and wine. The tableau dramatizes the individual reactions of the Apostles to Christ's startling statement. Leonardo divided them into groups of three, linking each group by gestures. Judas, the villain of the piece, is shown leaning back with his elbow on the table, excluded from the discussion.

under threat. It also announced a new stylistic trend that would characterize much of figurative painting in the sixteenth century.

The French invasion of Milan (1499) brought an end to Lodovico's rule, and his court was dispersed. Bramante had already moved to Rome, where he was establishing himself at the papal court. Leonardo went to Florence and later to France, where he died in 1519.

21

21. *Leonardo da Vinci*, Last Supper. *Santa Maria delle Grazie, refectory, Milan. Fresco. 1498.*

22. *Leonardo da Vinci*, Madonna of the Rocks. *Louvre, Paris. Panel transferred to canvas. Ca. 1485. Exploiting the potential of oil to outline and allow subtle changes of color, Leonardo's sfumato technique created an aerial perspective.*

22

CHAPTER 26

THE RETURN OF THE PAPACY

Art in Fifteenth-Century Rome

WHEN MARTIN V (1417–1431) returned to Rome in 1420, he became the first papal resident of the city of St. Peter's since 1309 whose legitimacy was recognized throughout Europe. For more than 100 years, the papacy had been the pawn of northern Europe rulers. At one point, three different popes affirmed a legitimate claim to supreme spiritual authority. Under these conditions, it was inevitable that the institution of the papacy suffered a severe loss of prestige. The return of Martin V to Rome, an attempt to revive the status of the papacy, also marked a major turning point in the city's fortunes. During the period of papal captivity in Avignon, Rome had stagnated both economically and visually. The fifteenth-century popes aimed at reviving the power of Rome and exploited the value of art and architecture to promote their cause. The projects undertaken in Rome ultimately reflected the character of the incumbent pope. Among the popes of the fifteenth century were an educated cleric (Nicholas V), a Sienese humanist (Pius II), a wealthy Venetian (Paul II), and a Franciscan friar (Sixtus IV). It was unlikely that personalities as diverse as these could agree on how best to present the image of a powerful papacy.

1

Thus, the art and architecture of fifteenth-century Rome inevitably lacked the consistent development seen elsewhere. Unlike other Italian cities, Rome was not a center of merchants and artisans. The papal court employed clerics for the transaction of official business, including many notable humanists. Equally dependent on the fortunes of the court were entertainers, prostitutes, innkeepers, and providers of luxury goods, such as jewelers, who served the population of pilgrims and important visitors to the Holy See. Any scheme to encourage more visitors had economic as well as spiritual benefits.

This was undoubtedly what Nicholas V had in mind when he revived the medieval custom of the Jubilee Year, announced for 1450.

Nicholas V

Pope Nicholas V (1447–1455) had applied his humanist education to a career in the Church. Influenced by a stay in Florence with the papal court, he appointed Florentine humanists to the Curia and employed Florentine craftsmen in his efforts to remedy the chaos of medieval Rome. Nicholas V spent papal

funds on widening streets, improving the water supply, mending bridges, and, above all, financing badly needed repairs at St. Peter's and other churches in Rome. Under the influence of Alberti, whose treatise on architecture was dedicated to Nicholas (1452), he planned a massive reorganization of the Borgo, between the Vatican and the Tiber, to create a more impressive approach to St. Peter's. The justification for this enormous expenditure appears in the decorative scheme for his private chapel in the Vatican. Both St. Stephen, who had been appointed a deacon by St. Peter, and St. Lawrence were

1. Perugino, Christ Giving the Keys to St. Peter. *Sistine Chapel, Vatican. Fresco. 1481. Decorated with scenes from the lives of Christ and Moses, which faced each other on either side of the nave, the cycle focused on the event that established the primacy of papal power.*

2. Fra' Angelico, St. Stephen Receiving the Deaconate and his Distribution of Alms. *Chapel of Nicholas V, Vatican. Fresco. 1448. In the architectural background to this scene, Fra' Angelico (ca. 1395–1455) adapted the heavy classical columns and entablature of the nave of Constantine's basilica of St. Peter's, markedly different from the elegant arcades of his native Florentine style.*

known for their generosity with Church funds in favor of the poor. The message was clear. St. Peter and his successors had received their authority directly from Christ, and the wealth of the Church should be used for the benefit of its members rather than for the self-glorification of individual popes or the luxuries enjoyed by the papal court in Avignon.

Pius II and Paul II

Nicholas V's immediate successors ignored this message. The humanist Pius II (1458–1464) concentrated his own energies and

3. Fra' Angelico, St. Lawrence Distributing Alms. Chapel of Nicholas V, Vatican. Fresco. 1448. Nicholas V's choice of the lives of St. Stephen and St. Lawrence carried a strong religious message: The wealth of the Church was not the personal property of the pope but should be used for the good of the people. The Roman authority forbade Lawrence from distributing the treasure, but he insisted it belonged to the poor. He was burned to death.

4. Palazzo Venezia. Rome. Begun 1455. Fortified and imposing, the palace was originally designed as the residence of the Venetian cardinal, Pietro Barbo, and enlarged when he became Pope Paul II.

5. Santa Maria del Popolo, façade. Rome. 1472–1480. Built as part of Sixtus IV's ambitious project for the renewal of Rome, the church reflected Sixtus's special devotion to the Virgin.

6

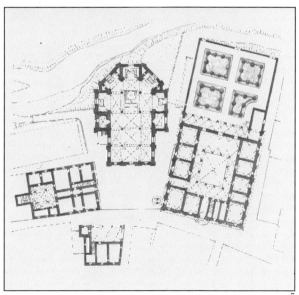

7

6. Bernardo Rossellino, Cathedral and Palazzo Piccolomini. Pienza. 1460–1462.

7. Plan of Pienza: the Duomo, in the center, is flanked by the Palazzo Arcivescovile on the left and the Palazzo Piccolomini on the right, with the Palazzo Comunale at the bottom.

the financial resources of the papacy on the reconstruction of his native village near Siena, Corsignano. The village was redesignated Pienza (from the name Pius) and, with an extensive development project, accorded civic status. Pius II persuaded other cardinals to build their own palaces there, but he was directly responsible for the two main buildings that appeared on the central square: the Palazzo Pizzolini (with a splendid hanging garden) and the cathedral. His humanist interests were reflected in the use of the classical orders on the façade of the palace. Pius's immediate successor was Paul II (1464–1471), a wealthy Venetian aristocrat who competed more directly with the other secular courts in Italy. His collection of antique gems and cameos was exceptional, even by the standards of his rivals in Florence and Mantua. To emphasize his new power, Paul moved the papal court away from the Vatican and St. Peter's to the palace he had built while a cardinal, the Palazzo Venezia. To reinforce the building's new function, Paul had it enlarged it and added a papal benediction loggia to the façade of the attached titular church, St. Mark's.

Sixtus IV and the Sistine Chapel

Paul II's successor was a complete contrast. Sixtus IV (1471–1484) was a Franciscan friar with a reputation for morality and piety. One of his first acts as pope was to dispose of Paul II's collections of antiquities, exchanging them for both financial and political gain. By promoting his own relatives to key positions at the papal court, Sixtus established a power base in Rome. Although he was open to the charge of nepotism, this allowed him to carry out his plans without opposition. His ambitious building program was aimed at promoting

9

8. *Melozzo da Forlì*, Sixtus IV Appointing Platina his Librarian. *Pinacoteca, Vatican. Fresco transferred to canvas. After 1474. Pointing down to his inscription, which described Sixtus IV's contribution to the urban renewal of Rome, Platina was presented as a member of the papal court along with Sixtus's relations. The tonsured cardinal was the pope's nephew, Giuliano della Rovere (later Julius II).*

9. Sistine Chapel. *Vatican. Begun 1473. Sixtus IV's most prestigious project, the Sistine Chapel provided a new setting for papal elections.*

10. Sistine Chapel, interior. *Vatican. Begun 1473. Before Michelangelo began his work, the vault was decorated with a star-studded sky. The religious significance of the building was reinforced by Sixtus's preference for early Christian architectural prototypes, including the opus alexandrinum pavement.*

11. *Sandro Botticelli*, The Temptation of Christ. *Sistine Chapel, Vatican. Fresco. 1481. Reinforcing the link with Sixtus IV, this scene included portraits of members of his court; the building in the background was his Ospedale di Santo Spirito, a charitable foundation for pilgrims and the sick.*

8

10

11

a powerful and successful papacy and included new churches, a hospital, and plans for extensive urban renewal. He also stimulated a major building boom by changing the laws on inheritance to allow cardinals and clerics to pass their property to their heirs.

For Sixtus IV, classical culture did not constitute an appropriate image for Christian society. Like his predecessors in the twelfth and thirteenth centuries, Sixtus revived the image of early Christian Rome, restoring many of the churches from that period. The same image was promoted in both the architecture and decoration of his major project, the Sistine Chapel. The walls of the interior were frescoed with illusionistic wall hangings depicting scenes from the lives of Moses and Christ and, at the upper level, by portraits of the first thirty popes, exactly like the decorative schemes of the old Christian basilicas in Rome. The general theme of the program was papal primacy, as expressed in the *Charge to Peter* by Perugino. Elaborate triumphal arches in the background deliberately refer to the culture of Ancient Rome. The inscriptions, however, reveal that Sixtus was commenting on its immortality, affirming that a Christian faith is greater than the riches of Solomon.

The message was a clear condemnation of contemporary Italian culture.

Changing Attitudes to Antiquity

Sixtus IV's warnings about the immorality of Ancient Rome had little effect on the growing interest in antiquity. The remains of Ancient Rome had been continually despoiled throughout the fifteenth century, as they had been since the fall of the Roman Empire. Given the lack of papal funds or a quarry of cut marble, who could blame Nicholas V for allowing his building foreman to remove 2,300 carts of stone from the

12. *Antonio del Pollaiuolo,* Tomb of Sixtus IV. *St. Peter's, Museo del Tesoro, Vatican. Bronze. 1484–1493. Commissioned by Sixtus IV's nephew, Giuliano della Rovere, the future Julius II, this massive statement of the new power and prestige of the della Rovere family was reinforced by the prominent display of their oak tree in the papal coat of arms.*

13. *Filippino Lippi,* Annunciation. *Santa Maria sopra Minerva, Carafa Chapel, Rome. Fresco. 1489. Like many Roman patrons, Cardinal Carafa employed Florentine artists for the decoration of his chapel. Filippino (1458–1504) was recommended for this job by Lorenzo de' Medici and stopped work on the Strozzi Chapel in Santa Maria Novella in Florence to take up this commission.*

13

14. *Bramante,* Santa Maria della Pace, cloisters. *1500–1504. Carafa's patronage of Bramante (1444–1514) helped establish the architect's reputation in Rome. His innovative use of classical orders was given full rein by Julius II.*

12

14

Colosseum in one year? The façade of St. Mark's was built with marble from the same source. The humanist Pius II was one of the few popes to attempt to preserve the ruins themselves; Sixtus IV concentrated his energies on preserving the monuments of early Christian Rome. Toward the end of the century, a more specifically antiquarian interest began to emerge, prompting a deliberate search for remains. The exciting discovery (ca. 1490) of Nero's palace, *Domus Aurea*, with its painted decoration still visible, gave artists a new vocabulary of classically inspired decorative detail, the so-called "grotesque."

Cardinal Carafa and Bramante

By the end of the century, this change of attitude was reflected in the architecture of the papal court. Cardinal Carafa was exceptionally wealthy and had commissioned Filippino Lippi to decorate his lavish chapel in Santa Maria sopra Minerva. His patronage of Bramante, newly arrived from Milan, marked a decisive turning point in the development of architecture in Rome, establishing antiquity as the primary source for design. In his cloisters of Santa Maria della Pace, Carafa's name was prominently displayed in classical lettering.

In imitation of the Colosseum, Bramante combined all four of the Roman orders in the same building. It was a major innovation that set the scene for the flowering of the High Renaissance.

15. Michelangelo, Pietà. St. Peter's, Vatican. Marble. 1498–1499. An early work in the long career of Michelangelo (1475–1564), the Pietà became especially revered for its exquisite finish and emphasis on psychological interpretation.

15

ONE OF THE PROBLEMS OF ASSESSING northern European art in the fifteenth century is the marked contrast with Italian developments over the same period. While Italian patrons were consciously reviving the culture of classical Rome to promote images of their new power and prestige, patrons in the north showed little interest in antiquity. There was no reason they should. The revival of antiquity in Italy was a deliberate attempt to create a style distinct from the culture of the northern courts of the late fourteenth century.

CHAPTER 27

PRINCES AND MERCHANTS

Northern Europe, 1400–1500

Rivalry between the French and English monarchies erupted periodically into a series of campaigns together known as the Hundred Years War (1337–1453). Royal funds that had been central to the creation of late-Gothic courtly styles were now directed toward military needs. The wealth of the patrons who dominated northern Europe in the fifteenth century was based on trade. The flourishing textile industries that benefited the Italian city-states were also the basis of wealth in cities of the Low Countries, such as Ghent, Bruges, Brussels, Louvain, and Antwerp.

1

Royal Patronage in France and England

Royal patrons in the fifteenth century tended to adhere to tradition and continued to construct and decorate highly ornate Gothic buildings in the styles established by their predecessors. King's College Chapel at Cambridge was completed by Henry VII (r. 1485–1509) with a fan vault that was spectacular in scale but distinctly traditional in style. Jacques Coeur, chancellor to the French king, emphasized his royal association by using his considerable wealth to fund a smaller version of a traditional royal palace. The duc de Berry, son of John II of France, continued the royal custom of commissioning elaborately illustrated manuscripts. In splendid miniatures, his extravagant *Book of Hours* illustrated the passing of seasons in activities such as hunting, feasting, and agricultural labor, which declared the prestige of its patron in images of abundance and industry. Minute attention to detail recorded both the opulent courtiers and the ragged peasants with equal skill. Another son, the duke of Burgundy, established his court at Dijon and built a monastery at Champmol that would become the family mausoleum. Broederlam's altarpiece for the monastery, with its emphasis on elegance and attention to detail, reflected the duke's close political links with the French court.

The Duchy of Burgundy

The impetus for stylistic change came with the progressive separation of Burgundy from France. A series of strategic marriages had brought the prosperous urban populations of the Low Countries under Burgundian control. These cities had close trading links with England and took its side in a critical phase of the Hundred Years War. They also provided more than half the income of the

1. *Jan van Eyck,* The Madonna of the Chancellor Rolin. *Louvre, Paris. Panel. Ca. 1435. The power and prestige of Nicolas Rolin, chancellor at the Burgundian court, was given visual expression in the opulent architectural setting, clothes, and other details.*

2. *Hôtel Jacques Coeur. Bourges. Begun 1443. Developed as a distinctly northern European style, Gothic remained popular in France, England, and the Low Countries while the revival of classical culture in Italy promoted a very different image.*

3. *King's College Chapel. Cambridge. Begun 1446, vaults 1508. Fan vaulting developed in England around 1350. Ornate, intricate, and expensive, it conveyed an image of wealth and power that remained associated with royal patronage until the sixteenth century.*

4. *Limbourg brothers,* August. *Musée Condé, Chantilly. Ca. 1415. From* Les Très Riches Heures du Duc de Berry, *this harvest scene depicted the rags of the peasants and the royal castle in equally minute detail.*

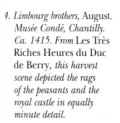

duke of Burgundy, Philip the Good (r. 1419–1467), an especially powerful incentive for the duke's attempt to assert his independence from the French crown. In contrast to the impoverished French and English monarchies, Philip's court flourished. His employment of Jan van Eyck as his court painter (1425) and occasional diplomat reflected his new power. Little is known of van Eyck's work for the duke, but the votive portrait of the Burgundian chancellor, Nicolas Rolin, illustrates Philip's adoption of a new court style in response to the growth of mercantile wealth in the cities of the Low Countries.

Van Eyck

A comparison of van Eyck's *Madonna of the Chancellor Rolin* (1435) and Broederlam's *Annunciation* reveals the remarkable developments that had taken place in the forty years between them. The precise observation of detail, common to both, was now extended to create a style that aimed at realistic portrayal. Elegant, sinuous figures dressed in ornately curving drapery and set in elaborate but unconvincing settings were rejected in favor of solid figures, their clothes hanging in angular folds, placed in a convincing space.

By analyzing the fall of light, van Eyck could use aerial perspective to create three-dimensional depth on a flat plane. The method was entirely different from that of his contemporaries in Florence, based on mathematical principles, but the goal was the same: verisimilitude. The use of oil paint allowed van Eyck to experiment with color and detail in ways not open to Italian fresco painters, who relied on tempera, and to faithfully render minute differences in the shades and textures of skin, fur, and rich brocade. Progress in the techniques of oil painting among the artists of northern

PRINCES AND MERCHANTS

5. *Master of Flémalle, Betrothal of the Virgin. Prado, Madrid. Panel. Ca. 1430. Round arches in the Temple at Jerusalem contrasted with the pointed arch used to frame Mary's marriage to Joseph and reflected the perception of Gothic as a Christian style.*

6. *Melchior Broederlam, Annunciation. Musée des Beaux-Arts, Dijon. Panel. 1392–1399. Courtly elegance and refinement were expressed by the Flemish artist Melchior Broederlam (active 1381–1409) in the ornate Gothic architecture and the sinuous poses of the figures.*

7. *Claus Sluter, Christ. Musée des Beaux-Arts, Dijon. Stone. Ca. 1390. The style of Sluter (active ca. 1380–1406) illustrated a developing sense of grandeur and solidity.*

7

5

6

Europe was of immense importance to subsequent developments in the history of Western art.

Mercantile Patronage

The new art patrons in northern European cities belonged to the mercantile class and had no interest in the expressions of wealth and power typical of courtly art. Whereas the sons of nobles and courtiers were educated in the ideals of chivalry, romance, and the art of war, the mercantile class took a more practical approach to education. Like their Italian counterparts, middle-class merchants in the Low Countries rejected the opulence and extravagance of court life. In response to the demands of this new class of patrons, a new style also emerged. The role of several artists in promoting the new style was a counterpart to that of Van Eyck at the Burgundian court.

Rogier van der Weyden was appointed as the official town painter of Brussels (1435), and Robert Campin was employed by the civic authorities in Tournai. A series of pictures from the early fifteenth century and attributed to the Master of Flémalle, usually identified as Campin, introduced new interpretations of traditional religious themes. The characters are presented in simple, unadorned interiors, and the values of contemporary middle-class life are reflected in the modesty of their clothes, the solid practicality of the furniture, and the presence of articles of everyday life. These middle-class interiors stood in marked contrast to the opulence of the Burgundian court as depicted by van Eyck, but the two artists shared an interest in spatial construction, figural solidity, and angular drapery. Other painters stressed emotional reality. Rogier van der Weyden's *Descent from the Cross*, commissioned by the Guild of Archers in Louvain, emphasized

8. Master of Flémalle, St. Barbara. Prado, Madrid. Panel. 1438. Mercantile patronage was reflected in bourgeois settings, simple clothes, homely details, and, above all, a greater naturalism in the treatment of the human body.

8

9

not only the humanity of the dead Christ, but also the torment of Mary and the grief of the onlookers.

The Master of Flémalle (Campin), van Eyck, and van der Weyden established the foundation of the new style, and their followers consolidated it. Civic authorities, confraternities, and guilds all employed artists to provide images that reflected their new status. The Confraternity of the Holy Sacrament in Louvain had a special interest in commissioning a *Last Supper* that centered on the institution of the Eucharist. Dieric Bouts's interpretation of this theme

had little in common with the more formal representations common in Italy. The simplicity and austerity of the setting, logical coherence of spatial construction, and framed presentation all contribute to the immediacy of the event and its importance to Christian faith. Bouts was among the painters employed to decorate the town hall in Louvain with scenes depicting the discovery and punishment of miscarriages of justice. The message these images were intended to convey was perfectly clear. They reflected the growing power of civic government and reinforced the responsibilities of elected

representatives. In contrast to the irrationality and unfairness of monarchical despotism, civic officials were obliged to uphold the concept of moral, rational government.

Van Eyck's *Arnolfini Marriage*

Mercantile patronage stimulated innovations in portraiture. Giovanni Arnolfini, a silk merchant from Lucca living in Bruges, commissioned van Eyck to paint a full-length double portrait of himself and his wife. This novel portrait type reflected Arnolfini's unusual desire to authenticate his marriage with a pictorial record of the event. Close

9. Rogier van der Weyden, The Seven Sacraments (detail). Musées Royaux, Antwerp. Panel. Ca. 1460.

10. Rogier van der Weyden, Descent from the Cross. Prado, Madrid. Panel. Ca. 1435. Commissioned by the Archers' Guild in Louvain, Rogier van der Weyden (ca. 1400–1464) expressed human emotion through poses, gestures, and facial expressions.

11. Hugo van der Goes, Death of the Virgin. Musée Communale des Beaux-Arts, Bruges. Panel. Ca. 1470. Hugo van der Goes (active ca. 1467–1482) consolidated the achievements of van Eyck, exploiting the use of oil to convey facial details and expressions.

11

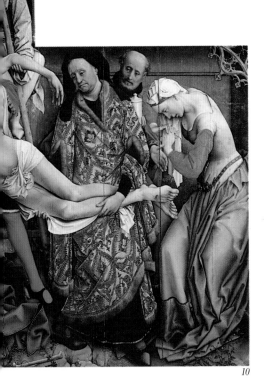

12. Hugo van der Goes, Portinari Triptych. Uffizi, Florence. Panel. Ca. 1477. Tommaso Portinari was the Bruges representative of the Medici Bank and commissioned a local artist, Hugo van der Goes (ca. 1440–1482), to paint this huge altarpiece, which was shipped to Florence to decorate the hospital of Santa Maria Nuova.

10

12

OIL PAINTING

The popularization of oil as a medium for mixing colors in the Netherlands during the fifteenth century is closely associated with the work of the van Eyck brothers, Jan (ca. 1390–1441) and Hugo (died 1426).

The procedure of mixing pigments with oils was indeed known since ancient times, but in Italy this technique spread rather slowly. In fact, one of the first persons to use this technique there seems to be Antonello da Messina (ca. 1430–1479).

But it was only in sixteenth-century Venice that this procedure became especially popular and widespread. Replacing the more traditional method of binding colors with egg yolk (tempera), oil proved more successful for the precise rendering of detail. Tempera dried relatively quickly, however, and the application of superimposed layers of oil paint was a more painstaking process.

The development of oil painting in northern Europe reflected the traditions of manuscript illumination. The luminous effects achieved with oil made it especially suitable for the realistic rendering of glittering jewelry, rich fabrics such as brocade and velvets, and, above all, skin tones.

Attention to scene details characterizes Flemish paintings of the fifteenth century; painstakingly depicted are not only details of clothes and domestic objects, but also certain aspects of the scenery (which can even be glimpsed at from windows) that act as a backdrop to the scene portrayed.

In Netherlandish art, a new kind of perspective was born: the feeling of depth was not established by the convergence of lines toward a vanishing point, but rather by subtle gradations of color, thus illustrating the desire for greater verisimilitude.

15. Hans Memling, Portrait of a Man. *Uffizi, Florence. Panel. 1480s. This portrait by Memling (ca. 1430–1494) was typical of the new fashion for nonidealized images that developed in response to the growth of mercantile patronage.*

15

13. Dieric Bouts, Judgment of the Emperor Otto. *Musée Royal des Beaux-Arts, Brussels. Panel. 1470–1473. Clear and concisely painted, this scene illustrated the efforts of the wife of one of Emperor Otto III's courtiers to clear her husband's name after he had been falsely accused by the empress and executed; the emperor ordered his wife burned at the stake. The story was used to underline the importance of loyalty to the state above family ties.*

14. Dieric Bouts, Last Supper. *St. Peter's, Louvain. Panel. ca. 1465. Utilizing the patterns of floor tiles to create a convincing architectural setting for his austere composition, Dieric Bouts (ca. 1415–1475) emphasized the religious significance of the scene with precise attention to comparatively sparse details.*

13

14

inspection of the mirror reveals two people witnessing the ceremony, which at the time did not require the presence of a priest. Objects in the room provided symbols of marital fidelity, notably the bed, the orange, and the little dog. Although the tradition of votive portraits nevertheless continued, this period saw the beginning of a new and very different approach to individual portraiture. Images of this material world began to replace those with references to the afterlife, and painters of the time exploited the new oil technique to enhance the lifelike reproduction of eyes, skin, hair, and clothes.

16. Jan van Eyck, Arnolfini Marriage. *National Gallery, London. Panel. Ca. 1434. Commissioned by Giovanni Arnolfini to record his marriage, this unusual double portrait was filled with symbols of marital fidelity.*

16

17

17. Quentin Metsys, The Banker and His Wife. *Louvre, Paris. Panel. 1514. Wealth was expressed not only in the coins, pearls, and rings being weighed by the banker but also in the illuminated manuscript held by his wife.*

THE SIXTEENTH CENTURY

After the cultural and artistic achievements of the early Renaissance which, throughout the fifteenth century, was characterized by relative political stability, the sixteenth century was marked by widespread restlessness and rapid changes that affected every aspect of Western civilization. The religious struggles, the Reformation, and the Counter-Reformation, are significant examples. Also during this period, the power of the fifteenth-century Italian city-states began to yield to the greater influence of the great European monarchies (in France, Spain, and England) and the papacy. In Rome, at the start of the century, the advent of Pope Julius II brought about a radical change in the arts, architecture, and city planning. To demonstrate the renewed prestige of the papacy, Julius II, with the support of extraordinarily talented masters such as Bramante, Michelangelo, and Raphael, developed a complex plan to remodel the city and some of its key monuments such as St. Peter's and the Vatican palace. Meanwhile, in Florence, the republic was breathing its last, and the Medici returned to the city (and art began to be linked strongly to the court). Venice continued its tradition of autonomy and maintained ties with the East, which was becoming increasingly rich in architectural and decorative achievements. Constantinople enjoyed a new splendor under Suleyman the Magnificent, while the Safavid Dynasty blossomed in Iran, and the Moghuls rose to power in India. In the meantime, Europe's royal courts were seething with foreign artists engaged in a fertile exchange of styles and ideologies.

	1480	1490	1500	1510	1520	1530	1540	1550	1560	1570	1580	1590	1600	1610

EUROPE

1483–1498 | *Charles VIII*
1485 | Bosch: The Garden of Earthly Delights
1498–1515 | *Louis XII*
1509 | *League of Cambrai*
1510–1515 | Grünewald: Isenheim Altarpiece
1515–1547 | *Francis I*
1517 | *Martin Luther posts the 95 Theses in Wittenberg*
1517–1518 | Leonardo da Vinci and Andrea del Sarto in France
1519 | *Charles V of Hapsburg*
1520 | *Martin Luther excommunicated*
1527 | Palace of Charles V, Granada
1540 | Francis I commissions the architect Sebastiano Serlio
1543 | Cranach: Portrait of Martin Luther
1546 | Square Court, Louvre, Paris
1550 | Goujon: Caryatids, Louvre, Paris
1551–1571 | Titian's works reach Spain
1556–1598 | *Philip II of Spain*
1563–1584 | *Escorial, Madrid*
1565 | Pieter Bruegel the Elder: Peasant Wedding
1567 | Treatise on Architecture by P. de l'Orme
1571 | *Battle of Lepanto*
1577 | El Greco settles in Toledo
1588 | *England defeats the Spanish Armada*

VENETO

1481 | Santa Maria dei Miracoli, Venice
1502–1510 | Carpaccio
1505–1507 | Dürer's second sojourn in Venice
1505–1510 | Giorgione: La Tempesta
1508–1570 ca. | Titian's career
1509 | *The League Cambrai defeats Venice at Agnadello*
1516 | Death of Giovanni Bellini
1549 | Palazzo della Ragione, Venice
1550–1594 | Tintoretto's career
1566 | Palladio: church of San Giorgio Maggiore, Venice
1566–1568 | Veronese: frescoes in Villa Barbaro, Maser
1570 | Palladio: I Quattro libri dell'architettura

FLORENCE AND ROME

Bramante: Tempietto, | 1502 San Pietro in Montorio, Rome
1503 | *Pope Julius II*
1504 | Leonardo, Michelangelo and Raphael in Florence
1505 | Bramante: Spiral staircase in Belvedere, Rome
Michelangelo: frescoes | 1509–1510 in the Sistine Chapel, Rome
Raphael working in the Vatican | 1509–1513
1510 | Bramante: Palazzo Caprini, Rome
Rosso: Deposition | 1521
1527 | *Sack of Rome*
1534 | *Michelangelo leaves Florence for good*
1536–1541 | Michelangelo: Last Judgment
1537 | *Cosimo I de' Medici, Duke of Florence*
1538 | Salviati: frescoes in Rome
1538–1564 | Michelangelo: Piazza del Campidoglio, Rome
1540 | *Pope Paul III recognizes the Society of Jesus*
1543 | Titian: Portrait of Paul III
1554 | *First edition of the Index of Forbidden Books*
1563 | *Council of Trent*
1546–1564 | Michelangelo: Dome of St. Peter's, Vatican

THE EAST

1494 | *Fall of Constantinople*
1502–1730 | *Safavid Dynasty, Iran*
1520–1566 | *Suleyman the Great*
1526–1605 | *The Moghul Empire is consolidated*
1539 | Sinan, architect at the court of Suleyman
1550–1557 | Mosque of Suleyman in Istanbul
1570–1574 | Mosque of Selim II, Edirne
1600 | Maidan-i-Shah, Isfahan

THE ELECTION OF A NEW POPE INEVITABLY inspires change. The repeated arrival of new figures, eager to stamp their own personality on the character of the papacy and with nearly absolute authority to do so, gave the development of the arts in Rome less stability than elsewhere. The election of Julius II as pope on November 1, 1503, marked a particularly radical change. His exploitation of the power of art and architecture as an expression of his papal vision was far more dramatic than that of his predecessors. The Venetian ambassador described Julius II as impatient, stubborn, and argumentative, but credited

JULIUS II AND THE HIGH RENAISSANCE

Rome, 1503–1513

him with grand vision. His papacy marks a period of major achievement in the arts, largely due to his determination to revive the power and grandeur of Rome as the center of the Christian world.

Julius II and the Rebuilding of Rome

The conclave that elected Julius II was one of the shortest in history. In choosing his papal name, the new pontiff deliberately recalled Julius Caesar, who was distinguished not only as a political figure but also for his achievements in the realm of art and culture. The authority of the papacy

was based on spiritual power, but this alone was not sufficient to compete in the political arena of Renaissance Europe. Julius II recognized that it was essential to establish a solid temporal base as well. The reforms he had in mind would require financial resources, so he minted a new coin, called the *giulio*, which stimulated inflation but at the same time raised revenues by as much as 30 percent. His military campaigns, although not on the scale of his namesake, had the purpose of expanding territorial holdings on the Italian peninsula. His greatest achievement, however, was the new architectural face he gave the city of Rome.

Roman life was centered in the papal court, which supported large numbers of church dignitaries and clerics as well as a variety of entertainers and traders in luxury goods, such as jewelers and goldsmiths. The seat of the papacy had been in Avignon from 1309 to 1377. After it was returned to Rome, the popes of the fifteenth century began to address the chaotic conditions that had descended upon the city, repairing and rebuilding roads, bridges, and churches (notably St. Peter's) and making major improvements in its general appearance. Julius II continued the reconstruction efforts, building the Via della Lungara and the Via

Giulia to provide better access to the Vatican. He had a grander vision than that of his predecessors, however, and recognized the need for monumental buildings to emphasize the authority of the Church.

Bramante and the New St. Peter's

Julius's decision to rebuild St. Peter's was opposed by conservative elements in the Church, who considered it unduly radical. Constantine's original basilica (ca. 320) was the visual symbol of the triumph of Christianity over pagan Rome; although it was now in serious disrepair, its age and

1. Raphael, Julius II. Stanza d'Eliodoro, Vatican. Fresco. 1512. This portrait of Julius II shows the pope as a direct witness to the Miracle of Bolsena (1263). The Venetian ambassador described him as impatient, stubborn, and argumentative but credited him with grand vision.

2. Bramante, Tempietto. Rome. Commissioned 1502. The classical combination of cella and peristyle, together with the appropriate and correctly proportioned Doric order, made this building a key monument in the revival of antique culture.

3. Caradosso, Medal commemorating Julius II's St. Peter's. Biblioteca, Vatican. Bronze. 1506. Caradosso (1452–1527) was a goldsmith and medalist from Lombardy who sought employment at the papal court, working for Julius II and his successors, Leo X, Hadrian VI, and Clement VII.

4. Bramante's plan for St. Peter's. Ca. 1505. Central planning was an aesthetic ideal but impractical for a religion whose liturgy was based on axiality. Bramante's plan was inevitably changed.

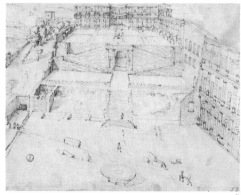

2

4

5

6

7

historical associations gave it immense power and prestige. In naming Bramante as the architect for the new St. Peter's, Julius II was giving his seal of approval to a revolutionary style. In 1502 Bramante had designed a tiny chapel for the king and queen of Spain on the site in Rome where St. Peter was said to have been martyred, beside the church of San Pietro in Montorio. Although the building followed the traditional circular form for a martyrium, Bramante broke new ground in his use of the classical form of cella and peristyle with Doric columns and a correct Doric frieze of triglyphs and metopes.

Instead of classical forms for the decoration of the metopes, Bramante used the attributes of St. Peter, such as the crossed keys. His use of the Doric shows that Bramante understood classical theory as outlined by the Roman architect Vitruvius and recognized that this order was the most appropriate for expressing masculinity and strength. Julius II clearly approved of this adaptation of the classical language of architecture to convey the Christian ideal. He was also well aware of the value attached by ancient Roman architects on scale and grandeur for transmitting the message on to future generations.

The plans for St. Peter's were certainly grand. A commemorative medal struck by the papal goldsmith, Caradosso, as well as Bramante's plan, indicated a design based on a Greek Cross surmounted by a vast hemispherical dome, with four towers placed at each corner. The scale of the building was manifestly Roman in conception. The same could be said about the choice of Doric for its articulation and the temporary shrine built by Bramante over the site of St. Peter's grave. But the main features of the design were unquestionably Christian in inspiration. Greek Cross churches, domes, and corner towers were essentially early Christian and

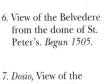

5. *Bramante,* Window in Sala Regia. *Vatican. Ca. 1504. Bramante (1444–1514) was educated in Urbino before finding employment at the Sforza court in Milan. His use of the classical language of architecture owed much to his knowledge of early Christian buildings in northern Italy.*

6. View of the Belvedere from the dome of St. Peter's. *Begun 1505.*

7. *Dosio,* View of the Belvedere. *Biblioteca, Vatican. Ca. 1560. This view of the Belvedere extension shows the division of the space between the old palace and the Villa Belvedere into three successive levels to accommodate the sloping ground.*

8. Apollo Belvedere. *Museo Pio-Clementino, Vatican. Marble. Roman copy of Greek original, discovered ca. 1498.*

9. Laocoön. *Museo Pio-Clementino, Vatican. Marble. Ca. 50 B.C.E. Discovered in 1506, this statue was immediately acquired by Julius II and transferred to the Vatican.*

10. *Bramante,* Spiral staircase in Belvedere. *Vatican. Begun ca. 1505. This staircase in the Villa Belvedere took visitors up a spiral ramp articulated by Doric, Ionic, and Composite columns that became increasingly decorative as they approached their destination.*

253

Byzantine. The central plan, nevertheless, posed practical problems for a religion whose liturgy attached importance to hierarchic processions following an axial plan. After the death of Julius II, the Greek Cross plan envisioned by Bramante was altered in a series of design compromises and finally replaced by a Latin Cross scheme. Bramante's plan also recalled the imperial Christian theme in its Doric-style window for the Vatican's Sala Regia, commissioned by Julius II, with its architrave broken by an arch —an old symbol of imperial power—which Bramante must have seen at St. Lawrence's in Milan and at Hadrian's Villa in Tivoli.

The Vatican Palace

As further visual proof of the power of the papacy, Julius II commissioned an enormous extension of the Vatican palace. The scale of the project made it the largest center of government in Europe and, at a practical level, provided badly needed space for the rapidly growing papal court. Bramante designed the extension in the form of two vast corridors, each housing papal offices (now the Vatican Museums) that would link the old palace with the Belvedere Villa, built by Innocent VIII (ca. 1487) on a hill to the north of St. Peter's. The corridors enclosed

an open space divided into three levels to take account of the sloping ground (now interrupted by the Vatican Library) and create a theater used for such entertainments as mock naval battles and bull fights. Bramante's interest in the classical orders was given full rein in the villa's spiral staircase, supported at different levels by Doric, Ionic, Corinthian, and Composite columns, following the same sequence as on the Colosseum. The staircase led visitors to the pride and joy of Julius's scheme: the antique sculpture court, an ideal setting for the prestigious collection of antique statues he had acquired (not always by the most

11. Michelangelo, Moses. San Pietro in Vincoli, Rome. Marble. Ca. 1515. Originally part of the tomb ordered by Julius II from Michelangelo, the statue of Moses illustrates Michelangelo's miraculous skill as a stone carver.

12. Sistine Chapel. Vatican. Ceiling fresco. Begun 1509. Julius's decision to repaint the ceiling of his uncle's Sistine Chapel was momentous. The choice of scenes from Genesis was made by Julius and his advisors, but the interpretation was Michelangelo's.

11

12

honest means), including the *Apollo Belvedere* and the *Laocoön*. All in all, the complex was undoubtedly the greatest single project in Rome since the fall of the empire. From its sheer scale and grandeur, one can clearly see how Julius II sought to imitate the great monuments of Ancient Rome. His intention in doing so was to create a symbol for the new Christian empire that would restore the splendor of antiquity.

Julius II and Michelangelo

In 1505 Julius II commissioned Michelangelo to design and carve his tomb, which he expected to be unprecedented in grandeur. The project was dropped the following year, presumably because the construction of St. Peter's consumed all available resources. It was revived after Julius's death but never carried out to completion; a few of the statues survive to the present day, including Michelangelo's *Moses*. These works provide some insight into Julius's vision and the sculptor's ability to realize it, and led directly to Michelangelo's commission to paint the ceiling of the Sistine Chapel in 1508. Julius's decision proved to be a critically important moment in the history of Western art. His choice of Michelangelo as the artist for the project was certainly unusual. Michelangelo had been trained as a sculptor, and this had a formative influence on his style, which has been described as "painted sculpture."

The original ceiling was decorated with gold stars on a blue background to represent the heavens. The work conceived by Julius would elaborate this theme with an epic narrative of the Creation, an innovation for ceiling decoration, and a series of prophets and sibyls who predicted the coming of Christ.

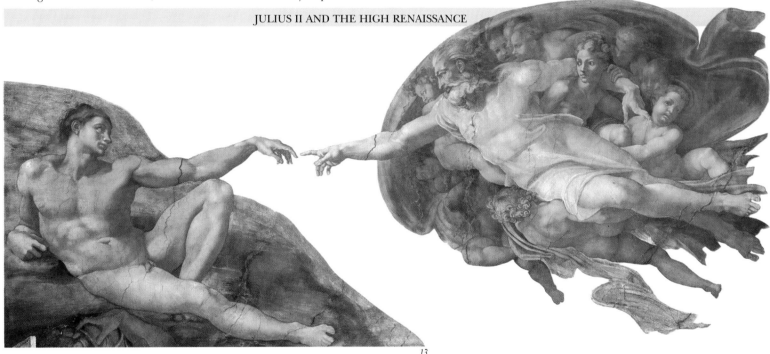

13

14

13. Michelangelo, Creation of Adam. *Sistine Chapel, Vatican. Fresco. 1509–1510. The dramatic moment just before God put life into Adam is stressed by the contrast between lethargy and action.*

14. Michelangelo, The Deluge. *Sistine Chapel, Vatican. Fresco. 1509–1510. Drama and movement were new features of High Renaissance art.*

15. Michelangelo, Delphic Sibyl. *Sistine Chapel, Vatican. Fresco. 1509–1510. The Sibyls, prophetic priestesses of Apollo, were adopted by the Christian Church to foretell the coming of Christ.*

15

RAPHAEL AND MICHELANGELO

In 1504, while Leonardo da Vinci was working on the Sala del Gran Consiglio in the Palazzo della Signoria, Raphael (then 21 years old) and Michelangelo (who was 30) were also in Florence.

The Florentine republic commissioned Michelangelo to create a large fresco representing the *Battle of Cascina* for the wall opposite the work that was to be done by Leonardo da Vinci. Neither work was ever completed, but both cartoons immediately became a model for numerous artists. In fact, later Ben-

venuto Cellini defined it as "The School of the World." Epitomizing the High Renaissance in art, the individual styles of these three artists were of immense influence on later painters.

Raphael (1483–1520) was born in Urbino and probably trained under Perugino, whose influence on his early works was marked. Employed at the beginning of the new century by wealthy Florentine

merchants to paint portraits and votive images, the young Raphael enjoyed a growing reputation that resulted in his move to Rome and the patronage of Julius II (1508). His style underwent a notable change in Rome, perhaps partly influenced by Michelangelo's Sistine Chapel ceiling but certainly in response to the intellectual, humanist atmosphere of the papal court.

Michelangelo Buonarroti (1475–1564) was first trained as a sculptor. Over the course of his quite long artistic career, he worked mainly in Florence and Rome, witnessing dramatic political and social changes that were reflected in major stylistic developments (see chapter 30). Michelangelo was always something of a loner and responded to the challenge of new ideas with unique artistic solutions. He was essentially a brilliant designer, but he was also a sculptor, painter, architect, and poet.

16

17

19

16. *Michelangelo,* The Holy Family (the Doni Tondo). *Uffizi, Florence. Panel. Ca. 1503–1504. This tondo was commissioned by Agnolo Doni to celebrate his marriage with Maddalena Strozzi. The complicated poses of the Virgin and Child were typical of the developing preference for complexity in early sixteenth-century art.*

17. *Michelangelo,* Madonna della Scala. *Museo della Casa Buonarroti, Florence. Marble. Late fifteenth century.*

18. *Michelangelo,* Battle of the Centaurs. *Museo della Casa Buonarroti, Florence. Marble. Late fifteenth century.*

18

19. *Raphael,* Maddalena Doni. *Palazzo Pitti, Florence. Panel. Ca. 1506–1507. The Florentine merchant Agnolo Doni commissioned Raphael to paint portraits of himself and his wife.*

In this way it would be possible to relate the ceiling to the wall frescoes and their theme of papal primacy. Michelangelo's interpretation of the *Creation of Adam*, dramatizing the moment just before God instills life into the lethargic body of Adam, was in marked contrast to tradition; a similar sense of drama imbues his depiction of the *Deluge*, in which the condemned of humanity are battered by a storm. As a deliberate reminder of his responsibility for the project, the Julius family emblem—an oak tree—appears throughout the ceiling; for example, a group of acorns appears just beneath the figure of Adam.

Raphael's Stanze in the Vatican

Following the custom of his predecessors, Julius planned the redecoration of a series of personal apartments in the papal palace. His private library, now known as the Stanza della Segnatura (the Papal Tribunal), was decorated by Raphael with four large frescoes representing the four spheres of knowledge—theology, philosophy, poetry, and jurisprudence. Traditional personifications of these subjects appear on the ceiling; the wall frescoes take a more innovative approach, gathering the masterminds in each realm into a single space. Each group is engaged in animated discussion, which at once brings visual unity to the collection of figures and symbolizes the Renaissance ideal of intellectual freedom. At the center of the *School of Athens*, illustrating philosophy, Aristotle and Plato gesture to indicate the sources of their inspiration: for Plato the ideal world, for Aristotle empirical reality. Other figures in the scene include Pythagoras, on the far left, writing in a book with his slate in front; and Euclid, on the right, demonstrating a principle of geometry with a pair of compasses. A similar pattern can be seen in the *Disputa*. At center of the picture is

20

22

20. *Raphael*, Stanza della Segnatura with the School of Athens. *Vatican. Fresco. 1509–1511. Decorating library walls with the portraits of famous men of the past was traditional, but the decision to group the masterminds of each sphere of learning in individual pictorial spaces and to represent them in animated discussion was a major innovation.*

21

21. *Raphael*, Ceiling of the Stanza della Segnatura. *Vatican. Stucco and fresco. 1511. The decoration of the ceiling included personifications of the four spheres of learning: Theology, Philosophy, Poetry, and Jurisprudence.*

22. *Raphael*, La Disputa. *Stanza della Segnatura, Vatican. Fresco. 1509–1511. The structure of this fresco was centered on the Host, reinforcing the fact that the Eucharist was the subject under debate in the scene.*

the Host, shown on the altar. The dialogue that ensues has both a heavenly and a temporal context: in heaven, Christ, Mary, and St. John the Baptist sit above various figures from the Hebrew Bible and New Testaments; on the ground, mortals discuss the theme of the Eucharist. The pope on the right with the book at his feet is Julius's uncle, Sixtus IV, who had written a treatise on that subject. The vivid scene on the left represents the moment of revelation. Here again, as in the Sistine Chapel, one notices Julius's autograph, in this case inscribed twice on the altar.

The concept of intellectual freedom embodied in these frescoes had important implications for the Reformation. The issue of the Eucharist, already an area of dispute within the Church, was destined to divide Europe.

Raphael at the Papal Court

Raphael's employment by Julius II established him as one of Rome's leading artists. It was probably Bramante, a distant relation, who brought Raphael to Julius's notice. Raphael's early career in Perugia and Florence was characterized by his

Madonna del Cardellino, painted for a Florentine merchant, Lorenzo Nasi. The marked change in style between his Roman paintings and his earlier work in Florence is usually ascribed to his familiarity with Michelangelo's ceiling figures. The strength and power of Raphael's later images, however, reflects no less the general atmosphere of optimism and power—both spiritual and temporal—in Rome during the early sixteenth century. Sigismondo de' Conti, an important figure in the papal court and private chamberlain to Pope Julius II, commissioned the *Madonna*

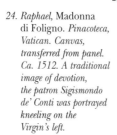

23. *Raphael,* Madonna del Cardellino. *Uffizi, Florence. Panel. Ca. 1506. Painted in Florence for the merchant Lorenzo Nasi, this image of the Virgin with Christ and St. John the Baptist was typical of Raphael's oeuvre before his arrival in Rome.*

24. *Raphael,* Madonna di Foligno. *Pinacoteca, Vatican. Canvas, transferred from panel. Ca. 1512. A traditional image of devotion, the patron Sigismondo de' Conti was portrayed kneeling on the Virgin's left.*

25. *Raphael,* Baldassarre Castiglione. *Louvre, Paris. Canvas. Ca. 1515. The author of a book on the ideal courtier, Castiglione achieved high status in the humanist courts of Italy. Raphael's portrait of his friend reinforced the image of secular intellect.*

26. *Raphael,* Cardinal Tommaso Inghirami. *Palazzo Pitti, Florence. Panel. Ca. 1510–1514. Raphael's skill as a portrait painter earned him numerous commissions at the papal court.*

di Foligno for the high altar of Santa Maria in Aracoeli, portraying himself in the position of supplicant to the Virgin with the help of St. Jerome, St. Francis, and St. John the Baptist. Cardinal Tommaso Inghirami, one of Raphael's advisors for the decoration of Julius II's library, preferred a more secular image of himself, writing in a ledger; only his eyes suggest his devotion. Baldassare Castiglione, the Urbino ambassador to Rome whose book *Il Cortegiano* (*The Courtier*) describes the ideal, secular life, looks straight at the viewer; it is the relaxed image of a wealthy and successful courtier.

Villa Farnesina

Those who had the wealth to do so preferred to commission architectural projects. Bramante's Palazzo Caprini set the style of the town palace for many centuries; among its characteristic elements were the use of the classical orders, a rusticated basement, and windows with pediments and balustrades. The most conspicuously wealthy member of Julius II's court was Agostino Chigi, a Sienese who held the favored position of papal banker. His *villa suburbana* was inspired by classical writings that describe the residences,

beyond the confines of the city, where ancient writers went to retire and relax. Chigi's house by the Tiber, the Villa Farnesina, was designed by Peruzzi and decorated with frescoes by Raphael, Sebastiano del Piombo, and Peruzzi. False architectural details in the room upstairs helped create the illusion of the *villa suburbana*, with views of contemporary Rome between false columns that imitated the use of different types of marble. If the expression of power and wealth through the use of rich materials and craftsmanship was unnecessary in the villa, a place of relaxation, Agostino Chigi made

27. Raphael, Galatea. Villa Farnesina, Rome. Fresco. 1513. Based on a scene in Ovid's Metamorphoses, *Raphael's fresco recorded the sea nymph Galatea in her cockleshell chariot surrounded by mythical sea creatures. The cupids aiming arrows refer to Ovid's story of the one-eyed giant Polyphemus, whose passion for Galatea forced him to kill her lover, Acis.*

27

use of real marble in his chapel at Santa Maria del Popolo, a more public statement of his status.

Julius II's successor, Leo X, continued many of Julius's projects but never had the energy or breadth of vision to continue Julius's plans for the establishment of Rome as a temporal power in Europe. The extravagance of the papal court, untempered by Julius's devotion to the institution of the papacy, was one of the factors that led inevitably to its decline and, ultimately, to the sack of Rome (1527) and the Reformation.

28

29

30

28. Bramante, Palazzo Caprini. *From an engraving by Lafréry. Ca. 1510. Also known as Raphael's House, this building was immensely influential and established a prototype for many later palaces.*

29. Peruzzi, Sala di Prospettiva. *Villa Farnesina, Rome. Fresco. 1516–1517. In the* villa suburbana *designed for Agostino Chigi by the Sienese architect and painter Baldassarre Peruzzi (1481–1536), this illusionistic scene of a loggia with views of Rome beyond is remarkably convincing.*

30. Raphael, Chigi Chapel. *Santa Maria del Popolo, Rome. Begun ca. 1513. Multicolored marble and complexity of design gave visual expression to the enormous wealth of the Chigi family.*

IN HIS HISTORY OF VENICE, DOGE ANDREA Dandolo (1343–1354) recounts that the city was founded by St. Mark and that various small lagoon settlements decided collectively in 697 C.E. to elect a leader called a "doge" (Venetian dialect for duke). Dandolo's mythical account was one of many that had evolved to explain Venice's origins, all of which stressed two points fundamental to the city's image: that it was Christian and that it was independent. The reality, of course, was more prosaic. Venice had long been under the authority of the Byzantine Empire, regaining independence only after the

CHAPTER 29

VENICE: THE IMAGE OF THE STATE

Venetian Art, 1450–1600

Lombard invasion and the withdrawal of Byzantine forces (ca. 750). With no land-based aristocracy, the Venetians exploited their links with the East and strategic position on the Adriatic Sea to become a nation of prosperous maritime traders. As the cities of northern Italy challenged traditional structures of authority in the twelfth century, so in Venice the power of the doge was progressively reduced. Subject to the control of city councilors, the doge became a figurehead of the republic. In 1323 the wealthiest and most powerful mercantile families took charge of the government, excluding all other

1

citizens from political office. The right to sit on the Grand Council became hereditary, and real power was invested in the Senate, the Council of Ten, and the magistracies elected from among their members.

Art and Propaganda

The Venetians were fully aware of the power of art as propaganda. One chronicler described how work was begun on the clock tower in St. Mark's Square (ca. 1496), despite a shortage of funds, to dispel fears that the state was on the verge bankruptcy. The prime images of Venetian power were the Doge's Palace and St. Mark's. Built on the model of imperial architecture in Constantinople, St. Mark's visually reinforced Venice's links with the Byzantine Empire. Indeed, the city saw itself as the heir of the imperial tradition. The church housed the relics of St. Mark, reputedly brought by Venetian sailors from Alexandria (829). Mosaics over the doors and inside the church celebrated the acquisition of these relics rather than the life of the evangelist himself. Venetian power was reinforced by other relics of the city's exploits, such as the four bronze horses looted from Constantinople (1204). The Doge's Palace, housing both government offices and prisons, was embellished with a new façade (see chapter 21) and a new entrance; the Porta della Carta was crowned with a statue of Justice, a common image of Venetian power. Its elaborately carved Gothic detail was originally gilded, giving visual expression to the wealth of the Venetian state. Gothic pointed arches were also used for the main floor of the courtyard, rebuilt after a fire in 1483. Classical ornament, so important elsewhere in Italy during this period, appeared only in the detailed decoration of the upper floors (begun ca. 1498).

1. Carpaccio, Lion of St. Mark. *Palazzo Ducale, Venice. Canvas. 1516. The background to this traditional symbol of Venetian power included the Doge's Palace and galleys to reinforce the Venetian context.*

2. Palazzo Ducale, courtyard. *Venice. Remodeling begun 1483. The classical elements on the Arco dei Foscari were taken from St. Mark's and reinforced the image of Venice as the heir to imperial Constantinople.*

3. Plan of St. Mark's Square, Venice.

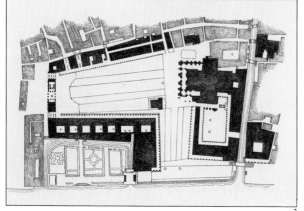

4. The Prayer Before the Discovery of the Relics of St. Mark (detail). *St. Mark's, right transept, Venice. Mosaic. Thirteenth century. The most prestigious church in Venice, St. Mark's was not a cathedral but the doge's private chapel. In function, style, and decoration it deliberately recalled Justinian's palace chapel, the Hagia Sophia in Constantinople.*

Classical motifs also decorated the dominant feature of the courtyard, the staircase, designed in response to a Great Council decision (1485) to create a more fitting summit for the doge's coronation ceremony and to provide a more prestigious setting for the reception of foreign dignitaries.

Palace Design

Venice in the fifteenth century had no real reason to revive the image of antiquity. The city had long promoted itself as heir to the imperial Christian tradition of Constantinople, all the more convincing since the fall of the Byzantine city to the Ottoman Turks (1453).

The pagan culture of Ancient Rome, moreover, was inappropriate to a Christian society. Patricians displayed the same lack of interest in antiquity for their private palaces as they did in commissioning images for the state. The main rooms of these palaces faced the Grand Canal to allow for maximum light; the windows represented an opportunity for the display of luxury. Built primarily as expressions of individual wealth and status, the palaces competed in ostentation. The Ca' d'Oro, or House of Gold, was originally covered with gold leaf.

Other patricians included two levels of decorative windows, corresponding to reception rooms inside. Typical of fifteenth-century palace design, the central arcades imitated the articulation of the Doge's Palace.

Although classically inspired ornament did appear, it was not until 1500 that Andrea Loredan adapted the classical orders for the façade of his palace. Even then he felt obliged to explain this pagan extravagance in an apologetic inscription at ground level, which stated that he was building for the glory of God rather than himself.

5

6

5. Palazzo Giustinian and Ca' Foscari. *Venice. Ca. 1450. The main thoroughfare of Venice,* the Grand Canal was lined with patrician palaces that competed with one other in opulent display.

6. Ca' d'Oro. *Venice. Begun 1424. Palace construction in Venice was a major undertaking. The cost of digging foundations was exceptionally high because of the marshy subsoil; piles had to be driven far down to reach solid ground.*

8. Santa Maria dei Miracoli. *Venice. Begun 1481. Despite the apparent classicism of this building, most of the details have their sources in St. Mark's. Its Christian function was reinforced by the cross above the door.*

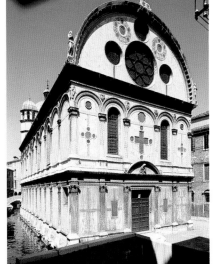

7. Palazzo Vendramin-Calergi (formerly Loredan). *Venice. Begun ca. 1502. Adapting the classical orders to emphasize the central windows, the importance of the piano nobile was stressed by fluted columns and a decorative balcony.*

7

8

Images of the Virgin

The Virgin was especially venerated in Venice as a symbol of the state, and her cults played an important part in state ceremonial. The legend that Venice had been founded on the day of the Annunciation (March 25) was an important feature of civic mythology, and the cult of the Immaculate Conception of the Virgin, which had aroused fierce controversy in the Church, was extraordinarily popular. Doge Agostino Barbarigo had been involved with the commission for Santa Maria dei Miracoli, itself dedicated to the Immaculate Conception; his votive portrait reflected both the official cult of the Virgin as well as his personal devotion.

The sons of Franceschina Pesaro commissioned the *Frari Triptych* from Giovanni Bellini specifically to commemorate their mother's devotion to the cult, referred to in the text held by St. Benedict. The gold mosaics behind the Virgin, often described as old-fashioned, were meant to be seen in a specifically Venetian context as a reference to the mosaics of St. Mark's. This altarpiece was typical in its combination of direct references to the wealth of its patrons, their religious beliefs, and their city.

It also illustrates the major changes taking place in Venetian art at a stylistic level. Bellini was one of the first Venetian painters to use oil as a medium for applying color, no doubt inspired by developments that had taken place in northern Europe (see chapter 27). His style was thereby completely transformed, reflecting closer attention to detail and the effects of light on different textures.

The *Scuole*

Tradesmen, professionals, and the rest of the middle classes were excluded by birth from

9. Giovanni Bellini, Frari Triptych. *Santa Maria Gloriosa dei Frari, Venice. Panel. 1488. The triptych was commissioned by the three sons of Franceschina Pesaro, who used their own names—Nicholas, Mark, and Benedict— and that of their father, Peter, in choosing the saints to be depicted on the side panels.*

9

10

11

10. Giovanni Bellini, Doge Agostino Barbarigo Before the Virgin. *San Pietro Martire, Murano. Canvas. 1488. Arguably the leading painter in late fifteenth-century Venice, Giovanni Bellini (ca. 1430–1516) exploited the use of oil to create a distinctive style that was a major influence on his pupils, including Giorgione and Titian.*

11. Giovanni Bellini, St. Job Altarpiece. *Accademia, Venice. Panel. Late 1480s. In a "Sacra Conversazione," the Virgin and Child with saints were incorporated in the same pictorial space rather than separated in individual frames, as had been common.*

political office. The potential for civic unrest was quelled in part by channeling their political and cultural aspirations into *scuole*, distinctively Venetian charitable organizations. The activities of the scuole were strictly controlled by the state. Founded as penitential movements in response to the growth of lay piety in the thirteenth century, they evolved into major public-welfare institutions that attracted considerable funds and dispensed them as relief for the poor, to pay for the funerals of members, and to ensure a dowry for their daughters. The funds were also spent on extravagant ceremonies and, above all,

on building and decorating their meeting halls. As patrons, the scuole were far from innovative; in special building projects no less than in day-to-day administration, they followed the models and standards of the Venetian nobility. Building façades provided a forum for competitive expressions of wealth and prestige. Their halls, like those of the Doge's Palace, were decorated with visual images of their own histories. For example, the prime relic in the Scuola di San Giovanni Evangelista was a piece of the Cross, but the Scuola commissioned a series of illustrations that depicted not the story of the Cross itself, but the

miracles associated with the relic and its acquisition. Like the mosaic in St. Mark's showing the arrival in Venice of the apostle's bones, this cycle reinforced the Venetian achievement rather than the power of Christian faith. Carpaccio and Gentile Bellini both set their miracles as subordinate events in minutely detailed panoramas of Venetian life, firmly establishing a Venetian context to reinforce their authenticity.

The League of Cambrai Wars

During the course of the fifteenth century, Venice considerably extended its domains

VENICE: THE IMAGE OF THE STATE

12

13

13. Scuola Grande di San Marco. *Venice. Begun 1487. The typical scuola building consisted of one large hall on each floor with a smaller adjoining room for more exclusive committee meetings. These interior divisions were clearly displayed on the façade.*

14. Gentile Bellini, Procession of the Relic of the True Cross. *Accademia, Venice. Canvas. 1496. Also commissioned by the Scuola di San Giovanni Evangelista, Gentile Bellini (ca. 1429–1507) (brother of Giovanni) disguised this miracle of the relic within a civic ceremony, minutely depicting St. Mark's and the Doge's Palace as well as conversations between members of the procession.*

12. Carpaccio, Miracle of the Relic of the True Cross. *Accademia, Venice. Canvas. 1494. Commissioned by the Scuola di San Giovanni Evangelista, Carpaccio (ca. 1460–1526) included portraits of the scuola members and other recognizable details, ranging from gondoliers to chimneys, to reinforce the reality of the event.*

14

on the Italian mainland. The policy of expansion encountered considerable opposition on the part of Pope Julius II, King Louis XII of France, and the Holy Roman Emperor Maximilian I, who, united in the League of Cambrai, resoundingly defeated Venetian forces at Agnadello (May 1509), captured the city of Padua (June 1509), and threatened Venice itself. Venice managed to survive and recover much of its lost territory, but the shock to its self-esteem was considerable. The victory was celebrated in three diverse images.

Giorgione's *Tempesta*, which has long puzzled art historians, was probably

16

15. *Titian,* Assumption of the Virgin. *Santa Maria Gloriosa dei Frari, Venice. Panel. 1516–1518. Commissioned by the Franciscans for the high altar of their church, this early work by Titian (ca. 1487–1576) made major stylistic innovations.*

15

commissioned by Gabriele Vendramin and commemorated the Venetian recovery of Padua, in which his family took part. The storm symbolizes the political upheaval; the patrician soldier and nursing mother provide powerful human symbols of war. State images of the victory were more explicit. The *Tempesta* also illustrates the important stylistic innovations made by Giorgione. His experiments in the use of oil led to softer outlines than those of Bellini and Carpaccio, and he abandoned the symmetry characteristic of their work. Titian explored these ideas further in his *Assumption of the Virgin*. While neither the subject matter nor the scale of this altarpiece was new, the interpretation and style were startlingly innovative, combining in dramatic and dynamic fashion the victorious mood of Venice and the final glory of the Virgin.

A New Image for the State

Increasing involvement with the politics of mainland Italy brought closer contact with the revival of Ancient Roman culture and the images it had provided for Italian rulers. The Venetians had shown little interest in adopting this pagan style as their state image, but their attitude changed dramatically after the victory over the League of Cambrai and the sack of Rome by imperial troops (1527). The wheel of fortune had turned, and Venice adopted a new state image, promoting the city as the sole heir of Ancient Rome.

After the sack of Rome, many intellectuals and artists moved to Venice; among them were the writer Pietro Aretino and the sculptor Jacopo Sansovino, both of whom were steeped in the classicism of the High Renaissance. Their new ideas found influential supporters, including Doge Andrea Gritti.

In this atmosphere of great cultural ferment came the decision to restore

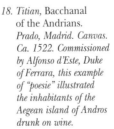

16. *Titian*, Pietro Aretino. *Palazzo Pitti, Florence. Canvas. 1545. Aretino was a leading intellectual figure in Venetian society and a friend of Titian. The portrait demonstrates Titian's ability to portray the personality of his subject.*

17. *Giorgione,* La Tempesta. *Accademia, Venice. Canvas. 1505–1510. The precise interpretation of this picture has provoked much debate, but the evocative landscape by Giorgione (ca. 1478–1510) clearly inspired many later artists.*

18. *Titian*, Bacchanal of the Andrians. *Prado, Madrid. Canvas. Ca. 1522. Commissioned by Alfonso d'Este, Duke of Ferrara, this example of "poesie" illustrated the inhabitants of the Aegean island of Andros drunk on wine.*

19. *Veronese*, Venus and Adonis. *Prado, Madrid. Canvas. Ca. 1580. Bought by Velázquez for Philip IV of Spain, this scene from Ovid's* Metamorphoses *by Veronese (ca. 1528–1588) demonstrates his ability to capture the different textures of brocade and human flesh.*

the political-administrative center of Venice. This would involve the creation of three new buildings, all designed by Sansovino, to express the new prestige and power of Venice: the Mint, the Library, and the Loggetta. The use of classically inspired architecture for such prestigious buildings illustrated a fundamental change in attitude. Following theories on the orders developed in High Renaissance Rome, the buildings were distinguished by the use of different combinations of the orders to reflect their function. The Mint, expressing strength and solidity through rusticated Doric, contrasted with the appropriately richer use of Doric and Ionic on the Library next door. The richest order, Composite, was used for the Loggetta, which was decorated with images of Venetian power. It was further distinguished from the other buildings by its use of extravagant building materials, combining the white Istrian marble used on the Library and Mint with a variety of exotic colored marbles.

A New Pictorial Language

This new interest in the culture of Ancient Rome had an immediate impact on painting and sculpture. Concepts of design, decorum, composition, and invention that had developed in High Renaissance Rome were codified into theories of art based on the classical ideal. Raphael and Michelangelo provided artistic models for imitation. Above all, artists now had a whole range of new subject matter at their disposal. Venetian artists, especially Titian, established a reputation for painting mythological scenes based on classical literature, such as Ovid's *Metamorphoses*. Most of these pictures were commissioned by foreign rulers eager to decorate their palaces with classical imagery as a reflection of their cultural status. Foremost among

20

21

22

the patrons of Titian's "poesie," as such works were called, were Duke Alfonso d'Este of Ferrara and Philip II of Spain.

Classical mythology was adopted as propaganda for the Venetian state as well. Allegory provided a new language for old themes, as the gods of antiquity became personifications of Venetian power. At the top of the ceremonial staircase where the doge received foreign dignitaries were Sansovino's statues of *Mars* and *Neptune*, symbols of Venetian military and naval strength. The fire (1577) that destroyed much of the earlier decoration in the Doge's Palace, including paintings by

Bellini, Carpaccio, Giorgione, Titian, and many others, was a strong impetus for state patronage. The League of Cambrai Wars and other recent Venetian achievements were presented as classical allegories. Veronese's *Apotheosis of Venice* illustrated the skill with which Venetian artists could present such improbable events in a convincing manner. These images provided important prototypes for later artists.

Portraiture

The Venetians were highly image-conscious, and portraiture flourished. A portrait could

be used to express the prestige, real or imagined, of the patron, and at the same time confer an aura of immortality. Titian's skill in this field led to commissions from statesmen throughout Europe. His portrait of the Vendramin family worshiping a relic of the Cross was not simply a votive image. It commemorated an ancestor, Andrea Vendramin, who had gained the family's admission into the nobility by helping the state in a financial crisis and donated the relic to the Scuola di San Giovanni Evangelista. Such public images were inevitably more formal and stereotyped than private portraits. Official portraiture

20. *Sansovino*, Loggetta. *Venice. Begun 1537. Facing the entrance to the Doge's Palace, this loggetta was designed to give the young patricians a place to congregate. The most ornate of the buildings commissioned for the renovated Piazzetta, its sculptural decoration reinforced Venetian power and prestige.*

21. *Sansovino*, Mars and Neptune. *Palazzo Ducale, Venice. Marble. 1554. Jacopo Sansovino (1486–1570) worked in High Renaissance Rome before moving to Venice (1527), where he became a key figure in the development of classical architecture and sculpture.*

23

23. *Titian*, Vendramin Family. *National Gallery, London. Canvas. Early 1540s. This portrait of Gabriele Vendramin, his brother Andrea, and Andrea's male children illustrates Titian's skill at composition.*

24. *Tintoretto*, Madonna and Child with St. Sebastian, St. Mark, St. Theodore, and the Treasurers. *Accademia, Venice. Canvas. 1567. This votive image of Michele Pisani, Lorenzo Dolfin, and Marino Malipiero together with their clerks was typical of portraits commissioned to commemorate a term of office in Venetian government.*

22. *Veronese*, The Apotheosis of Venice. *Palazzo Ducale, Sala del Maggior Consiglio, Venice. Canvas. Ca. 1585. Venice borne aloft and crowned by Victory provided a fitting image for the main Council Chamber in the Doge's Palace.*

24

developed dramatically in the sixteenth century as a visual expression of the community standing that Venetian society attached to political office. Invariably votive, these portraits reflected the importance of tradition in enhancing the prestige of office. Tintoretto's many portraits of civic officials also illustrated the role of clothes as a symbol of status in Venetian society.

Unlike Titian, Tintoretto was not part of the intellectual elite of Venetian society, and his best commissions came from the scuole. Founded as religious institutions, the scuole did not adopt the images of antiquity used by the state. Although Tintoretto's style reflected the changes that had taken place since 1500, his subject matter was traditional. The Scuola di San Rocco commissioned him to paint fifty-six canvases to decorate the rooms of their meeting halls, choosing scenes from the Hebrew Bible and New Testament with particular relevance to charity. The three canvases commissioned by Tommaso Rangone for the Scuola di San Marco continued the traditionally Venetian theme of commemorating the arrival of that saint's relics in Venice. The drama of Tintoretto's interpretation of the discovery of St. Mark's body by Venetian sailors is heightened by the asymmetrical composition and his skill in exploiting the effects of light.

Palladio

Venetian trade had been seriously affected by the growing power of the Ottomans and the fall of Constantinople (1453). During the sixteenth century, the state encouraged the development of uncultivated land on the mainland to exploit the potential of agriculture as a new source of wealth. Patricians acquired estates and built villas that functioned as rural retreats as well

26

25

25. Tintoretto, Discovery of St. Mark's Body. *Brera, Milan. Canvas. 1562–1566. Tintoretto (1518–1594) exploited the use of perspective, pictorial composition, and light effects to enhance the dramatic moment of the discovery of the saint's body.*

26. Tintoretto, Crucifixion. *Scuola Grande di San Rocco, Sala dell'Albergo, Venice. Canvas. 1565. The bulk of sixteenth-century Venetian art was religious. Tintoretto painted exceptionally fast, and his style was considerably less finished than Titian's.*

Giangiorgio Trissino's decision to give a modest stonecutter named Andrea di Pietro della Gondola (1508–1580) the benefit of a classical education was a significant one in the history of architecture.

Trissino took the young stonecutter to Rome (1541), where he studied the remains of antiquity, gained introduction to the wealthy elite of Vicenza, and acquired his classically inspired name, Palladio. Contact with Trissino's circle led to prestigious architectural commissions, notably the remodeling of the Town Hall (Basilica) in Vicenza (1549) and a series of palaces for the city's nobility.

Palladio's designs established a formula for the adaptation of the language of classical architecture to the needs of his sixteenth-century humanist patrons. He exploited the use of the classical orders, rustication, and regular proportions and published his ideas in a treatise called *I Quattro libri dell'architettura* (*The Four Books on Architecture*, 1570).

Palladio's success in Vicenza encouraged commissions from rich Venetian patrons eager to build old-style villas on their mainland farms. These in turn led to important projects in Venice itself, where he took over as the city's leading architect after the death of Sansovino (1570). His designs for the churches of San Giorgio Maggiore and the Redentore ingeniously adapted the classical pediment to reflect the height of the interior nave and lower flanking side aisles.

Andrea Palladio's solutions to palace and villa design were enormously influential. Taken up by later architects in England and America, his ideas inspired the development of the eighteenth-century country house.

27

27. *Palladio*, Villa Capra. *Vicenza. Begun 1550. Palladio's innovative combination of a classical temple façade and dome as a formula for villa design was enormously influential.*

28. *Veronese*, A Barbaro Lady and a Nurse. *Villa Barbaro, Maser. Fresco. 1566–1568. Veronese exploited his skill at illusionism in the Villa Barbaro with informal portraits of the Barbaro Family. Here the family nurse is directing her mistress's attention across the room toward two children and a dog teasing a monkey.*

28

as farmhouses. The development of a style to suit the new aristocratic country house was largely the work of one man, Andrea Palladio. The son of a miller, he moved to Vicenza and did his apprenticeship as a stonemason. The Vicentine humanist Giangiorgio Trissino (1478–1550) took Andrea under his wing and educated him in the culture of Ancient Rome. Palladio established his reputation with buildings in Vicenza, adapting classical designs to modern functional needs. His pleasure villa for Paolo Almerico, known as the Villa Rotonda, was a major innovation whose combination of a dome and temple façade would prove enormously influential in later centuries. Palladio's designs for the Venetian patriciate included farm buildings in the porticoes, while the main block expressed the prestige of its patron by the use of classical orders and a coat of arms in the pediment of the façade. In contrast to the extravagance of their palaces on the Grand Canal, the mainland villas were simple in design, materials, and ornamentation. Stucco was used as a cheaper alternative to marble, and interior decoration was appropriate to the rural setting. Veronese's cycle for the Villa Barbaro included scenes of classical mythology and portraits of the Barbaro family.

The new image of Venice was an enduring success. The works produced by its artists and architects found many imitators. Paintings by the likes of Titian and Veronese became collector's items and established a formula for the depiction of classical mythology that profoundly influenced later generations. Palladio's designs set a similar standard for the interpretation of classical architecture. Above all, Venice created an image of culture whose power of inspiration continues to the present day.

29

30

29. *Palladio,* San Giorgio Maggiore. *Venice. Begun 1566. Palladio's Venetian patrons also found him commissions in Venice itself, including this prestigious church across the lagoon from the Doge's Palace.*

30. *Palladio,* Villa Emo. *Fanzolo. Late 1550s. This plain Doric villa was built for Leonardo Emo, who took up farming after a career in Venetian public service, experimenting with land reclamation and agricultural renovation.*

INDEX OF NAMES AND PLACES

Page numbers in boldface refer to pages in this volume.

W

X

Y

Z